The Afterlife and Beyond

From the Author Of . . .

Understanding Life After Death – An Exploration of What Awaits You, Me and Everyone We've Ever Known

" . . . Basically, the book is aimed at helping the reader in 'living life to the max"' – something much easier to do when we are less fearful and see meaning that goes beyond this life. The open-minded reader should find much food for thought in this book and be nourished by it." – *Michael Tymn, author of The Articulate Dead*

Available on Amazon in Kindle or paperback editions:
https://www.amazon.com/dp/0692529179/

The Afterlife and Beyond

An Examination of Life After Death by an Out-of-Body Explorer

First Printing - 2018

Dedicated To . . .

So much of my family has crossed over in recent years. Most recently, my father who passed just last week (as of 08/12/18). So, this book is, of course, dedicated to my mother, brother, and now father. A dedication that transcends beyond a typical dedication to deceased loved ones, because my transitioned family members are among the people who teach me about the afterlife. Literally speaking, my mother is the one who kept me encouraged to finish this book due to our late night conversations in the out-of-body state. Further, I must thank the board of the Afterlife Research Education Institute (www.afterlifeinstitute.org) including Craig Hogan, for bringing me to speak at the Scottsdale symposium now two years in a row. The Zammits (www.victorzammit.com) for continuing to be the main face of afterlife education on the Internet, now going on almost 20 years (and also a major supporter of my work.) I must thank KAren Swain—as we were able to work together successfully to release *Awakened by Death* which was an amazing project. And, of course, all the regular contributors to *Afterlife Topics and Metaphysics* who keep that forum as the most dynamic place for afterlife related critical discussion on the Internet.

Dear Ian;

Thank you for your support! Let me know your future OBE adventures.

Sincerely

Contents

Preface

First, I'd like to give special thanks to everyone who's waited patiently for this book. This book was originally advertised at the end of my 2015 release *Understanding Life After Death* with the title "Understanding Spirit Communication." Ambitiously, I believed I would have the next book finished within a year's time. Soon, I was entertaining e-mails or Facebook messages weekly asking when the sequel was coming out. And I'd respond with a lot of inaccurate postponements.

Then, in 2016, things blew up in my life. My mom passed away, which is obviously horrific and tragic—but it was also the beginning of a whole new chapter in my life in regard to my studies into life after death—as it turns out my mom is exceptionally talented at cross-dimensional communication. For a period of time, she'd visit me while in an out-of-body state as many as three times per week. Contacts faded, but she remains nearby if I ever need her. The last time I spoke to her was in a semi-dream state a couple of weeks ago—she lectured me a little about a girl I was dating at the time ("Cyrus, you should at least post about her on social media instead of keeping her secret. Maybe put a photo of you guys together on Facebook!")

It took another year of allowing this saga to unfold before I felt comfortable fleshing out some of these experiences in a book. In that time, I also continued out-of-body travel whenever I could, allowing me to continually learn and discover new things. Then, suddenly, last year one of my older brothers unexpectedly died. Although my contact with him was not a fraction of the frequency of my mother's contact, it still compelled me to postpone the book to hopefully learn yet more about the afterlife.

The book was also sidetracked by a "side project" that turned out to be incredibly important—*Awakened by Death* which is the collaboration between myself and KAren Swain. This book features some of the best near-death, after-death and out-of-body stories ever told. However, getting that book launched required another momentous effort—especially while juggling www.afterlifetopics.com, the *Afterlife Topics* Facebook group (and that group's sometimes grueling admin duties,) my freelance publishing and editing career, and my day job when I'm back in the USA!

And so, the book remained in limbo for a long period. With pieces of drafts sitting around my computer collecting digital dust, I finally settled down during a recent Southeast Asia excursion to finish it all. Sitting on a couch near my condo's balcony overlooking the concrete jungle of Jakarta, I feverishly worked to meet a late August deadline. And thus, we've arrived to the finish line. The creation of a book that I hope, above all, will assist people's anxieties about death and to show that facts and objectivity are aligned to much greater hope for all of us.

I write this as another study is revealed attempting to "debunk" near-death experiences through a study that shows a one second electrical discharge in the brain shortly before death. Despite the fact this study is highly unverifiable and there is zero evidence that the energetic release is enough to even amount to a single conscious experience, skeptics are clinging to the study to announce with new fervor "there is no life after death!" and those without education are buying the narrative. It's almost as if the materialist lobby gains some perverse pleasure out of destroying people's hope with misinformation. And so, even if this book's readership is limited to a niche audience, it's not being released fast enough.

I understand my tonality is not for everyone—and I even had one (rather puritanical) person block me on Facebook because he despised my occasional use of colorful language. So be it. I am neither a fan of censorship nor self-censorship and trying to please everyone is a habit I shrugged off years ago—and this has assisted my life greatly. The stress of trying to make everyone happy, or not making hard stances or disagreeing with people when necessary, is not a fraction of the stress caused by keeping thoughts and feelings internalized. In this "New Age" field I encounter a sordid amount of misconceptions and ideologies that I feel require addressing, even if that means making a few people mad in the process. That's part of what I do and I know in my heart it's necessary.

Finally, I give a special thanks to YOU—it's sometimes a rough ride staying motivated. However, the fans of my first book came out of the woodwork to tell me how much my research helped them—sometimes on deeply personal levels. So anytime I experience issues related to drama on my Facebook group or one-star reviews by critics or people ex-communicating me because my afterlife studies conflict with some religious belief, I remind myself of the enormous benefit of my work—and how extremely important it is to roll with the punches.

Enjoy the book!

I – Life After Death Affects Us All

After speaking candidly to my father upon my mother's death in 2016, we began to use the present tense about her existence. That's because we came to find she'd visit both of us on the same exact mornings, making her far from a thing of the past. We could even comment on her latest style of clothes.

"I'd never seen her wear anything quite like that plaid dress before. It was quite astonishing," my father said.

"Well, the thing about that other dimension is I'm pretty sure the designer clothes are free," I pointed out.

My father, wracked by mental illness and narcissistic tendencies, went on a downward spiral beginning in 2008. As of writing this, he's still in this realm. I don't know for how much longer.[1]

Substance abuse, including alcoholism, led to the dissolution of millions of dollars of property. I grew up on two ranches—both quite lavish. By my late teens, my old lifestyle had become a thing of the past. Of course, my father's involvement with organized crime provided a silver-lining to our sudden descent into poverty, because at least it would mean he'd no longer have the money to affiliate with such people. Growing up not knowing whether or not a Mexican cartel is going to cut off your head because your father couldn't pay a debt is not a fun way to spend your carefree years.

By the time I was getting the hell out of Arizona, my parents were in a rental home with no water. The home was festering. Putting time and money into the situation barely helped as how can you help people who won't help themselves?

When my mom, a woman who was once a reputed wildlife artist, came down with liver failure after years of alcoholism and self-destructive behavior, it was entirely expected but still horrific.

My dad ended up in a mental hospital after she passed. However, as a master charmer and manipulator, he talked his way out of that situation. He ended up back in the house with sewage accumulation and no running water. I'd visit and find him collapsed on the ground in a pile of his own piss, his blood alcohol at absurd levels.

Due to my stable income at my day job, I was able to sweep through and provide enough finances to get my father moved out of that place. Removing him from that environment was something that helped,

[1] On July 29th 2018, after writing this, my father was found dead on the floor of his rental home in Tucson, Arizona.

as it separated him from the memory of my mother and the little floor mattress where she grew sick and ultimately died.

Little did my father know, my mother was going through her own ordeal.

In 2014, I began the ability to leave my body (as recounted in my 2015 book *Understanding Life After Death.*) I was the first person to greet my mom after her death. She had awoken in a replica of the old family ranch in the desert (long ago foreclosed.) I was already very familiar with this location because I'd appeared in this house dozens of times during out-of-body episodes.

Whenever this happens, I "wake up" in my bed. There is little difference compared to this dimension. I can get out of bed, explore the environment, and perform experiments. I've been known to cram things in my mouth, pinch or cut my skin (to test for the existence of pain,) leave notes for next time (or for others to read) and test the consistency of my astral body. I do this because, at the very least, I like to call myself a paranormal researcher. And having the opportunity to be "me" in the so-called "spirit world" is exhilarating despite how short-lasting many of these experiences are.

When my mom appeared back home, she was freaked out that she had suffered an amnesiac episode.

"One minute I was in the hospital, and it was a terrible experience. You won't believe how much that feeding tube hurt me. You guys should have never taken me to that hospital. And now I'm back at home. What's going on? I guess I'm having dementia."

So, I'd appear there, spend time with her, wake up and return the next night. One thing I couldn't explain to her was that she was dead. This, I assumed, I'd leave to the "professionals." She wasn't in the correct state of mind to handle such information.

Next, she ended up in a rehabilitation facility. She was administered because, unfortunately, she was still suffering from deep, dark habits and alcoholism. Before her admittance, and upon discovering where she was—the astral world with a different set of operating physics—she realized she could start conjuring things with her mind. Whether alcohol or anything else she wanted, it was available to her, and contrary to popular misconceptions about the afterlife—the same operating physics of our bodies persists in astral replica bodies—which is good news for those like me who love eating, dancing and sex—but bad news for people with substance-abuse habits.

Obviously, this wasn't healthy. She was admitted by a team of highly trained professionals who not only rehabilitated her from many of these mental issues carried over from the Earth plane, but they taught her the nature of the other side and how to expand her consciousness to appear back on our plane to make contact. My mom was already a kind of psychic on this world, so she learned fast. She became very talented.

As soon as she learned to do this, she was warping into my bedroom. Laying still on the bed, I could feel her enter the room. By shifting focus to my astral body's vision, I'd see her and could physically feel her as solidly as any other real experience. She would sit with me, hug me, and we could chat. These visitations became a weekly occurrence.

Next, she started a campaign of constant contact with my father, who began receiving visitations sometimes several times in a week. As she did for me, she'd appear in his room or even manifest her voice in an audible way with a short burst of a message. (A most recent one occurred December 24th, 2017. Her voice manifested in his kitchen as "Merry Christmas!")

And so began a shift of focus to the primary issue: my father.

My mom found herself teamed with my grandmother (deceased, my father's side) and my aunt (deceased, also my father's side) in an attempt to provide constant ADC (after-death contact) experiences. The goal: to lift up my father's spirits, expel the grief and help him get his broken life back together. Their theory was that the mere realization of their continued existences would bring some happiness back to his life. I, of course, could also make direct contact with my mother and discuss this overall strategy.

In addition, when communicating with my mom, we'd also discuss the conditions of the afterlife. For me, aside from fulfilling personal curiosity, I was intent on relaying information to readers in the Facebook group *Afterlife Topics and Metaphysics*—a community I started in 2015 with the goal of discussing—and sometimes debating—the conditions of the other side.

Did the strategy work? Almost two years since my mother's death my father became fully aware of an afterlife, no longer in a strict Biblical sense nor an abstract New Age sense. He's now very aware of a cadre of loved ones who've worked to stay in touch with not only him but also me. He even uses accurate terminology these days; such as other dimensions and realms (rather than "heaven' or "hell.") And so, it dawns on us that the family is still together; despite mere differences of dimensional barriers. The situation is far from fixed, but I'm certain the combined effort saved him from further decline and perhaps reduced (to some extent) his alcoholism.

My father had other experiences, too—perhaps more frequently than I have. My father tends to keep hidden the more rattling, amazing or disturbing experiences of his life, but I managed to pry some details about an event that occurred shortly after her crossing. Apparently, my father claims he had an out-of-body episode and my mom—accompanied by some specialist—provided my father a secret phone number. He said he dialed it (upon waking up in THIS world)—and spoke to my mom for a few minutes beyond the dimensional barriers.

My father never mentioned this story again—and refuses to talk about it— but due to my knowledge of unbelievable advancements in cross-dimensional technology—I did not have a hard time believing such a thing *could* be possible.

Of course, one's natural skepticism and "boggle threshold" may create a gut reaction against such claims. That's understandable. However, for how much longer will stories such as these remain beyond belief? As we speak, based on the reports from members of the Afterlife Topics Facebook group and the reports of prominent instrumental transcommunication researchers like Sonia Rinaldi—there's an extraordinary increase in technological communication occurring around the world—with people receiving text messages, Facebook messages, voice messages, and telephone calls from the other side. In Rinaldi's case, she produces direct communication with not only deceased people but living comatose patients who are outside their bodies and capable of communicating with family members again. You can listen to one of Rinaldi's telephone experiments at the ATRANS website (http://atransc.org/sonia-rinaldi-telephone-itc/.) Rinaldi claims much of the work is co-facilitated by electronic voice-phenomena pioneer Konstantine Raudive, along with Nikola Tesla—whom oversees a transmission station. When I spoke at the 2017 Afterlife Symposium in Scottsdale, Arizona—Rinaldi also attended, presenting clear and concise audio of Tesla's voice.

This represents just one area of information that is creating breakthroughs in the subject of the afterlife—pushing this information "beyond" the scope of what it once consisted of and into mainstream consciousness. My experiences with my mother (as well as my brother who passed away more recently) have eliminated all doubt for me—but I hope many others have opportunities to have their doubt reduced or eliminated. And, in the event the afterlife begins concrete scientific recognition—what implications are in store for society? That very question is what this book will explore.

As for my mom, she is always grateful that I was there for her shortly after she crossed over. It's been a rough ride. It hasn't always been positive flowers-and-sunshine. People think we die and are wiped of all our problems. The reality is this is not the case. However, the other side is outfitted with advanced specialists, mentors, teachers, and doctors the likes of which we cannot imagine. And so, anyone who dies is in very good hands.

With my mom, it's an ongoing process and she's far from entirely healthy, but she's come a long way and I'm quite proud of her—her death on this plane was very important for her growth as an individual and I feel no grief at all, given she's still in my life and finally has a life of her own after years of being in an abusive, co-dependent relationship with my father.

On the astral Earth, she enjoys art, the beach, and taking care of foster children who die on this side. She still maintains, in my opinion, psychological issues—and we even argued a few weeks prior to writing this which was very exhausting. Nonetheless, I'm happy people stay themselves on the astral—warts and all—until they develop themselves on their own pace. And I'll happily take my mom's sometimes ridiculous arguments and temper flare-ups if it means she's still herself—why would I want her as anything else?

(Please note: as a researcher, I deal in objective evidence. What I report about her conditions in the afterlife was cross-corroborated through a powerful medium with no awareness of my out-of-body episodes. I've further been able to completely prove communication with the deceased during other OBEs, which I'll discuss later in this book.)

The strategy implemented by these loved ones on my father was ultimately related to breaking down a mortality paradigm. The other side recognizes our ignorance as an excellent learning tool; however, it's obvious to anyone in higher density spectrums that the Earth plane is vastly imbalanced. Perhaps through a combination of the willful and unknowing spread of ignorance, the vast majority of people are asleep. This ignorance spreads fear and a general malaise against our very existences. To make matters worse clandestine powers exploit our ignorance so they may use our resources and leverage power. This phenomenon applies to a number of topics; the least of which is the extra-dimensional properties of ourselves.

Imagine the possibilities if this information were finally disclosed as publicly recognized knowledge.

For Fence Sitters Reading This

Not everybody has the privilege I've enjoyed. From astral experiences in real, mind-bending locations to direct, physical contact with deceased loved ones—there is no room for doubt in my mind. And so, the afterlife has become a personal mission—if I can help to reduce the grief of death in just a few people's lives, I'll have accomplished my work.

However, for what I imagine are many people reading this, it's not a topic one can get behind with absolute certainty. Further, attempts to "understand" the afterlife (as I strung together in my first book, *Understanding Life After Death*) often creates more questions than answers—and more than a few conflicting reports that leave readers confused about this most important of all subjects.

There are two things I can therefore offer: my personal experiences interacting with these higher-density dimensions known by our primitive society as "the afterlife," and an assortment of objective resources for afterlife information and evidence that can be researched. There is also a greater body of evidence that exists on the edge of this spectrum, concerning topics from non-materialist biology (discussed later) to psi and extraterrestrials. These are different subjects but are linked together to form a unified picture of our true nature.

Amidst all these subjects, and so many books about differing perspectives and subjects, I maintain one distinct point of view: the best information is obtained from actually being on the other side (astral projection) or communicating directly with "spirits" and asking them critical, analytical questions (whether through astral projection, a powerful mental or physical medium, two-way EVP technology, or an ability like clairaudience.) This is how I obtain my information. As a result, some of the information I receive is notably different from other areas of writing in this field. And, unsurprisingly, I attract non-fans who become furious that I call into question deeply-held beliefs; be they religious, dogmatic or concerning a very narrow perspective of an afterlife. As we'll discuss in the pop-spirituality chapter, I've argued with people who've had certain styles of near-death experiences—or read a great number of New Age books—who allege my experiences and communication is invalid as, after we die, we all become formless orbs of energy and exist in a non-physical space or hyper-dimension

I've had lengthy discussions with "dead" people in the astral environment—sometimes in their homes or restaurants or even once during a group discussion in a hotel—and it's interesting to hear how they describe such ideas as, essentially, urban legends. It's not to say there isn't truth behind outlandish afterlife claims. After all, everyone has vastly different experiences. Your death experience depends on countless factors, including your existence prior to incarnation. For some people, the more stranger circumstances post-death are completely true—whether ascending to non-physical realms of pure fractal shapes and energy or becoming a giant space jellyfish. But just because your neighbor Tom died and became a galactic octopus creature, does not mean this will happen to you, nor will it happen to the vast majority of people who cross over. It just so happens Tom's soul family was that of tentacled space monsters.

My experiences interviewing the deceased lit the fire under my feet to hopefully spread some semblance of an accurate education on the afterlife—despite the enormous difficulty in such a task where thousands of years of preconceived ideas paint so many different pictures.

Since the purpose of this book is to help prime people on the afterlife and the philosophies that go beyond it, I feel it is my *duty* to report information that is factual. While I believe people have legitimate experiences that reinforce personal views, direct communication has revealed a vast myriad of experiences, with a preponderance towards continued existence in Earth-like realms, where we retain our human forms and identities. I believe most of us know in our hearts that this is true, because often during the dream-state, even non-astral practitioners may experience "astral dreams"—bits and pieces of memories of a prior or concurrent existence on the astral domain. How often do these dreams include formless states of existence? By contrast, a frequent dreamer may recall grandiose environments that feel like other worlds—and dynamic adventures from within such realms. In a dream discussion group on Facebook I attend, I often hear people talking about places they couldn't imagine came from their subconscious minds—floating islands traversing seas of clouds dotted with ornate cities—cold, icy realms with palaces seen glimmering in the snow—golden plains with temples and ancient, wise teachers. I contend all these environments listed are actual realms in the multiverse that a dreamer is merely obtaining little pieces of data about.

Sometimes, these pieces of information—fragments of dream memories—can last a lifetime. Mark Twain famously referred to a young woman he'd remember from dream environments—often meeting her in different situations or with different appearances, but they could always recognize each other. So profound was this subtle yet real relationship that he penned a short story about her titled "My Platonic Sweetheart." At the end of the story, the main character contends "Dreams are deep, strong sharp and real, whereas reality is a vague, dull and tinted artificial world."[1]

And dream contact is merely the start of experiences with "the other side." It's a gateway—a small window interpreted by our limited brain—yet even the dream—often muddied by subconscious ideas and hallucinations—can feel more "real" than our present reality. And that's because on vibrations higher than our own, thoughts and emotions become even more vibrant, and connections with others become stronger, more real, deeper. That is the nature of life on a higher spectrum, and how it can be incalculably better. The best analogy I can personally use is that of being a child. Some experiences as a child seem much more resonant with us in our memories, and we can never quite return to that state. For instance, being a child in a forest and being in wonder at nature. As an adult, we may return to the same stream or grove and enjoy the environment but fail to experience the deep connection we remember as children.

As a natural state of mind, this is how people operate on astral levels that represent frequencies higher than our own. It does not mean that life is shockingly different—on a visual appearance, we will see people on the astral Earth leading familiar lives, working jobs, having parties, banquets, weddings and so forth—but on a mental, emotional level it's a richer experience. This is why religions have interpreted the other side to be "heavenly" because it's much more robust than our current lives.

This is not to say there is no dark side, though. In fact, later in this book, I dedicate a whole chapter to the dark—a reality we cannot deny. While our emotional experiences are much richer, it seems it can operate in a reverse way, too. Given an issue is entirely psychological and not related to a physical (brain-related) problem, I have found no evidence that we do not carry these mental states with us. That is the nature of healing centers in the afterlife that is so commonly reported.

The duties performed in such centers cannot be underestimated, as problems of the mind can become exaggeratedly profound on the astral levels. It can result in a manifestation of chaotic elements in the environment, or even a person being plunged into chaotic realms, cut off from help. Professionals work hard to prevent these situations from occurring, with psychiatry being a field of great importance. I have a personal hypothesis that one reason we choose to incarnate in this world is that the lower-density environment actually allows for a more subdued emotional level—which may be necessary for growth and personal development. Returning to a heightened state of existence from such a subdued existence is the source of the incredible feeling of contrast that people who have spiritual experiences attest. Yet, it may come with certain psychological dangers, as well.

All of the above information may be compelling, but a fence-sitter needs proof, and for that, you may require your own experiences. To experience "the other side" you can practice OBEs (there are many guides to assist with this,) or perhaps you could even find a nice cottage in the forest to retreat for a week or two, to focus on meditation and trying to reach out to powers beyond. In the hustle and bustle of a modern city, the vibration is far too askew for the other side to make easy contact. However, deep in nature it's much easier—which is why so many more people report supernatural experiences in such locations (my father sometimes tells the story of a spirit of a Native American who materialized in front of him when he was camping in the woods in the 1980s.)

In lieu of your own experiences, please see the concrete, objective evidence for the afterlife available in numerous books besides this one. You can start with my prior book, *Understanding Life After Death* (if you like my writing style and want to keep reading what I have to say, that is) but I also suggest *Life After Death: Some of the Best Evidence* by Jan Vandersande, *A Lawyer Presents the Case for the Afterlife* by Victor Zammit, *Surviving Death: A Journalist Investigates Evidence for an Afterlife* by Leslie Kean, and there are many more. This particular book, however, is an attempt to go deeper into the rabbit hole than the entry-point of analyzing the evidence. At a certain point in my own journey, I realized there was an endpoint to the research and the personal experiences. I was no longer stuck trying to prove to myself that it was real, but I fully accepted its reality, and this provided the opportunity to focus energy elsewhere and beyond.

II — Disclosure and Changing Paradigms

Living With New Realities

My experiences with the afterlife are personal and cannot be "proven," however, sharing stories of the afterlife—something we've done in earnest at the *Afterlife Topics* Facebook group—can change lives. That's why I wanted to begin this book by discussing part of the saga with my mother. And, that's just the tip of the iceberg in relation to my own adventures with the other side. It's these experiences that keep me motivated to continue my work because I understand the vastly positive effects such information has on both individuals and society at large.

Nonetheless, I foresee a rocky path toward the acceptance of the afterlife on a much greater level. As evidence accumulates (not just the anecdotal kind, but scientific as well) we see the penetration of the information into the populace. And with it, unavoidable questions: How will society process the information? What will a post-death world look like? What is accurate afterlife information that can be taught universally? What more can we learn about the physics of the afterlife to enhance our education? What technology can be created (or improved) to facilitate communication? (For instance, EVP, ITC, the work of Rinaldi and others who focus on the technological side.)

More and more, the afterlife seems to unravel itself into society through a self-initiated disclosure process. Disclosure is, of course, the revelation of something that is already true but was kept hidden—either intentionally or because of ignorance. It's up to people in the afterlife research field—including readers like yourself—to be part of that disclosure process.

We know a disclosure doesn't occur by wrapping the topic around a sledgehammer and beating people's heads with it. We also know it's a very slow process. People have to gradually learn to accept the information, and sometimes it takes a new generation to actualize a major idea change.

Although anecdotal, I personally feel major strides have been made in the last twenty or so years. Organized skeptics still exist who try to keep a stranglehold on afterlife information—especially through tools like Wikipedia—a site managed by the Wiki-approved *Guerilla Skeptics* who are the self-proclaimed arbiters of allowable information. However, these attempts at censoring the afterlife disclosure process are too ineffective to contain the robust information. Namely, because afterlife-related topics are just too fascinating and relevant for the general public to willingly ignore. To the disappointment of the enemies of afterlife information, people keep studying and learning.

Even the late Stephen Hawking—in his later years—began writing and hypothesizing about very "out there" topics—like "shadow people" and the existence of parallel dimensions. Hawking was a staunch afterlife-denier, but I'd like to believe this opinion had started to change before his death. I've seen other noted materialists taking a slightly more moderate approach as well, including skeptic Michael Shermer. I sometimes wonder how many people are secretly in this field but afraid to go public lest they face an academic backlash. We'll explore—and tackle—modern materialism and skepticism in depth in Chapter 10.

Parallels to the UFO Field

I am now positive that times are changing, and it's exciting. The word "disclosure" has taken a greater emphasis in the latter half of the 2010s—although in relation to the UFO field and not yet so much about our multi-dimensional existences. Nonetheless, surprisingy, these types of "para" subjects have relationships to each other—and I see important parallels developing between the recent, impressive strides in the UFO / extraterrestrial world—and the subject of humanity "waking up" at large.

In December 2017 UFO disclosure went viral. That's because one morning in the week leading up to Christmas, the New York Times broke the story of a Pentagon-operated UFO research program funded to the tune of 26 million, operating from 2007 to 2012 (and allegedly still going in secret.) The now-famous footage of a U.S. fighter jet chasing a bizarre craft that defied physics was released. This was followed by interviews with former Pentagon officials (namely Luis Alezando) testifying to not only the existence of the program but his personal belief of an extraterrestrial origin of UFOs.

The 24-hour news cycle finally decided (or perhaps someone decided *for them*) that it was time to run with the story of ETs. For at least two weeks this story was blasted on every major news outlet almost every day, with the same choppy 42-second video clip of the alleged ET craft being played again, and again. Although this was far from the most impressive UFO footage ever released, it had the Pentagon's seal of approval, and the message was displayed loud and clear: UFOs (or

"UATs" as they decided to rebrand them with the bizarre moniker of "threats") are real.

To date, this book could be vastly outdated because recent announcements have hinted at ongoing Pentagon-affiliated UFO footage releases, with more to come in 2018—all via the questionable *To the Stars Academy* spearheaded by Blink 182's Tom DeLonge. By the time you're reading this, who knows what developments will have burst onto center stage.

My main interest, however, concerned the sociological impact of what became dubbed the "soft disclosure." Decades of hard programming into the population to reject or even condemn the so-called supernatural had received its first bit of unraveling. Although I'm not entirely sold on the nature (or honesty) behind Tom DeLonge's soft disclosure, the social effects were undeniable.

At the time, I worked a funky part-time job on the west-side of Los Angeles, promoting cars for Honda by doing community service, smiling and waving at cameras (maybe you saw me on TV.) The reason for such odd jobs on my part is because of the dark truth of entrepreneur authors: it doesn't always pay the bills, despite the impression you may receive after a good round of publicity. However, mingling with Los Angelites and out-of-work actors was a good opportunity to hear what "regular folk" were talking about while standing around the coffee machine.

As I rarely hit "muggles" over the head with information about my secret life in supernatural studies, I'd consider myself a bit of a covert agent. I was quite surprised then to find what some people were saying about the UFO soft disclosure.

A woman I worked with who was typically uninterested and unknowing of the topic said something quite telling: "I'm not sure what to think anymore. UFOs aren't supposed to be real, but if they are real and aliens are real, well I guess life's a lot different than I thought."

This was the greatest thing I'd heard all year: A genuine public reaction to a soft disclosure. Even though UFOs have never been my main interest or field of study, this reaction represented a crossing of the gulf between the mainstream and the "outer limits" of which subjects like the afterlife are also included.

The reaction was an example of the possibilities of how disclosures could radically redefine how "regular folk" see their reality; which would open the floodgates of greater consciousness. Whether one wishes to subscribe to the wider conspiracy theories of suppression of truth or not, it would be reasonable to assume far-reaching or society-changing information would be kept from the masses to maintain order. This would be justified as for the people's own good. After all, humankind is likely not mature or sensible enough to take drastic information easily without collapsing cherished institutions.

The afterlife field, unlike the UFO field, is not dependent on clandestine government entities to make the revelation. Instead, it's dependent upon reasonable people to do the appropriate research and be willing to expand parameters. Unlike UFOs, which are spurious and hard to pin down or observe, practically anyone can explore out-of-body episodes or contact with the other side—at least, those people dedicated enough.

The only thing stopping the "afterlife" from becoming common knowledge are our limitations. Even so, integration into this idea I hypothesize will be easier than predicted. That's because many of us already believe in contact with the "beyond"—via religion. Although religion creates a crude (at best) interpretation of these other realms—it has at least planted the idea firmly into consciousness. In my work, I've found many people have adapted objective afterlife data with their religious

Astral Experiences: Proof Positive

I will attempt to pepper this book with my more memorable personal experiences in out-of-body states.

One that stands out is the time I appeared in a familiar territory: the astral version of Phoenix, AZ.

I found myself, as coherent as I physically exist normally, outside some commercial buildings. I entered a club that catered to fans of MMA fighting and other sports. A patron explained that on the astral side, you won't sustain long-term injuries; and so, people can battle each other to their heart's content.

Behind the bar, I met a young man with a winning smile who was serving drinks. I interviewed him about his motivation to work in such a place, his life on Earth before he crossed over, and his full name.

When I returned to my dimension, I immediately pulled out my laptop and loaded Facebook. I entered his name—and his face appeared. A Facebook memorial page for a young man from Arizona who had taken his own life 6 months prior. It was his same face, same smile.

I ended up in contact with this man's mother. At first, she was highly skeptical, but through a moment of synchronicity we encountered each other again almost a year later, and she told me how she saw a medium who verified my story—that her son had indeed taken to working a bar in the astral!

beliefs as the best way to comprehend the subject. This is, of course, also a serious issue because such an approach can skew the information, create wishful thinking or even inaccurate and terrible notions (eternal hellfire.) Nonetheless, at least religion is a place for people to start, and the deprogramming from religious thinking can gradually occur in light of objective data.

When a Paradigm Really Changes

The point of this book is to talk about a world that's finally changing in considerable ways—and what we must expect for not only your individual life but society as a whole. The data about the afterlife is spreading faster and faster—whether the scientific data about near death-experiences and consciousness provided by doctors like Sam Parnia and Stuart Hameroff, to pop culture ghost shows (of varying quality, but they still get the message across,) and an acceptance of personal experiences—that it's OK to talk about near death-experiences, out-of-body experiences, and visits with deceased loved ones.

The New Age realm has been talking for decades about a "New Earth"—in fact, the very term "New Age" refers to a kind of shift in thinking that will rapidly evolve our species. Terms like the Age of Aquarius or "ascension" of humanity were widely used among the spirituality community leading up to 2012. Personally, I felt nauseated by all of it because I knew in December, 2012 if anything out of the ordinary happened, I'd find the nearest straw hat and eat it with a bottle of Tabasco sauce.

"But, you're so negative Cyrus, you'll be proven wrong in 2012, I assure you!"

And I don't blame these people for wanting a sudden supernatural event to happen—life on this planet is a pain in the ass. We have to watch most of our loved ones die of terrible diseases like cancer. Our looks fade. Far too often our jobs suck. Many people feel empty and alone. Despite the fact a major solution is being nicer to everyone around us, people become angry about their problems and then attack each other—not the smartest behavior, I must say.

And so, we cling desperately to a bit of hope—that a supernatural force will come down and wipe everything clean so we can start fresh. Whether it's the rapture, ascension or the Age of Aquarius, these ideas have been embedded into our psychology for a long time.

Don't get me wrong—despite my criticism, I still admire the inconsistent, rambling work of David Wilcock (*The Ascension Mysteries*, 2015), who is the primary researcher of all things related to human cosmic shifts. His work is always fascinating, and although perhaps mired in uncertainties and a lack of concrete evidence to satisfy skeptics, there appears to be truth hidden in the details.

David Wilcock is such a guilty pleasure that I've binge-watched most of *Cosmic Disclosure* and *Wisdom Teachings* on the "spiritual Netflix" Gaia TV. He's a funny, clever and dedicated host who I'm sure is a lightning-rod of subconsciously channeled information. And hell, maybe he really is the reincarnation of Edgar Cayce (they sure look the same physically.)

It's very hard to encapsulate Wilcock's endless body of work in a couple of paragraphs, but, to greatly simplify things: Wilcock and others in his field believe mankind is on the verge of a breakthrough. Due to a combination of government-approved releases of information, the ending of systemic societal brainwashing (spurred on by the recently toppled "powers that were",) a vast migration of advanced spiritual souls into Earth bodies ("indigo children",) and being on the verge of a celestial energy shift in this sector of the galaxy—humanity can expect everything from immediate connections to the other side (our world and the astral Earth practically merging together,) a widespread emergence of telepathic powers, and our graduation to a space-faring civilization complete with anti-gravity and multi-dimensional technology to allow easy vacations to Zamarak VI or whatever alien planet we want to visit.

Needless to say, these ideas have people in the "Spiritual Awakening" community excited. And as much as I loathe elements of the New Age world—I hope I'm still a "team player" in that I absolutely want these ideas to be true. The problem is—repeated attempts to solidify exact dates seem to fly by the wayside, with the most embarrassing obviously the 2012 fiasco (which Wilcock was the biggest cheerleader.)

In an attempt to understand why so much information from "beyond" is a dud, I found myself taking note of a few points brought up by David Wilcock's highly controversial insider, Corey Goode.

Corey is one of the primary insiders focused on by Wilcock's addicting-to-watch *Cosmic Disclosure* series. He claims that since a child he has worked as a government empath for liaisons with extraterrestrials and that all upper echelons of society are highly aware of everything from multi-dimensions (life after death) to traveling space and communing with aliens. His stories (combined with the stories of other alleged insiders like Tony Rodriguez) put to shame some of the best science fiction I've read. They give Frank Herbert and Isaac Asimov a run for their money. And of course, it's more exciting to watch because of the possibility some—or all—of the information is true, as at least some attempts to objectively verify the claims is provided (the late William Tompkins, an esteemed former Navy engineer, is presented by Wilcock to verify many of Corey's claims, as well as other insiders.) The attempt to combine evidence behind the data creates a little endorphin rush that hooks viewers, but it's still not so convincing to skeptics.

While Corey isn't easy for everyone to digest—claims of time travel and a Reptilian-alien controlled cabal put many viewers off—he did a good job of summarizing some very important philosophical points about why the cosmic humanity shift is so elusive—and I suggest people heavily invested in this subject to revisit Corey's work and take note of why the "energy shift" appears to be going nowhere.

To greatly paraphrase from various episodes and interviews, here are some reasons there appears to be no 2012 ascension event happening, no cosmic shift, no solar event or any of its other names (this is not to say it won't someday happen, but it's just...er...*constipated.*)

- It's up to US to create a paradigm shift in society. Aliens or multi-dimensional entities can't do it for us. If they did, it would interrupt our free will. (Think *Star Trek* folks: Would the Federation land on a planet and reveal next-level ideas to a less-advanced race, providing them powerful technology? Hell, no.)

- There's an existence of parallel timelines. A timeline exists where humanity does "wake up" and evolves to the next level—but sadly, a timeline also exists where we stay completely ignorant and humanity further declines. Nothing is set in stone because it's up to human free-will to choose knowledge over Kim Kardashian and excessive SnapChat usage (guess which of these options humankind, at least people back home in California, typically chooses.)

- To manifest the reality we want, we have to take action. Sitting around and hoping for aliens to land won't do it. In the same way, the afterlife won't reveal itself by some mystical power.

- When a major shift really begins happening, and information about everything from advanced technology, aliens, cover-ups by the elite to yes—the reality of our existences as multi-dimensional entities who completely survive the superficial process of bodily death—is revealed, it won't be a "kumbayah" moment. Rather, we can expect a tumultuous—even violent—period as humanity tries to adjust.

And therein lies the problem I've noted for years in the New Age world—a constant need to find shortcuts and fall back to lazy thinking. To point out in a less-than-polite way the behavioral issues I see among folks in pop spirituality communities:

- A "give me" attitude—wanting enlightenment served on a golden platter, no work required.

- Dubious afterlife beliefs that bypass personal responsibility ("When we die, we ALL become angels ascended to a higher sphere, regardless of our actions or consequences on Earth. Even Hitler is an archangel, sitting on a cloud playing the harp.")

- Double standards and misinterpretations of ideas like the Law of Attraction ("You want lots of material goods and wealth in your life? That's selfish! I want lots of material goods and wealth because I am seeking abundance through the Law of Attraction. Big difference.')

(I rant more about the New Age community in Chapter 6 *Reconciling Pop Spirituality and the Afterlife*.)

It's no surprise then that pop spirituality has clung to the idea of aliens landing and providing all the secrets, or a spiritual shift one day emerging and suddenly everyone is an angel flying around with wings and dropping fairy dust on people.

The hard truth, as Corey Goode accurately points out in his lectures, is the *personal* path to any kind of spiritual "awakening" is grueling. While many people believe they can just use their thoughts and become instant enlightened gurus via meditation or yoga retreats, the truth is that spirituality is a silly terminology for a much more complex subject known as *self-development*. And, real self-development is not easy. It involves doing work that people don't always like to hear about—and that's not as marketable as promising fulfillment through nothing but meditating on a mountain or practicing yoga in Nepal. Our real development requires experience with other people and facing ourselves—versus running away from ourselves.

In Summary

The world will benefit in innumerable ways from a disclosure of life after death (among other topics,) but it's up to us to materialize such a situation. The extreme fear in our society over the death and dying process is a mostly socially constructed affair. It's a monumental challenge attempting to piece together thousands of years of social conditioning to reimagine death and the possibility that it's not the end. The New Age movement has imagined various scenarios of a sudden awakening of mankind and consciousness shift; however, these ideas suffer from a fatal flaw of believing that some higher power will descend from the heavens and perform all the hard work for us. With a bit of critical thinking, this idea becomes less feasible. Whatever work must be done to bring humanity to the "next level" is up to us.

III – Understanding Life After Death – A Rehash

In the next two chapters, we'll explore a quick run-down again of objective evidence of the afterlife—in case you forgot, never read the first book, or have lost track of the overwhelming amounts of research and work—followed by my analysis of what the afterlife is like and what it means for you and me.

What is This Afterlife Business About, Anyway?

Probably the biggest mistake made in this field of research is assuming a single subject represents the evidence for life after death. In fact, there are numerous—dozens—of individual subjects that detail the evidence. As retired lawyer Victor Zammit (www.victorzammit.com) frequently points out, it's not merely one area of evidence that constitutes something akin to "proof," rather, it's the entirety of all the evidence put together.

Studying the evidence can change minds about our existences on this mortal coil. Although the evidence by itself seems to hit a plateau for most people; as without direct experience and contact, merely reading other people's anecdotes or research is not always enough to bust into a new paradigm of reality.

Nonetheless, without first-hand experience, the research by itself still represents the closest a layperson can get to understanding this extremely important topic. For me personally, in the days before my own experiences, highly influential books included *A Lawyer Presents the Case for the Evidence* (Victor Zammit,) *Hello From Heaven* (Bill and Judy Guggenheim,) *Evidence for the Afterlife* (Jeff Long,) *Mindsight* (Kenneth Ring, regarding perception among blind people during out-of-body states,) *The Afterlife Experiments* (Gary Schwartz,) and the documentary *Calling Earth* that recounts phenomenal electronic communication and experiments in contact with the other side. I also suggest any and all literature related to the Scole experiments in England—highly verifiable physical mediumship experiments.

I devoured a lot of this material because it all pointed in the same direction: survival of consciousness after death, which I surmised was a marginally important topic given it affects literally everyone alive.

Over the years, I also wrestled with the skeptical points of view, of which one exists for every possible subject. And, in many ways, I'd always consider myself to be a "skeptic," as I'd avoid surrendering my beliefs over to any particular subject, always leaving room for doubt versus becoming a true believer—a path to irrationality. This also represented the "plateau" mentioned earlier—without my own experiences (like those I recounted at the beginning of this book,) the information remained in a theoretical realm, and I was forced to still consider the alternatives of post-death *non-existence* as a lingering and real possibility.

Today, I'm no longer within that paradigm, because as mentioned before—beginning around 2014 I began incurring regular out-of-body episodes. This included: encountering deceased people in astral worlds whom I could objectively verify the existences of upon my further investigation, detailed communications with deceased loved ones, the ability to verify objective details in this world while separated from the body, and encountering distinguishable individual personalities in this state that were clearly not figments of my mind.

While I do not know when—or if—you'll have your own convincing experiences—whether out-of-body episodes, direct contact from beyond, or (hopefully not) a near-death experience, anyone can still learn about the afterlife through objective evidence. And so, I'll provide provide quick summaries of the best topics for exploring life after death. If this book has left you boggled up to this point, it may be wise to set it down and delve back into the research before going further.

The Best Areas of Evidence

Afterlife Laboratory Experimentation

Although a generalized topic, I am referring in particular to the work of Gary Schwartz. I would suggest reading *The Afterlife Experiments, The Truth About Medium* and *The Sacred Promise.*

What sets Schwartz' research apart is that it includes triple-blind experimentation processes, high-tech laboratory equipment, and strict protocols to verify communication occurring with the beyond. Further, it is always evolving, to a point where skeptics virtually cannot keep up with his research.

At the 2017 Afterlife Symposium in Scottsdale, AZ, Schwartz demonstrated various new experiments. For instance, relaying objective information from a spirit contact and a medium completely isolated from the details of the communication. This included using psychic artistry to verify the identity of a contacting spirit.

Earlier experiments included the use of a $20,000 photon detection unit to confirm the manipulation of light in a completely sealed environment, with photons occurring at precise points when the spirit team agreed to manipulate the completely dark room. To date, no skeptic can account for such an experiment's results short of lazily declaring fraud.

Apparition Experiences

One of my favorite subjects concerns the phenomenon of "deceased" people appearing, albeit briefly, in our own realm. Far from a hazy or dream-like hallucination, this involves a "spirit" materializing, in flesh and blood, in front of a person.

The group I created in 2015, *Afterlife Topics and Metaphysics*, has too many awesome experiences posted for me to encapsulate so easily, but here's one good example of the types of experience that is frequently reported. This was by a group member named Lynn Owens, posted in 2016:

> "Saw my mum about twenty years ago. I was wide awake and had got up to adjust curtains. It was light in the morning and I got back into bed, only to see my mum who'd died in 1981 sitting next to me in bed to the left. She looked about thirty years younger and was wearing a white dress. By the time I registered surprise and gasped out, she was gone. ... [I] never knew her as a young woman because she was in her forties when she adopted me but it was her alright. I have never forgotten it because I loved my mum." (Afterlife Topics and Metaphysics, 2016.)

Apparitions like this case are a rarer form of after-death contact, but there's a long history behind them. The Society for Psychical Research has archived reports such as a case documented by parapsychologist Hanz Holzer of nine people witnessing the materialization of a husband sitting by his dying widow's bedside, allegedly visible for 30 minutes at a time.

Apparitions are often unexpected. My father recounted how, in early 2018, my mother materialized in the kitchen. He claims he spoke to her several minutes, holding her arm the whole time and stunned by the idea she was physically solid, made of flesh and bone. After she claimed she was out of energy, she simply disappeared.

Death-Bed Visions

Like every subject listed, this could be a life-long area of study. Death-bed visions are when those close to death begin seeing loved ones who were deceased. Researchers recount that such visions sometimes result in the revelations of people who were not known to be dead (like a relative the family had lost contact with.) This topic also goes hand-in-hand with accounts of terminal lucidity and shared-death experiences. For resources about death-bed visions, I'd suggest books by terminal care nurse Penny Sartori.

Evidential Mediumship

Many have the wrong impression about mediumship, as they believe it consists entirely of TV personalities throwing generalized guesses out at people in an audience. Further, there's no denying a large amount of ineptitude among mediums who cannot provide accuracy to save their lives. However, a real phenomenon exists of highly talented, evidential mediums who can provide anomalous information.

For an example of such mediumship in action, please see this link: https://youtu.be/g74znWzyRTU (A Medium Conducts a Reading With a Non-Believer.) This video was part of a series of experiments performed by Donna Moncrieffe of the Medium 7 project that established the validity of some mediums. In the linked clip, we see a demonstration of the true power of real mediumship in effect—and how it can shake the foundations of a person's skeptical or materialist belief system. Unfortunately, true mediumship is a rare power, and it's unlikely to be found at a cornerstore psychic. When experiencing the real thing, it's unmistakable, going far beyond the scope of what a mentalist or cold-reader would be capable of.

Personally, an experience in 2016 with medium Susanne Wilson, shortly after my mom passed away, verified to me beyond-the-shadow-of-a-doubt the authenticity of some mediums, as she provided personal protocols established to prevent cold reading and was able to provide extremely specific, detailed information that was unavailable to any third party (ruling out hot-reading.)

EVP and ITC Research

Electronic voice phenomena and instrumental transcommunication are popular subjects in the field of ghost-hunting, but many are unaware of the more sophisticated research into this field. In my own experience as admin for the group *Afterlife Topics and Metaphysics*, I've been stunned by members of the community carrying on regular communication with deceased loved ones via normal recording software. Although often hard for outsiders to decipher, even private users will occasionally receive a Class A communication—a direct message in a deceased person's voice that is clear to any third-party listener.

Brazilian ITC researcher Sonia Rinaldi is perhaps the most reputable researcher in this field. Rinaldi claims direct communication with deceased personalities like Nikola Tesla who, according to her, have established multidimensional communication channels from their world.

While this is a big claim to make, she also offers a more practical claim that can be verified by outside parties—Rinaldi allegedly uses EVP tech to reunite family members with loved ones who are in comas. Understanding how "the other side" operates we learn that no one is necessarily confined into their bodies in this world, and people who are comatose in their Earth body may still have active lives happening in astral states. She even claims she can provide communication to the parents of autistic children who do not normally communicate.

For further research, I suggest the documentary *Calling Earth* which is usually available for free viewing on sites like Vimeo (give it a Google search.)

Near-Death Experiences

The most well-known of all afterlife studies. Near-death experiences consist of a wide field of research concerning a phenomenon experienced by millions of people. In approximately 9% of cardiac arrest patients have a near-death experience, according to a University of Southampton study[2]. Such persons will report an anomalous experience including, but not limited to: leaving the body, encountering deceased loved ones, entering an idyllic otherworld, encountering a Light / feeling the presence of God, being told of a grand design for their life, being sent home or choosing to return home, and other aspects.

Near-death experiences are so prevalent that researchers believe they've helped to shape history. Even *The Tibetan Book of the Dead* and other ancient texts (including *The Egyptian Book of the Dead*,) draws heavily on NDEs, and they likely helped shape mythology about the death process and virtually all religious beliefs about what happens when we die.

Near-death experiences are, however, not the be-all, end-all of afterlife research. In my personal view as an amateur researcher, this topic creates a limited perspective due to the personal nature of such experiences. Some NDEs represent a curious, if not questionable, type of experience—for instance, entering highly fundamentalist religious environments or being given strange messages or prophecies that fail to come true.

This may be due to a psychedelic nature of NDEs. They appear to be equal parts genuine afterlife experiences and potentially subjective DMT-inspired trips, as well. As a result, I suggest not drawing major conclusions about the nature of the afterlife from any one particular NDE. Rather, read them on a collective basis.

I suggest the book *Evidence of the Afterlife* by Jeffrey Long. There is also ongoing research by cardiologist Sam Parnia to verify NDEs as able to produce veridical perception outside of the body and occur when a patient is truly clinically dead and without brain-wave activity. Famous examples like the Pam Reynolds case include verified brain wave non-occurrence during the midst of the experience.

Out-of-Body Experiences

Of course, it's not necessary to be near-death to go out-of-body. OBE practitioners can induce these experiences independently, and often provide the most detailed and sometimes mind-blowing accounts of what the afterlife is like. This subject is all too familiar to me, as it was the sudden occurrence of OBEs that thrust me deep into this field.

OBE research can contain fairly advanced information about the afterlife that crosses most people's boggle-thresholds. If, however, you're ready to take a plunge—I'd suggest to begin with Jurgen Ziewe's *Multidimensional Man* where he breaks down the nature of the afterlife throughout excursions into realms beyond the imagination.

OBEs are a complex subject—and one which we'll continue tackling in greater detail in this book. However, most people can experience this phenomenon for themselves with a level of practice, including the manipulation of sleep states and the obtainment of lucid dreaming—a stepping stone to entering real (non dream-like) environments. To anyone who is talented at recovering awareness while sleeping, entering the OBE state is only a breath away. However, certain physical barriers may interrupt the experience. This includes sleep paralysis (a potentially frightening experience) and strong sensations (electrical, whirring, whooshing, etc) which have the potential to induce panic and prevent the full bodily disconnection.

There are many techniques on the web to research about practicing this state; however, I'll recommend one technique for readers to practice right away: set a soft alarm. Not loud enough to wake you up, but soft enough that you can hear when sleeping. If you want to be ambitious, make the alarm a recording of your own voice saying "Awareness now." If you can hear this as you sleep, you'll be cued to "take the steering wheel" of your sleeping experience. When conscious of yourself during the dream state, instead focus your mind back to your body and attempt to lift your arms up. If your body is paralyzed from sleeping—you'll discover the limbs you're lifting are now your astral (etheric) counterparts and not your normal arms or legs. The first time I performed this feat and watched my astral replica hand disconnect from my physical hand—and then I made a fist and felt the "pins and needles" like I hadn't used my etheric hand in a while—and I felt blood flow into this parallel limb—I knew in a proof positive way everything I had studied was real.

Out-of-Body Perception

If it is truly possible for a person to leave their body, then logically this state should be independent of physical conditions like blindness, and wouldn't they be able to recount specific details?

This has long been considered a "holy grail" in supernatural research. And, there's results to be shown. I suggest the book *Mindsight* by Kenneth Ring which explores near-death experiences among the blind, including the blind at birth, who allegedly incur sight for the first time after awareness shifts from outside of the physical eyes. In fact, the area of near-death experience perception is one of the best places to explore this subject.

Although there's been a lack of modern experimentation in regard to out-of-body perception from a healthy (not near-death) state, a lab experiment by parapsychologist Charles Tart in the 1970s demonstrated some evidence of out-of-body perception in an anonymous female college student named Miss Z, who apparently identified a string of hidden numbers in a room.

On a personal note, I'd like to add that as an out-of-body practitioner, it's very hard to identify objects in this environment in the OOB state. This is because usually within moments of leaving the body, I'll find myself in an entirely new environment. The "near-Earth" state can also be modified and different in appearance from our own world (I'd liken it a little bit to the show *Stranger Things* and the so-called *Upside Down* mirror reality.) Nonetheless, I've been able to sustain myself in the near-Earth state before, long enough to identify objective details, including a roommate's activities in another room. These amazing experiences have provided for me solid proof of the objectivity of OBEs.

Phone Calls from Dead People

This may sound surprising, but there's an increasing amount of reports of people receiving direct electronic contact from deceased loved ones. These reports date back at least to the 70s with the book *Phone Calls from the Dead* (Raymond Bayless.)

In the modern era, I've heard reports in the *Afterlife Topics* community of cell phone calls, text messages and anomalous Facebook messages from deceased people. Often, based on the reports I've gathered, a person will receive a scratchy phone call from an unknown number, and they will be able to make out the hushed voice of a loved one before the call ends.

I am often surprised by how common these reports are. Currently, I'm writing this in a city called Kuching on the island of Borneo, and the other night I was talking to a young Peruvian tourist who recounted a story of a friend who received a voicemail message from a deceased family member. Almost wherever I go, stories like this crop up, and I can't help but think electronic messages are becoming much more common.

In one case I investigated, a deceased member of an afterlife-related Facebook group continued posting lovely photos of sunsets long after his passing. Some suggested he found a way to time and automate continued photos, or a loved one had access to his account; however, the frequency of these Facebook-related contact stories does make me pause a little to consider a paranormal explanation.

I investigated a most unusual case in 2017 of an allegedly active Facebook account of a deceased person. She had been posting in *Afterlife Topics* and providing fairly insightful analysis. Later, another member told me he believed the account belonged to his deceased spouse (from an internet-based relationship.) I contacted this person and engaged in various long conversations. She claimed she was operating the Facebook directly from the afterlife dimension within a "transitionary" realm to help people who recently cross over. She made various wild claims such as "possessing" the bodies of relief workers in war-torn areas like Syria as a way to assist in humanitarian causes.

Despite how engrossing her story was, and our long conversations together, sadly I could not verify this person's true identity or whether or not she was actually dead. I eventually had to conclude it was all a wildly imaginative work of fiction. Nonetheless, it was an interesting investigation to place into my little personal archive (and who knows? It's a crazy, crazy world.)

Physical Mediumship

In my 2015 book *Understanding Life After Death* I go into much detail about 20th century direct-voice medium Leslie Flint. However, even in the modern age, there are still mediums who claim to be able to produce tangible, physical phenomena inside of séance rooms. Mediums include David Thompson out of Australia and Scott Milligan from the U.K.

Among all para-subjects, the reports of physical mediumship are among the wildest and hardest for "muggles" to wrap their brains around. For instance, sitters of Milligan's seances have reported the presence of animals from the spirit world materializing into the séance room—including once even the presence of a baby elephant! Personally trusted afterlife researchers, like Sandra Champlain (*We Don't Die Radio*,) have vouched for the authenticity of Milligan. However, I have not investigated this matter to make any definitive conclusion.

There's deep layers of information in this field, including reports from lesser-known physical mediums and highly accredited researchers. I'd suggest the book *Life After Death: Some of the Best Evidence* by physicist Jan Vandersande who exclusively investigated physical mediumship for decades, which included the compilation of highly evidential photographic records. Jan presented his work at the 2017 Afterlife Symposium and also appeared on the show *Coast to Coast* with George

Noory, revealing much of this information to large audiences for the first time.

Famous physical mediums from yesteryear included Rita Goold and Minnie Harrison, both of whom deserve proper research to help fully understand this subject. I suggest the book written by Harrison's son, *Life After Death: Living Proof* as an excellent account of what it was like living amidst this most unusual phenomenon.

Another one of the best reported physical phenomena was The Scole Experiments. I'd suggest reviewing the *The Scole Report* which is the several-hundred page long documentation of the phenomena. Highly investigated by independent researchers and scientists, Scole represented some of the most documented physical experiences of all time, including the materialization of spirit personalities, the conjuration of spirit lights, the development of film within sealed containers (and held by investigating scientists to rule out fraud,) and many other exciting incidences. For more information, see: http://www.victorzammit.com/evidence/scole.htm.

Remote Viewing

Among all subjects, remote viewing is the only field widely explored by governments for security purposes. Remote viewers can relocate their consciousness to virtually any area imaginable, beyond the scope of space and time. A trained remote viewer could, therefore, pose a national security risk—or could be used to infiltrate rival governments.

To understand remote viewing at a glance, it's very important to understand the professional protocol in place. Remote viewing is NOT a person merely using their imagination to come up with various facts and ideas about a subject. Rather, a strict guideline is used that the viewer is NOT aware of the details they are attuning to. They may be given, for instance, a series of coordinates or a location on a map, or something even more vague.

In one of the most unusual cases, a remote viewer employed by the CIA was once, as an experiment, asked to remote view the distant past of the planet Mars (millions of years ago.) Using typical protocols to remain blinded about the details of the viewing, he began to describe the existence of an ancient Martian civilization and subsequently his report became an official CIA document. To read the report, see the following link at the CIA.gov website:

https://www.cia.gov/library/readingroom/docs/CIA-RDP96-00788R001900760001-9.pdf.

The existence of remote viewing, by itself, blows up the materialist paradigm and demonstrates that consciousness is more than the brain.

Shared-Death Experiences

According to NDE pioneer Raymond Moody, and his book titled *Glimpse of Eternity*, a loved one or family member may experience the death process alongside the dying person. This experience may include seeing the tunnel to another world open, encountering the presence or visual appearance of deceased people, or even a sensation of leaving the body. Such anomalies may even be witnessed by hospital and nursing staff.

When Moody began this research, he once again changed the face of afterlife studies by adding a whole new layer of afterlife phenomena, and a new subject grounded in objectivity and verifiable documentation. I suggest picking up a copy of his book to learn more.

Reincarnation Research

This is another topic too vast to understand within a couple of paragraphs, so I suggest if you're interested to launch into a full analysis of the subject beginning with the extensive research conducted at the University of Virginia by Professor Ian Stevenson.

The 20+ years of research by Dr. Stevenson included highly detailed evidence supporting this subject, including the verification of birthmarks and pre-birth memories among children who couldn't possibly have access to such knowledge.

I also suggest the following link to an ABC news story about a boy who was born with full memories of a deceased WWII fighter pilot: https://abcnews.go.com/Primetime/story?id=132381&page=1.

Like many other subjects, reincarnation is something also firmly rooted into people's personal experiences. Pre-birth memories are far from uncommon. While I remain skeptical of certain past-life regression phenomena (a lack of protocols, potential client-patient expectation fulfillment) I have no doubt people may experience memories from prior—or perhaps even concurrent—lives.

Spirit Artists

Spirit artistry is fascinating because it becomes extremely hard for skeptics to refute a phenomenon that is demonstrated fully on tape. For instance, there's video documentation of spirit artist Rita Berkowitz entering trance and drawing two different portraits at the same time, one with her left hand and one with her right hand—with her eyes closed.

Meanwhile, psychic artist Luiz Gasperetto has been recorded creating a detailed painting via his toes with his foot placed under a table. Far from unprofessional thrown-together paintings, the end results of blindly using his toes is still high-quality and professional. Gasperetto claims to channel famous deceased painters, and the works are themselves of a caliber of quality reminiscent of the alleged channeled artist, including names like Rembrandt, van Gogh, and others. It would be quite an achievement for a skeptic to explain how even a trained artist of vast talent could create consistent paintings under such conditions

For a detailed list of painting mediums, as well as YouTube footage of their abilities in action, please see the following link: http://www.victorzammit.com/evidence/Painting%20mediums.htm.

Putting Evidence Together

There is so much more that can be explored: psychic detective work, spirit doctors, the cross correspondences, transfiguration mediumship, ghosts / poltergeists and similar subjects, and still much more. This chapter was just a glance—no—a *glance of a glance* to help refresh those reading as we begin to explore more complex areas concerning the afterlife (and beyond.) It literally would take volumes of books, however, to give the afterlife subject justice.

In my first book, I explore several of these subjects in much greater detail. However, to make room for discussing other subjects related to the afterlife—including important subjects like the details of our lives on that side—I must limit the exploration of the evidence in this book. As I always do, I suggest Zammit's site as a good fundamental starting point to learn about the different subjects. For those who are fence-sitters about all of this, it's always important to step back and keep reviewing the evidence until one feels comfortable enough to delve deeper into the rabbit hole.

IV – The Nature of the Afterlife

Trying to Make Sense of the Facts

Once we are primed in the evidence of the afterlife, the next struggle is figuring out what the afterlife is truly like and making sense of reality—objective reality—versus pop cultural interpretations, theories, philosophies, religions, and all types of mental clutter that blocks us from understanding this big, crazy topic.

There is no subject in the world as mired by speculation and misinformation than spiritual worlds or the afterlife. It wasn't until I began studying the best sources of direct spirit communication and contrasted them with my own experiences, that I began to draw more definite answers about the lives and conditions of people in higher densities. Trying to tackle what the afterlife is "really" like is necessary or else all of the evidence listed in the prior chapter becomes a big blob of uncertainties. We see this general ignorance made manifest in pop culture. Consider all the TV ghost hunters who believe they are addressing phantasms or non-corporeal boogeymen as opposed to real, living people in other dimensions (which is more like what the evidence suggests.)

There may be no other way to grasp these topics short of those two crucial factors: direct (and verified) spirit communication, and personal experiences (which is the only way to get past the "knowledge plateau" I spoke of earlier.) Beyond these areas, there exists a library of people making stunning claims. And, so many of these claims are not backed by reputed sources—they are, in essence, speculation that is highly contradictory in nature. And yet, when we delve into reliable channels, the contradictions stop happening—or are at least reduced. Consistent information is a telltale sign that we're closer to the truth.

Many sources of bad information are often created with good intentions but suffer from the arrogance of the human condition to explain everything away in "black / white" thinking or they attempt to be more knowledgeable than everyone else by discovering the "real" answers—only those "real" answers are intermixed with millions of other "real" answers and don't have much value.

As an example, one of my readers recently contacted me feeling troubled after hearing a presentation by Tom Campbell (*My Big TOE.*) Campbell appears to have a few unique ideas about the other side: that *all* deceased people have transcended into realms far beyond who and what they once were—their old consciousness disappears and they are replaced by a type of "VR simulation." This idea seems to be an attempt to reinforce Campbell's famous VR / simulation theory of life. He therefore proposes the deceased loved ones we meet when we die are illusions created by the database of God to provide comfort, but our real loved ones are inaccessible.

However, to make this claim, he needs to account for the endless stories of after death contact or encounters with deceased loved ones during NDEs. Although I've not heard Campbell make the claim, I've heard his supporters propose that the entire astral world must, therefore, be a fabrication also—a big computer simulation trying to dupe us when we die, shortly before we are ushered into a reincarnation cycle or we merge back with Source consciousness, ending our old personalities.

Obviously, the idea that all our loved ones are mental illusions is not a very nice thing to imagine for those of us desiring to see our deceased family and friends in the afterlife. It's also a completely rubbish idea to me. As an out-of-body explorer, I can verify with complete certainty that most of us who transition are still ourselves—and we may stay in astral realms that are not alien to our senses but real, living, breathing continuations of the Earth. There is no Akashic record illusion needed.

Once, quite upset after hearing some of Tom Campbell's ideas, I astral projected that night and struck up a conversation with a flamboyant gentleman with a noticeable lisp who lived on that side (likely in the astral version of West Hollywood which was near my current Earthly residence at the time.)

"Are you real, or just like a computer simulation? How do I know you're a literal person? You could also be in my mind."

The man looked aghast. "You have what I'd call a dandelion heart—so quick to fall apart! It's common for people who have recently crossed over, or anyone who's come here from the Earth plane, to believe these ridiculous things about us. It's just paranoia, that's all it is!"

Another example of a widespread superstition is the internet conspiracy theory that "the Light" is, in fact, a trap created by the archons (groups of powerful, celestial extraterrestrials who siphon the energy from mankind.) So, when someone dies and encounters the "divine light" commonly reported, it must be resisted or else you are thrown into the "reincarnation trap"—forced to return to earth to become another energy battery for the archons to devour.

While this claim seems ridiculous, I also understand a little how it came about. Near-death experiencers on the internet often speak of sudden unyielding devotion to "The Light"—a near obsession that blots out every other goal or experience ("Even the love of a mother for a child pales in comparison to the love of The Light," is something I hear frequently.) Maybe some hear these reports and conclude if "The Light" separates mothers from their children—it isn't something to be trusted. I get why people feel this way. However, I remind myself that these ideas brought back from NDErs are just people's subjective interpretations. Even someone who had an NDE isn't necessarily a paragon of wisdom afterward. For instance, I've heard people who've experiences NDEs claim the Light gobbles all of us up into "permanent bliss" that never ends. I don't believe either interpretation (the Light is evil or the Light gobbles us up) is true. These are both examples of afterlife superstition.

In my view, pessimistic models of the afterlife (whether Tom's idea that deceased loved ones are illusions or that the Light is going to eat / force us to reincarnate) are also related to deep-seeded ideas of death being a finality or that the individual, harkening back to materialistic beliefs, is still somehow lost (the idea that death is "the end" is deeply rooted.) These odd accounts have created a veritable minefield of dubious sources that can potentially confuse a person at best—or at worst ruin their hopes. I've coined the term **fatalistic spirituality** to refer to spiritual philosophies that are ultimately hollow and promote an end-result no better than materialistic oblivion.

Death, at least for those "regular folk" I've spoken to, can be as simple as one moment being where you are—dying—and the next moment being brought out of your body, still solid and "normal"—and taken to a new world surrounded by friends and family. They wouldn't know anything about these out-there claims, and they certainly laugh at the idea their worlds are fake and their personalities illusions!

Immediate Differences and Similarities in the Next Density

When I first began leaving my body, I felt exuberant as I discovered this apparent normality. Similar to a depiction from the 2016 film "Doctor Strange"—I'd find myself casually relaxing in my astral body as my Earth body slept. At a certain point, I'd grow tired of listening to my body snore, and decide it was time to go back. As uneventful as these experiences were, they were the most transformative. It gave me opportunities to observe my astral body and perform experiments.

Natural questions would arise like, "If I'm in an etheric body, do I have taste buds in my mouth?" and so I would place my fingers into my mouth and suck on them. I discovered both saliva and taste (although this experiment was a bit gross—it was acceptable in the name of science.)

Does my astral body have genitalia? The answer was yes. Would I feel pain if I hit my hands together in karate chop motions? The answer was yes. And on and on my experiments continued until I could only conclude that the astral body is a replica of the Earth body.

However, despite the replicated nature, some elements—perhaps cosmic laws about the nature of the astral body—appeared unchangeable.

Notably was a change of interior physiology. It took numerous bedroom excursions before I realized one important difference—I wasn't breathing. If I made a conscious effort to breathe, I could. However, when in a relaxed state of mind, as our bodies normally breathe in an automatic fashion our astral bodies do not—there is no need for breath to sustain it.

A second notable difference involved communication. Although I could seemingly speak if I wanted to, as my experiences evolved and I began having encounters with other inhabitants of this dimension, I would find that communication was a mixture of English "verbal" communication and telepathic mental exchanges.

This style of telepathic exchange is both familiar and easy to perform, and also quite alien to the uninitiated. Imagine for a moment that you wish to tell your roommate who lives upstairs that you picked up the mail. You would not have to shout from the bottom floor or hike upstairs to find him. Instead, you could simply focus on his existence for a split second and *think* to him the message. Potentially the entire block of information can be "uploaded" to the recipient as a single thought.

At the same time, this style of communication has differences that are still hard for us to fully understand in our current forms. What I discovered was that our thoughts, as they exist currently, are *muted.* In other words, the voice in our heads is more a silent whisper. When we communicate telepathically, the whisper becomes "loud" and audible as if we were speaking normally using our vocal cords. As a result, we may not realize we're communicating via this new method at first—it may "sound" like we are speaking as we normally do. It's only upon more careful consideration that one realizes their lips were not moving. The telepathy is also apparent when the information comes in an entire chunk of data as I mentioned before.

Even if a voice sounds right next to you, it's clearly telepathy when the voice is projected across a distance In one experience, a woman in an astral neighborhood greeted me from about a block away. As we walked together through the neighborhood, her voice was no less audible as she walked alongside me—no different from when she spoke to me from a distance. During our walk, our lips did not move. The communication arose as a simple matter of her detecting my consciousness and sending me messages (she was guiding me to a friend's house—a doctor—because she thought I was acting extremely peculiar.)

This rudimentary telepathic communication also seems to be the baseline method, and our minds can advance to even higher techniques. During my first encounter with an "advanced" (higher density) spirit human, our communication consisted of both telepathic-verbal communication and the exchange of mental imagery to "illustrate" the words. However, "exchange" may be an improper word as it was a one-sided affair; I lacked the acumen to transfer images back to him. This illustrates the notion that not every skill in higher density planes is immediately fulfilled without practice.

Regarding Manifesting and Materializing Objects

As the mind obtains greater power over physical reality, it can also begin to manipulate and shape objects. There are countless sources of information about this phenomenon, but I'll cite an old and detailed text to explain it concisely: *Autobiography of a Yogi* by Paramahansa Yogananda. One of the original, greatest astral travelers of the 20th century, Yogananda recounts meeting with his guru from a higher, more exalted astral (afterlife) realm. Many details are revealed by this guru as he explains:

> "Every astral object is manifested primarily by the will of God, and partially by the will-call of astral beings. They possess the power of modifying or enhancing the grace and form of anything already created by the Lord. He has given His astral children the freedom and privilege of changing or improving at will the astral cosmos. On earth a solid must

be transformed into liquid or other form through natural or chemical processes, but astral solids are changed into astral liquids, gases, or energy solely and instantly by the will of the inhabitants." (*Autobiography of a Yogi – Chapter 43)*

As realms become less dense (more exalted or of a finer dimensional quality) so the mind and physicality blend to a greater degree. In practical terms, it becomes easier to shape and modify physics using thoughts. On this realm we currently exist in, it may be possible to perform feeble attempts at telekinesis, but in the realm that Yogananda's guru described, you can quickly materialize, de-materialize or alter objects around you.

In *Life in the World Unseen* the communicator, Monsieur Hugh Benson, describes a type of exchange economy that occurs as a result of the natural ability to manifest objects. Benson points out that not every item conjured is of a perfect quality, as it depends largely on the passion and knowledge of the creator. As a result, a person with exquisite knowledge of jewelry may create a brooch of greater quality than a layperson; and would thus be a more "valuable" object. For this same reason, the expertise of architects or engineers is still required to build certain structures, even if steps are reduced through the manifestation process. Interestingly, it can be argued that we exist currently in the same condition. In this way, although it requires time and physical effort to produce objects, they're ultimately manifestations of our mind and talent. The difference is that in our realm to turn thought into physical reality, we must go through the arduous effort of using our hands to sculpt or build.

This is not to say this is the sole form of construction, and that the "old fashioned" techniques do not also exist or have merit. During the Leslie Flint seances, a great variety of communicators from the astral side spoke for decades through a crude ectoplasmic voice box to sitters. As is so often the case, the information presented was highly consistent with all other areas of afterlife research, including the specific details of the conditions of their world. Many reported the commonality of manifesting and materializing objects, although it's never described as an ability that interferes with nor replaces the natural world. A working-class Englishman who passed on, identifying himself as George Harris, appeared through a Flint séance in the 1960s and described how buildings in his realm are created using bricks, and the bricks were likely made in kilns. In his mind, there was no severe difference between the Earth's physics and his, and it would seem he preferred more "Earthly" methods, even turning his nose up at the conjuration practiced on higher realms (which he felt was performed with less love and care.) Below is part of the transcript of this conversation (courtesy the Leslie Flint Trust):

> "I very interested in building and I like my job. But here it's like a different... We do build... We do build with materials and things that are real and solid and all that but... Of course you don't do it for money. You don't do it for... you know, because you've got to do it. You do it because you like doing it, because you get pleasure and happiness out of it. Course, I've been told by some of the people that where I am it's very sort of um... Well, I suppose you'd call it, you know, 'early stages' you know. That's why we have to build, as you say, you know. But they do say, you know, on them higher planes as they call it that everything's created by thought. Well! I suppose it is. I don't know. Can't make 'ead or tail of it, myself. Where I am it's as real as real can be. You have materials and you work with materials. You create, as you say, with materials. Oh, I've seen practically a replica of, oh, many things which were common on your side. People don't just sort of sit and think about something and there it is. Wouldn't be much pleasure in that. I should think that's a lousy way of carrying on, myself. I think unless you have to make some effort towards it and build for it and work for it... After all that's the only real pleasure and happiness, I think, as far as I can see is... is... being, you know, sort of creative, you know; doing it with your own... you know... effort like. And all this business they talk about these high places I've heard them like talk about... make... I don't know. Can't cotton on to that at all."

I like to highlight this transcript because it shows how it's arbitrary to claim a higher density realm is "better" than a lower density. Our friend George Harris is not attracted to the practice of building matter via thought. He likes to get his hands dirty, use solid stuff—bricks and mortar—and make every inch by hand to put as much love into the work as possible. And who can blame him? I'm not a builder, but I feel exactly the same way. It provides me a lot of relief to know such practices are still available and no one is pigeon-holed into one type of realm.

My mom even jokingly told me once that materialized food wasn't as good as places that really cook it. This revelation told me a lot about the nature of "more physical" versus "less physical" and how it's utterly pointless trying to argue one is better than the other (in particular, so many I talk to who argue that a more physical realm must be some terrible punishment according to Spiritualist doctrine. No. It's all based on our preferences. This concept is not controversial among people actually in the afterlife who enjoy all types of experiences and realms.)

In my own experiences, I've found myself in realms perhaps slightly lower density than those described by Yogananda's guru, or even the more pastoral worlds described by Flint's communicators. In the "Second Earth" I've explored, the manifestations of the mind are subtle, and the world is even more physical—albeit still far less dense than our current dimension.

Despite my best efforts, I've never been able to materialize an object or change matter too greatly. However, I have been able to move and levitate objects (similar to *The Force* from Star Wars, I suppose.) I've also levitated from the ground and been able to fly to an extent, which actually impressed a few onlookers—indicating these mental abilities are not always practiced in the astral Earth realms—which may explain why I see peoples still driving automobiles (I've been in a taxi before in the astral Los Angeles, which is—by the way—a much prettier city than our density's LA. It looks almost European-style.)

The subconscious mind also seems to have a greater physical effect on the environment. For instance, a person's mood can be reflected in their outer appearance—and a dark or unhappy mood seems to age a person—while a bright and happy mood physically creates a luminous effect around a person (and enhances their natural beauty.) This interesting phenomenon has been observed by me many times, and it was described in fuller detail in Jurgen Ziewe's *Multidimensional Man.*

After my mom passed away, I was given a tour of an astral hospital for new arrivals who died in particularly difficult ways and required care (my mom included.) In this hospital, it was brought to my attention that traumatic thoughts in the minds of the patients would sometimes manifest physical objects around them; requiring the patients to be placed in isolated care lest their psychological effects pose a threat to others around them. As an example, you could imagine a victim of a fire so traumatized by the experience that they begin manifesting flames as the memories remain so embedded into the psyche. Such a situation would require counseling and healing to help lingering traumas from the Earth-density to be fully eradicated.

In summary, in higher density realms thoughts have the power to become things. As explained by Yogananda's guru, the molecular composition of matter on that side (sometimes called lifetrons—by various sources) is flexible to thought in far greater ways than here. And so, with enough concentration, you can finally create that Bentley—given you're already a heck of a skilled car mechanic and you know what you're building. However, the difficulty of accomplishing such a feat depends on the density-level of your natural environment. Astral earth-like conditions pose more difficulties; while levels above that realm are easier and easier to manipulate via thoughts. Whichever density you live on is up to a combination of personal preference and mental ability to reach that particular plane—and there's no shame whatsoever in those like George Harris who find physical realms to be more creative and with greater opportunities than thought-responsive environments.

(As an addendum, I'd like to point out in Jurgen Ziewe's *Multidimensional Man* he recounts a story of a car being materialized straight from the Akashic, and even without prior mechanical skills, it had a fully working V8 engine after the hood was popped. So, it's debatable whether mechanical knowledge is always needed to "summon" an object.)

The Realms of the Multiverse

It's a mistake to assume the next density is pure energy, dream-like, formless, or even the clichéd term "non-physical." It may also be a mistake to assume that when we speak of realms being "created" by collective thought that they exist beyond the bounds of nature or a general structure of a universe (as occurs here.) Rather, it's my own personal hypothesis that everything exists *altogether* in the vastness of the cosmos. Our planet has gradients of "afterlife" dimensions, and those dwelling astrally in fact still exist on the "planet Earth" in a certain form. Perhaps even planets uninhabitable on our frequency bear life on parallel frequencies.

In other words, the space you occupy right now has an astral gradient that may look very similar. You can lay down, go "out-of-body" and become aware of the astral density gradient around you, leading to an astral projection experience.

This astral gradient, within the astral earth, is just one layer in a very big cake. This layer, itself the size of a planet and populated by millions (if not billions) is still just one layer. By focusing your consciousness and raising your vibration, it's possible to go a layer upward to an even "higher density" version that's even more thought-responsive. You're still on a particular planet, in a particular location, but now the layer has changed yet again. The building you were in may or may not still exist in this location—and if it does, it may become more beautiful looking if you are entering a higher density domain. These higher planes become more rarified, and the environment begins to resonate closely to us. We don't merely see a beautiful scene of nature (like a forest) but we feel the trees, the earth, etc. These "heavenly" realms are as much about the aesthetic appearance as the incomparably higher levels of consciousness we possess when inhabiting such places, allowing us to enjoy and resonate with every detail in a way that must be experienced to understand. Such higher layers, corresponding to our consciousness, also means we are aligned to the state of consciousness known as our "higher self" and thus our soul collectives. Although we are still our same individual selves, as we move to the greater astral realms, we are also aware of a massive interconnected chain of souls that form who we really are, in addition to awareness of countless lives we've possessed throughout our elemental existences.

Now, as we ascend to a new plane, there will be a new population of different people inhabiting this environment. Although layers are invisible to each other, the interaction between people or the environment on different layers is the explanation behind "ghostly" phenomena—one layer bleeding into the next.

A layer may go above even "heavenly" environments, slowly becoming more and more alien to our senses. I've only visited Earth-like gradients, but other out-of-body explorers (like Jurgen) have gone up the chain into much "higher" realms that involve greater unified consciousness levels. Eventually, it seems possible to reach realms so thought-responsive there is no difference between thought and manifestation—the composition of such an existence is beyond whatever we may currently imagine.

Sometimes these uppermost gradients are called mental planes, but I believe mental planes may also consist of accessible non-physical states of consciousness that are not so difficult to enter and are commonly experienced by out-of-body explorers. I liken a basic state of mental existence similar to using the Internet. On the web, we have no physical bodies but are interconnected to the entire world around us, allowing a vast potential of communication and exploration. Mental planes are so similar to our Internet it's almost as if the Internet is a clunky version we created to satisfy such a desire. I do believe "advanced" souls spend most of their time in purely mental states but will still sometimes manifest themselves on a physical astral spectrum. Maybe for the purposes of performing a lecture, visiting friends and family who are not connected to such a mental existence, or just enjoying some physical exploration of new places.

Unlike other writers, however, I prescribe no greater importance on the mental planes. Everything is based upon preference and context. Deciding to dwell entirely on a mental spectrum and avoid the astral-physical realms seems unrealistic. There are concepts inhabitants of mental planes feel they *must* learn from physical existences in both our Earth-level and the Earth-like astral levels. Likewise, people from our world and astral worlds aspire to enter mental planes because those individuals feel there are experiences they *must* learn from such conditions. And generally speaking, in my experience, an advanced spirit swaps between both state of existence as easily as thinking about it. Any attempt to say "We must all aspire to escape astral and physical conditions and return to the purely mental worlds" is proposing a type of fundamentalist belief. For some reason, Earthlings trying to explore these topics like to pigeon-hole themselves or argue that one thing is so much better than the next thing. It may be our limited psychologies.

For a very long time, spiritual teachers have tried to install this pecking order to existence. The problem with this "order of importance" is people forget that all of us already exist on a higher-consciousness level in these advanced realms (as our so-called higher-selves)—but willingly choose to inhabit "lower" density realms for the purposes of experiences, creativity, adventure, contrast (more negativity is not necessarily *negative*) and so forth. So those authors who dismiss astral and physical realms as "useless" compared to more superior conditions are, to me, immature and naïve about the nature and complexity of reality.

They also forget the vast potential of the astral cosmos. The astral world is not merely people wandering around a few replicated environments of our own Earth. Far from it. The astral domain represents where the majority of all lifeforms dwell. According to reports and theories, it's incredibly vast.

Yogananda's guru explains this in greater detail (*Source: Autobiography of a Yogi)*:

> "There are many astral planets, teeming with astral beings," Master began. "The inhabitants use astral planes, or masses of light, to travel from one planet to another, faster than electricity and radioactive energies."
>
> "The astral universe, made of various subtle vibrations of light and color, is hundreds of times larger than the material cosmos. The entire physical creation hangs like a little solid basket under the huge luminous balloon of the astral sphere. Just as many physical suns and stars roam in space, so there are also countless astral solar and stellar systems. Their planets have astral suns and moons, more beautiful than the physical ones. The astral luminaries resemble the aurora borealis—the sunny astral aurora being more dazzling than the mild-rayed moon-aurora. The astral day and night are longer than those of earth." (*Autobiography of a Yogi*).

Admittedly, these detailed accounts from Yogananda are difficult for a neutral researcher like me to digest. A universe a hundred times larger than ours is a spectacular claim—given our universe contains billions times billions of stars. It means the astral side is unfathomably big.

However, it still makes more sense to me than previous hazy, dream-like descriptions of the astral state where it's implied that every realm is entirely created by thought rather than holding any position in space. The "phantasmagoric" description would imply that there is nothing if one should dig into the ground, and nothing if one should journey upward into space. Instead, it would be a kind of fairy-tale realm enshrouded by mist and not existing on a planet or in the heavens. An enclosed realm locked within people's minds. These ideas have always made me feel uneasy. Yogananda's description liberates this perception. Also, astral residents I've spoken to would find the fairy tale description a bit ridiculous: nobody argues that they're not inhabiting planets in space.

I sometimes default back to something my mom told me twice, on separate highly physical, lucid astral encounters: "*It's quite normal to me here. At night, I go to sleep. I wake up in the morning.*"

Insecurities that the other side is alien to us or our human existences end subside when I remind myself of my own experiences.

The people on the other side I've personally encountered say with certainty they are still human and residing on a planetary system.

The Really Weird Stuff: Time and Multi-Locality

One cannot have an education about life in astral conditions without touching on commonly reported properties of multi-dimensional consciousness. Something that seems to occur on all levels that I've seen—even "lower" astral Earth conditions. For instance: being in multiple places at once or transcending the boundaries of time.

To be honest, this is the area I've struggled with the most. In the afterlife research circles, it's common to hear something that's almost a platitude: "*Time does not exist on the other side.*"

Professor Gary Schwartz, who conducts elaborate experiments related to spirit communication, went on a memorable rant about this at the 2017 Afterlife Symposium in Scottsdale, AZ. To paraphrase, "I hear again and again that time doesn't exist in the afterlife. How is that possible? I am a musician, and music is related to the rhythm of vibrations measured in time. If there is no time, there can be no music, yet we hear about amazing music on the other side. So, how can we say time does not exist?"

So, where does this "no time" concept originate from?

I'd harken the idea back, in part, to the highly influential website *near-death.com*. This website (which itself seems to transcend time as the site design is identical to how it looked in 1999) compiled a great deal of quotes from near-death experience survivors in an attempt to piece together higher concepts. The *Time* page includes quotes from popular NDE accounts, including those of Betty Eadie, Jayne Smith, Kimberly Clark Sharp, and others—and includes the following summary written by the site's author:

> After death when we enter the spirit realm, it feels as though we were there just a moment ago. Our time on earth seems like only a brief instance. Time in the spirit realm does not exist. By getting rid of the illusion of time from our minds, we have the power to expand our consciousness. We will realize that we are already living in timelessness right now. This means a person can remain in heaven for eternity if they desire before deciding whether to return for another earth life. In the spirit realm, if we desire, we can travel

> instantaneously from the beginning of earth history to the end. We have the power to grow forever. We are powerful spiritual beings.[3]

One of the first things I noticed about this paragraph when I first read it probably 15 years ago is the obvious contradiction: How can you exist somewhere "eternally" before deciding to return to Earth life? The very word "before" denotes time and space. One thing occurs *after* the prior thing. A sequential order of events. So, by definition, you cannot be in one state "eternally" and then move into another state. Something is obviously lost in translation.

Probably where people are going awry is interpreting this information to mean, quite literally: *There is no time so existence is a giant mash of everything happening at once, incomprehensible by us and a giant chaos dimension.*

It's interesting when I pick apart afterlife views rationally; and I hear these beliefs literally fleshed out. It makes me realize that a lot of people repeat information without spending much time to think about what they're saying.

This is not to say, however, that the "time" issue is irrelevant. In fact, consistent afterlife data from numerous sources report either a lack of "time" perception, a higher perception, or a different style of "time and space" than we are used to. In fact, in my astral experiences, one of the early things my mom told me was, quote, "There's no time here anymore like we're used to!"

That statement, however, is not the same as "time doesn't exist." In my own experiences in the astral state, **one event still precedes the next event**. If I put a piece of chocolate in my mouth and eat it, the chocolate existed in a non-eaten state, an action is implemented whereby it's eaten, becomes mush, and is swallowed (then I assume is converted directly to energy, or whatever becomes of digestibles in the astral body.) So there was a clear *before* and *after* series of events. By its simplest definition this is the existence *time.*

What may be radically different, however, is our perception of time and how we relate to it.

A big factor is the sensation of memory. In our lives here, memories that are older appear "distant." Have you ever considered *why* a memory is distant? Somehow, this relates to neurology. A neurologist may say the synaptic connections are "old and rusty" and so memories from when we're three-years-old are going to feel extremely hazy and distant compared to memories of a movie we saw yesterday.

If we remove neurological limitations, memory would be a very different experience. If our astral brains function perfectly (which I presume they do) then a memory from three-years-old will be crystal clear like with any other memory.

Next, we toss into the mix accounts of the so-called Akashic record, where we can mentally attune ourselves to any event in history and potentially even relive it. So, a memory from eons ago would not only be crystal clear, but we could effectively enter a trance and place ourselves back in that state, reliving that moment as solidly as a normal experience.

A third factor is then the lack of entropy. In our world, a castle from 1,500 years ago will be little more than a foundation and some ruins. On the other side, such a castle may exist perpetually with no reason to assume it will ever fall apart.

When we place these three factors together it's easy to imagine that existence no longer feels like an endless path, leaving prior events behind in the shadow, linked together by fading memories and impermanence. The alternative sensation is permanence among all events. Did you have a fun night out doing whatever things we do on the astral dimension? This memory is now a crystal-clear episode that's permanently recorded into the substrate of reality, which can be replayed or simply remembered and imagined at any moment.

There are also reports that this Akashic effect of replaying prior events can be taken a step further, involving literal time travel and the ability to reconnect with events from history, relive them, and take them into new directions via the creation of a parallel timeline.

All of this taken as a whole means that our perception of reality is quite different, and certainly not for the negative. Our Earthly perception would appear very morose by comparison, where moments fade away, and we are bound by what could be described as *linear* time—forced to go along on a singular path, leaving behind past experiences as fading memories doomed to be lost. An alternative to this doesn't so bad, does it?

Bi-Location

Another discovery I made was that it's possible on other planes to exist in multiple places at once.

When I first experienced this, the thought came to mind of my short-attention-span habits where I browse the Internet with multiple tabs open at once. Similarly, I've had astral projection experiences where I appear to be having concurrent experiences and pressing a mental "alt + tab" to switch between them.

Subsequently, I had a conversation with my mom about this, and she explained two things to me: "Yes, we bilocate to multiple places at once and it's near impossible for people from Earth to comprehend this" and "There are currently four versions of me at once." Because I'd experienced a taste of this first-hand, it wasn't entirely outside of my ability to comprehend it.

I have also wondered if this ability has any limit. It may explain why so many near-death experiencers report meeting Jesus. If these reports are true, and it really is Jesus, how can Jesus be in so many places at once? Well, via multi-dimensionality, maybe there's hundreds, thousands or even millions of versions of the same consciousness operating in many spaces at one time.

When little kids ask how Santa Clause can visit every home in the same night, we reply "magic." Well, maybe multidimensional physics is the "magic" we'd be referring to.

What Do People Do All Day in the Afterlife?

I cannot finish this chapter without addressing, at least in some way, the topic of lifestyle. Because among all New Agey spiritual books, it's a topic sorely missing, yet distinctly human. How many books with the moniker of "Light" (Going to the Light, Returning to the Light, Embraced by the Light, the Light this, the Light that,) address the obvious issue of what day-to-day life is like on the other side?

The lack of information is sometimes steamrolled over by platitudes ("We all exist happily in the light of God,") or misrepresented concepts ("Time does not exist, so it doesn't matter what we do, we are doing everything at once") that leave students of metaphysics boggled, perplexed, angry and sometimes jaded against the afterlife subject altogether.

Fortunately, this bad information is more of a reflection of our own shortcomings of comprehension. I don't believe for a moment that the other side is devoid of lifestyle and existence. Including, but not limited to, the human experience.

It's tempting to believe the human experience ends at death. In fact, some people probably desire this outcome—especially people who have not had particularly pleasant human experiences. This *fatalistic spirituality* is the likely reason behind the pushback I receive against my research into human and Earth-like afterlife worlds: "I don't want to be a human again, I want to just get away from it all."

This feeling is the result of trauma. Lives of depression, abuse, and hardship bring about a jaded perspective about human life, and polarity in regard to ideas of the hereafter: a need to create an existence as alien as possible by comparison to our hardships on this life.

But is this the most rational perspective? What I've discovered is the human existence, on this plane, is…if nothing else, a bad imitation of how it's meant to be. The human existence could be a very beautiful thing: consider all of the best elements of your life, including time spent in your youth, or having a family, or that great vacation you took to Fiji. In between the things we find terrible: jobs we dislike, freaking out if that lump is cancer, the grief when people die, there's a lot of amazing elements to life on Earth. In the astral Earth, those amazing elements are magnified and supremely enjoyable while most of the very sour elements are minimized or eliminated entirely.

This is not to say the astral Earth is just roses and daisies all the time. The "perpetual happiness" notion is one of the biggest misconceptions I've personally discovered, which is an idea I blame solely on Christianity—the idea of "heaven" where all problems and woes are eliminated. Far from it, the nature of the human mind will become dissatisfied at times. This dissatisfaction is a catalyst for growth and change. I've never met in an astral experience people with painted smiles, existing in perpetual joy like some never-ending drug trip. Instead one will discover all manner of characters, personalities, and moods—including negative situations.

I'm always curious why people would desire it any other way. I am reminded of the Toby Maguire / Reese Witherspoon movie "Pleasantville" where the protagonists enter an obviously astral replication of a favorite 1950s "Leave it to Beaver" style TV show, likely created by inhabitants desiring an escape from any semblance of negativity. This, of course, created a "black and white" realm of extreme predictability and a fear of emotions. While the residents were "happy" it was a kind of fear-based happiness with limited growth, a stifling of potential and a background sense of morbidity. The protagonists, of course, help the populace rediscover emotion and "color"—sometimes involving moods like anger—helping them to escape the confines of their strange astral demiplane.

Despite the clear warnings from this movie, that I assume most people at this point have watched, people still desire Pleasantville-style situations in the afterlife. Meanwhile, artists, poets, writers, filmmakers and other creative types loathe the idea of the gradient of color being removed and being in a situation where emotions on the other end of the spectrum are forbidden.

The astral Earth I've experienced, however, is far from a Pleasantville-existence. And this could be why I am drawn to it more than idyllic "Summerland" type situations reported by other astral explorers or encountered in some near-death experiences. Contained within the astral Earth are the best, adventurous elements of our lives here—while still possessing the "nitty gritty" elements. From hotels and street markets, to strip clubs and biker bars, I've encountered almost everything we find in this world—with major differences being much of the populace is aware they're "dead"—and there are occasional surprising manifestations of "magical" mental power like teleportation, thought-forms, and a visitor or two who knows how to fly.

For this reason, at least in the astral Earth environment, we can answer the question of lifestyle by simply looking around this world. What we see around us here still exists over there, although with certain industries that are markedly different upon closer examination. For instance, we may not find the existence of restrooms for the reason that astral biology doesn't require our physical-realm waste-removal processes. I have also been told there are fewer mirrors as most people can learn to displace their consciousness and look at themselves from any angle. Further, aging and the threat of permanent death is no longer an issue—we can rule out a life insurance industry and nursing homes.

We'll also find a great emphasis on fun, fantasy-fulfillment, and leisure. As an example, in 2017 I found myself in astral London as a tourist. I noticed a lot of emphasis in the city on Harry Potter-culture and magic. I attended a magic workshop that involved the use of spell-casting via magic wands. This is one small example of the type of activity that would be impossible on this side due to our rigid physics. And of course, artistic desire, fantasy-fulfilment and "fandom" plays a big role in the creation of such places. I daresay when most "geeks" die and find themselves in this environment, their first order of business is to recreate things that were never possible in this world. I can only imagine what astral Tokyo is like.

From a sociological perspective, we'll, of course, find differences in behavior among residents. I often note that the astral Earth is like a giant party by comparison to here, and that's a simplistic albeit accurate perspective. There are fewer reasons for people to take anything very seriously,

Astral Experiences: A Violent Prank on the Astral Earth

Is the astral Earth an entirely safe place? Free of care or concern? This is tempting to believe at first, but some experiences hint otherwise.

One afternoon on a street corner of astral Phoenix (there are astral equivalents of all locations from our world,) I was standing near a crosswalk when I noticed a smirking woman in a burgundy dress. Unsure of what she was doing, I noticed her kneeling down and tending to small robotic insects that I assumed were some kind of toy.

In fact, she was releasing these automatons on the unsuspecting populace. These large electronic ants would chase pedestrians, violently biting at them—leaving people running and screaming.

Out of curiosity, I decided to grab one and teleport back to my astral home to inspect it. This was a huge mistake. The exact nature of these insects went far beyond mere wind-up toys to harass people. They were designed to create as much havoc as possible.

For instance, an attempt to trap the creature caused it to activate a replication technique where it would copy itself. An attempt to damage it physically resulted in the creature "evolving" to a more powerful version.

After the experience, a friend on the astral remarked, "If just one of those things were released on the Earth plane, it'd have taken a small army to stop." This also demonstrated the importance of security / law enforcement in rowdy parts of the astral.

which means, generally speaking, the population is much more laid-back. My personal observation is that there's a sense of open-ended socialization and trust. In a neighborhood, it's not particularly unusual to walk into somebody's house and visit them. If you're in a hotel or apartment, you'll find many doors open with people listening to music, drinking, and essentially "partying"—and they're generally more than happy to bring in completely "random" visitors to join the fun. I find this sense of socialization almost anywhere I go.

This behavior makes sense when you consider how a sense of threat and danger is reduced by either a lack of death or a transformation of what death means. One thing I've not discovered is the possible consequences of physical destruction—can a person be a victim of violence on the astral Earth? Due to the presence I've seen of both security and law enforcement, and having once been the victim of a violent "prank" on a street corner (see the side box above for more info,) my sense is that yes—damage can be inflicted upon others. However, what I believe is removed is long-term consequences: for instance, the permanent physical destruction of the bodily vessel. Physical pain can be inflicted, as can violence, and thus regions must still be moderated or governed, but no one can be permanently eliminated through physical violence as we experience here.

Further, I would assume on "higher" planes where the frequency is based more on love, these types of issues are not apparent. (Of course, for the sake of adventure and storytelling I prefer the gritter parts of the afterlife—even if that means there's a threat from less than savory characters.)

In Conclusion

You may have found this chapter very surprising, if not hard to fathom, and my descriptions have angered more than a few people who insist the astral world MUST be nothing else but fluffy bunnies, fairies and unicorns. And certainly, I am sure unicorns and every other manner of fantastical creature can and does exist on that side—but the experiences of most astral travelers (I am one voice among millions) will testify to the full breadth of the spectrum of that side. This is why it's important to leave most preconceived ideas at the door and understand the nature of the so-called "afterlife" (the greater multiverse) is that everything we can imagine, exists. And, that includes not only a perpetuation of the human experience (no, we do not all become merely orbs of light floating around) but the same shortcomings among the human population that exists here (such as a desire to release nasty robotic insects on people for laughs.)

At the same time, this doesn't rebut your favorite descriptions from your favorite authors. There are many different realms. The places I hang around represent a realm where a majority of human inhabitants go—especially those attached to Earthly existence. Perhaps you're more interested in the realm described by famous NDEr Dr. Eben Alexander where he rode on the back of a giant butterfly through a pristine forest. Or maybe you want to experience the "The Light"—the phenomenon where some entity (presumably our higher self representing "God," but who can say?) envelopes you in blissful light and love, and you just remain in that state forevermore (until you get tired of it, I assume.) Maybe that's what some souls legitimately want. Some people authentically are only "visiting" this realm and want to return to a primordial state of existence, and I can't judge those who desire to disappear into this type of realm. The notion has attracted many followers who resonate with this perspective. It just doesn't resonate to me (and hopefully it never will.)

Nonetheless, the fact remains that the "afterlife" is an extremely limited terminology for the multiverse that extends beyond this one single, rather ridiculous little realm. This world around you right now is not the full story. Many realms exist. And in those realms, this fact of the existence of a multiverse is common knowledge. **We are the weirdos—the troglodytes who haven't evolved to understand the true science and the true physics**. Ask people on the astral about our civilization, and they'll shake their heads—more than relieved they've gotten away from the ignorance and bizarre nature of the Earth-plane. Perhaps, however, with education and diligence, we can begin to learn from our brothers and sisters in our closest astral neighborhood and begin to learn about the true nature of reality—catching up with the knowledge that everyone else—across the spectrum of countless universes—understand as common knowledge.

Why is it we are so ignorant? This is a question I'll leave for a future discussion.

V – The Secret of Astral Projection

In this short chapter, I want to take a moment to touch on the most surprising personal revelation about "the other side" which, in my opinion, takes the subject to a new level—beyond our current understanding of the afterlife and in an unexplored territory: how "astral projection" really seems to occur.

To help understand the concept of astral co-existence, I'll turn to William Murray (author of *Love After Life*[4]) who has maintained a relationship with his wife, Irene, after her passing. William, more than anyone I know, has been committed to building a bridge to the other side. Often this has been through meditation and guided visualizations, but things began to take a turn. In a post on Facebook dated the 20th of July, 2018, Murray made an announcement:

> For the past year, ever since my wife and soul-mate, Irene, crossed over, I've been trying to achieve a full transdimensional interaction with her - fully sensory, fully real. We've accomplished a lot of contact and good interaction in the past year, but it's always been the goal for full, 100% real visitation in some form.
>
> Early this morning I laid down for one of our usual "transdimensional" efforts, where I begin with a prayer, affirmations and visualizing her with me. What happened next has never happened before. While we were having a "visualized" conversation, while I was fully conscious and aware, I transitioned to being somewhere else.
>
> Instead of being in bed, I was sitting on a couch in a room in a different house. Irene was sitting on the couch with me, and our conversation was the same - a seamless transition. It looked, sounded and felt 100% real. No "dream-like" or imaginary quality to it whatsoever.
>
> The transition felt so normal and natural, it didn't even register for a few minutes. Then I realized everything around me was real. I realized I was actually seeing and hearing her, actually talking and interacting. I just watched and listened as she was talking about the kids and other things, and walked around the room doing other things during part of the conversation.
>
> When she paused, I said, "Hey, you know what's great?" She looked at me quizzically. "We're having a completely new

> conversation!" I spread my arms out with a knowing and happy smile on my face.
>
> A look, with a big smile, came across her face, as if realizing that I was actually, consciously there with her - fully. (This made me think later about how Cyrus Kirkpatrick has commented that, to people in the astral, he looks and acts as if he's not fully, consciously "there" when he is focused "here", in his waking state - if I remember that right, Cyrus.) She immediately came over and wrapped me up and gave me a big, long, hard, passionate kiss. I could feel two things - that I was transitioning back to my body in bed, and that she was kissing me so hard because she wanted me to know, for sure, that it was really her, and that it was **real**.
>
> I didn't "wake up" because I never lost consciousness - I just became aware of still lying in my bed, and I could still feel her lips on mine.
>
> So, all our work and effort has paid off - we actually did it! To tell you the truth, I never really believed it would happen, but I was never going to stop trying. I NEVER would have been able to do this without all the afterlife information, resources and support I had access to when Irene first crossed over and since. To Victor Zammit, Wendy Zammit, Susanne Wilson, Cyrus Kirkpatrick, Jurgen Ziewe and everyone else working on getting this information out - Thank you SO much! Irene and I greatly appreciate it and it has made ALL the difference! We are so happy and excited!
>
> For all of you who are trying to regain or increase contact with loved ones who have crossed over, all I can say is - just keep trying, don't lose hope or faith!

What William describes is classic astral projection. He also discovered the elusive revelation that some astral practitioners (myself included) have arrived at—that beyond the out-of-body experiences in one's bedroom, when a person "warps" into an environment on the astral side—full of faces staring back at you—you're entering into a parallel version of your life. A secondary version of you existing independently on the other side. This concept dovetails, of course, with the bilocal nature of life in the afterlife (as explained in the prior chapter.) To summarize: some of us are living here and there at the same time.

This idea adds a new dimension (figuratively and literally) to what astral projection is. Rather than imagining "leaving" the body, it could be considered a period of "merging" with another version of yourself. Temporarily your mind, the one limited by the parameters of the brain, reconnects with your astral "double."

In early astral projection experiences, in a replica of my home, I realized I was looking at evidence of a second version of "me" (who is really the "only" version of me, but our minds have been displaced.) There were dressers full of clothes and various other belongings. As I sorted through all these possessions, I could try and piece together clues about what this other life consists of. A bustling, dynamic life that, while intimately connected to me, also remains almost entirely hidden from my conscious Earth-plane life, with cherished memories locked away so long as my consciousness is trapped in the Earth body. As I browsed the evidence of my other life, I couldn't help but get emotional. Soon, the experience ended, I awoke in my Earth body, with my consciousness again displaced between my two separate lives.

Implications

The clearest implication is an extremely oddball phenomenon that, for lack of better terminology, I call "Earth possession."

Imagine for a moment you are having a grand old time on the astral Earth (or just "the Earth." On the other side, they would simply call the astral version of Chicago as "Chicago"—nobody uses terms like "astral" except for us and our Earth-plane sensibilities, but I digress.) You are on a porch enjoying your fourth glass of iced tea (easy to indulge when you don't have to urinate) with some neighbors when suddenly your Earth-based incarnation decides to start astral projecting. You spit out your tea, stare at your neighbors bug-eyed, and declare "OH MY GOD! I'M OUT OF MY BODY!"

Your neighbors react with a smirk and a laugh. But they know to be gentle because they understand some of these facts of life that we do not. Namely, that people's consciousnesses are often split apart into different realms. In this case, an incarnation in a lower realm may become aware of its higher counterpart, causing a temporary lapse of awareness, with both minds converging together and memories perhaps being swapped in favor of Earth-plane thoughts.

"Are you OK, Jim?" (Presuming your name is Jim) one of the neighbors asks you (telepathically, of course.)

"Ugh," you rub your head. "Sorry about that. I decided to reincarnate, and so I have a version of myself living on the Earth plane. Sometimes he gets cocky, and our minds blend together. I think they call it astral projection."

"Don't worry about it, Jim. In fact, my incarnation is really a reincarnation originating from where an even higher version of me exists, and sometimes I project to that level and do the same thing to that persona!"

(That dialogue was fictitious and does not represent anything but hypothesis.)

As strange as this scenario may seem, I do believe there is truth to it because in all astral experiences where I seemingly appear amidst a pre-existing situation, I am faced by people aware that I am astral projecting and "possessing" the body of their friend or family member.

For example, one time I had an astral experience in a rather lavish hotel in the downtown area of a city. A gentleman was with me who offered a

Astral Experiences: Waking Up Astrally

As discussed previously, while some OBEs involve directly pushing up out of your body, others involve "merging" your consciousness with an existing, parallel life on the astral side.

When this happens, it's like I suddenly have a conscious snapshot of my parallel life. I may "wake up" in my bed. Only, it's my bed on the other side. It can be jarring, because the experience is always real and normal like it is here. I may get up, drink a glass of water, and explore my bedroom a bit until I return to my other Earthly bedroom.

I may find myself in foreign environments—hotel rooms, hostel rooms, apartments, or some luxurious castle I am spending the night at. During periods when going OOB was prolific, going to sleep would mean never knowing what type of bed I would reawaken in.

To those wondering, bedrooms are just like here. There is no difference, albeit bathrooms may contain a sink and washroom but no toilet. On the astral plane, food is processed and absorbed directly as energy. No waste disposal is necessary and parts of the body become inert.

chuckle as he said, "Whenever you go on these spells Cyrus, you don't even remember who I am, your best friend!"

Another example occurred when I asked my mom the following:

"When I come to you on your side, after the experience ends for me do I just poof—disappear like some character on Bewitched?"

"No," she responded, "in fact you stay right where you are."

One time I astral projected in the middle of having sex. I couldn't help but think maybe I was ruining the experience a bit for my other self—especially after I announced to her loudly "I'm astral projecting!"

In summary, **many of us exist simultaneously on the astral plane. Therefore, astral projection is actually the convergence of our Earthly and astral minds. Temporarily, we are a whole entity again.**

So Why Do We Meet Deceased Loved Ones?

And now we arrive at an inevitable philosophical roadblock: if we exist as these parallel selves, why then do we encounter our loved ones to greet us after we die? As the stories go, they often arrive in a kind of tunnel accompanied by the perception of heavenly light as our minds adjust to a higher vibration. But why? Shouldn't we just reacclimate immediately to our parallel lives if we reacquire full memories?

This is certainly a paradox and one I haven't quite figured out. Shouldn't experiences like NDEs involve immediately remembering your life on the other side without any fuss or difficulty? Why do people appearing in astral conditions feel like they've "discovered" it for the first time? Why is this different from OBEs? Why would deceased loved ones appear to greet you?

The first possibility I can think of is that **not everyone has a parallel life on the other side**. Perhaps the majority of people do not, and as a result, a majority of people who die must be greeted when they cross over and must acclimate to the afterlife. A person living on the astral who has reincarnated (has divided a portion of their consciousness to exist simultaneously on the Earth-plane) will simply rejoin with their greater self upon death on the Earth plane (I would fall into this category.)

A second possibility is that **the fractured consciousness does not reunite with its old self or it takes considerable time**. This is a scarier thought because it suggests the life I lead on the astral, of which

I sometimes regain memories about, would be severed from my consciousness and the "Earth Cyrus" would now be the commanding consciousness. My memories would have to be "rediscovered" while friends and family on the astral would have to work with me like an amnesiac patient until I regained information about who I am / was.

My opinion? It's probably more likely the first possibility. What I expect will happen to me when I die is I will appear on the other side, as I have during many OBEs, but I will be highly cognizant of all my Earth memories and that I had just crossed over. I will have full, crystal clear memory of my life on the Earth side, but simultaneous full awareness and memory of my life over there.

What gives me some anxiety is how different my "astral self" could be by comparison to how I am now. Here, I go out-of-body and see evidence of my dual life. I can look through my belongings and clothes and so forth, and everything suggests many similarities. On this planet, I travel and stay in hostel dormitories to meet other travelers. On numerous occasions, I have found myself out-of-body in similar hostels. One time, I awoke to the sound of shuffling around and people talking in Mandarin. I was staying at a hostel and a group of Chinese tourists were locating their bunk bed in the dark. Yes, life on the astral can be as wonderfully mundane as this.

However, the idea of merging together both versions of myself is intimidating: Despite my similarities, what will still change? How will I handle remembering my entire life on that side? Will it take away from the experience of "discovering" life on that side? Will my personality change significantly? While for others the afterlife is a first-time experience, I will be arriving as a trained veteran.

A third possibility also exists, and now we are getting too esoteric for comfort…

I have entertained the idea that there are multiple dimensions / layers. My astral experiences may be occurring in some parallel dimension that is disconnected from the afterlife "I" will experience when "I" cross over. That a separate version of "me" exists in a parallel astral universe that is not connected to what I will encounter when I cross over.

This idea seems logically possible, if not convoluted, but the reason I generally reject this idea relates to my deceased relatives. The same place I appear in the out-of-body state appears to be the same realm my mom inhabits. I've even had "astral friends" from that life hang around at my mom's place trying to find me or say hello to me.

More recently, my mom said, "There's a young lady here who says you're her soulmate from a past life and she appears to be waiting patiently for you to die to be fully reunited again." I then met her—a rather attractive woman with platinum blonde hair. I found this experience curious because it dovetails with my larger questions: If I have a parallel life on that side, why would she have to wait for me to cross over to reunite with her? I really should have asked this question, but only after I returned to my body did I remember the paradox (and my brain promptly scrambled.)

My conclusion is there must be something I don't understand yet, maybe related to issues of not being "fully" manifested on that side. Perhaps she waits for me because my existing ties to this side limits my existence. Maybe I only appear in the afterlife while I slumber on Earth. Maybe she's not permitted to be with me until my reincarnation is finished. Maybe we are together and she was talking specifically to the amnesiac Earth-plane Cyrus. I don't know.

As a side note, this experience (with the platinum-haired "soulmate") was confirmed with a woman I met in Jakarta, Indonesia in summer 2018. Our relationship was (more or less) platonic, yet we became close enough that she'd visit 2-3 nights a week and we would sleep in the same bed together. Among other things, she was a medium, an empath, and a psychic who could predict distinct details about very near future events via dream messages. As far as her mediumship skills, she would often babble messages from the beyond in half-asleep states. One night, she started mumbling, "Cyrusss…. A woman is here… she says you're her soulmate from a past life…" This, of course, was an exciting way to confirm this woman's existence as my "soulmate"—patiently waiting so very long for my return (yet, I don't even know her name.)

In Summary

An understandably confusing topic. If we exist simultaneously in the afterlife, how much of our memories do we retain? Why do our loved ones greet us after we die as if it's our first on that side instead of us just reappearing among them? There must be an explanation that hasn't been fully hashed out yet.

One more possibility is maybe because our consciousness has been split, we exist in a more ghostly and unattached existence on the astral. It's not until we rejoin our Earthly consciousness do we become whole again, and this is why people patiently wait for their loved ones to "return."

Or what if it involves parallel timelines? What if the astral Cyrus has already fully lived the Earth-plane life—living and dying in my current life, and he now exists in the "future" on the astral plane, while the "me from the past" astral projects into my future self's mind? In this case, I'd die and still be entering the afterlife for the "first time." Yet, if this were true, why do my astral abodes often match where I live on the Earth plane? (e.g.: Los Angeles.) Ugh, this is getting more convoluted than a late-season episode of *Lost.*

I could probably sit here and speculate all night—it won't do much good. So, if you're in contact with any deceased people and you'd be interested in asking them deeper questions about this matter, please e-mail me: cyrus@cyruskirkpatrick.com with your findings. In the meantime, I will continue to probe into this subject and hopefully report my findings over a *AfterlifeTopics.com.*

.

VI – Reconciling Pop Spirituality and the Afterlife

> "...so many souls of the earth world are almost shocked to be told that the spirit world is a solid world, a substantial world, with real, live people in it! They think that that is far too material, far too like the earth world; hardly, in fact one step removed from it with its spirit landscape and sunshine, its houses and buildings, its rivers and lakes, inhabited by sentient, intelligent beings. This is no land of 'eternal rest'. There is rest in abundance for those who need it. But when the rest has restored them to full vigor and health, the urge to perform some sensible, useful task rises with them, and opportunities abound."
>
> Monsieur Hugh Benson

The afterlife, as a real place, is no longer a hidden or mysterious concept. As early as the late 1980s, Oprah Winfrey began interviewing guests who experienced NDEs (near-death experiences). Combined with the earlier efforts of Raymond Moody's first books, the public at large (especially in Western culture) began to adopt the idea that the afterlife is a real place and it's independent of the concept of collecting points on your favorite religion's scorecard—until one is rewarded with the ability to sit in a big cathedral and worship a man with a beard *for all eternity*.

Whether through the rise of near-death experience literature or the New Age movement, a new idea took root that upon death we move through an expansive tunnel toward a luminous and intelligent "Light." We experience oneness—perhaps with the whole cosmos, and certainly a merging with God, the "Creator" or "Source Consciousness." We may reunite with our loved ones, but the details of what happens after these reunions are hazy, at best. A choice is made and we are thrust back to our bodies, forced to grapple with an experience that shakes our foundations.

While millions experience the above example through near-death experiences, the mythology surrounding these experiences influences how we encounter and communicate with the so-called other side. We are all familiar with TV shows where a medium is looking around the premises of a supposedly haunted house, speaking with some bravado to the unseen spirits that they must "go to the Light." Upon questioning this technique, the medium may say, "Well, a spirit is lost, Earthbound, until they merge into the Light and rejoin with God and their family members, who are now angels in heaven."

"What happens next?" A particularly prying questioner may ask.

"Well, they are with God. They are happy, forever."

"What if they did bad things in life?"

"They will be healed."

"Okay, well that sums that up."

And so the medium continues on with her method, and the conversation is shut off. A more cynical person may follow-up with, "Won't being with God and angels get boring after a while?"

"No," she'll say, "Impossible when you are One With God."

What occurs next is a combination of indifference among the followers of the New Age belief system, who accept these concepts as universal truths, and perhaps malaise among the general public.

The malaise stems from the fact that this picture, as it's commonly painted, is strikingly similar to Western Christianity, a field that our increasingly atheistic population has less tolerance to believe. In fact, there's no doubt that the New Age-movement has meshed with Western Christianity. Today, we can supplant "Saved" with "Going to the Light." A similar proposition where a low-effort physical action (moving toward a geographic territory as opposed to making a verbal commitment) has high-yielding metaphysical consequences (a removal of responsibility of negative actions in life or whatever predisposed the soul to spook people in a 1800s attic in the first place.)

Whether we are Saved by Jesus or we Return to the Light, these descriptions compromise our attempts to figure out our legitimate afterlife conditions. It creates a false dichotomy that one is either exalted or troubled. It also misrepresents the nature of consciousness and souls. It reinforces the most fundamental misunderstanding that someone who exists outside the Earthly body is an alien or divine creature. Ghost hunters on popular TV shows rarely interact with the alleged hauntings as if they are normal people existing on a different frequency. Instead, they address them as "entities" that must be spoken to as such.

"Why are you still in this lighthouse? Why have you not gone to the Light yet?" the ghost hunter asks, not considering that maybe they already did "go to the Light" and just prefer the nice scenery of the lighthouse, or that there's an adjacent astral equivalent world, populated by perfectly happy, non-ghost like spirit people but the lighthouse is experiencing a bit of "astral bleed through."

I hear this dichotomy in action among readings by various mediums. A concerned loved one may ask, "My husband . . . has he gone to the Light yet?"

"No," the medium will say, "Your husband hasn't found the Light yet. We must pray for him." (Or pay the medium an extra $200 to help the husband "go to the Light.")

The client will gasp, they'll hold a séance, and try to send him into the Light where he can fulfill the Judeo-Christian concept of merging with God. This process, of course, ends his Earthly-driven existence and immediately converts him into an angelic form. He will be outfitted with a pair of wings and a harp and will be ready for his eternal existence on a cloud.

I hate to be the bearer of bad news, but based on my personal interactions with "the other side," the residents of parallel planes think we're a bunch of lunatics for believing these types of things.

Redefining the Afterlife Based on Evidence

Since embarking on my personal journey of experiencing astral realms, and after a thorough analysis of numerous objective areas for the afterlife (documented in my 2015 book, *Understanding Life After Death*,) my view of the other side has become much clearer.

In that clarity, I recognize that pop culture—ghost hunters, ghost whisperers (and sometimes dog whisperers,) Hollywood afterlife shows, and even some popular near-death experience literature, is all steeped in religious interpretations that fester in our collective psyche. Concepts of being saved, or not saved, linger. Accurate representations of what the afterlife is like are missing. Death remains mysterious and beguiling. And when something is mysterious and omnipresent, it's guaranteed to generate fear.

While "going to the Light" and crossing over are true occurrences, it's only a small piece of the puzzle. Near-death experiences, now reported in the millions and given serious attention by medical professionals, report a high percentage of death experiences that involve meeting the Divine Light. And, certainly, there are troubled "spirits" who haven't found their way and appear—for one reason or another—to co-habitat with us in old lighthouses and Grandma's attic. But, it's a mistake to think of all spirit people as either existing in heaven playing the harp, or haunting houses because they're "earthbound." The reality of how life exists in the astral, as well as non-physical dimensions, is different, often unimaginable, but can be conceptualized through the examination of evidence.

In regular pop literature, it's hard to find the truth behind what happens to us "beyond the Light." To figure out the truth it's necessary to go deeper—into the realm of direct spirit communication—and learn from the lion's mouth of their conditions and lifestyles. In most of my work, this is my purpose. With dedication, it's possible that you, too, may be able to communicate directly with this parallel dimension and obtain personal insight about what awaits us after death—bypassing inaccurate pop ideas altogether.

McSpirituality

Unfortunately, for thousands of years, the afterlife has been a source of wish-fulfillment. Whatever we desire in this life we project onto the possibility of a mystical after-existence. The atheist-materialists project a desire for oblivion and non-existence from the Earth's pains, while the highly religious project a desire for moral superiority and vengeance against those who doubted.

In between, we find newer, modern examples of wish-fulfillment. The New Age movement, complete with its popular bookshelf aisles and crystal conventions, projects the desire for an afterlife of instant gratification and happiness—where self-development and responsibility are nullified through the purification by "the Light." In this interpretation, reinforced by sporadic teachings of alleged channelers and occasional episodes of Oprah, even a murderer is given a blank slate at death. This happens because Source consciousness turns all who die into enlightened, non-physical beings, beyond all boundaries of time or space with unlimited consciousness in a realm of eternal love.

One classic example of the New Age community gone awry is the notion that Hitler is an angel on a cloud. This claim originated from two sources I'm aware of: author Rob Schwartz and the *Channeling Erik* mediums. The internet psychic community was soon abuzz with claims that Adolf Hitler was not only purified of all his transgressions, but he was a type of archangel sent to Earth to aid us in our growth process.

(Isn't it interesting how the revelations made by social media psychics seems to correspond identically to things written by trending authors? Hmm.)

"It is impossible to have negative experiences in the afterlife," some of these people claim. "God turns all to love. Everything becomes pure love."

"But didn't Hitler spur a movement that resulted in the cruel suffering of millions? He was free of personal responsibility even after creating genocide and being filled with hatred against Jews?" A rational person may ask.

"Yes, but all is for a greater purpose, a greater good. Even Hitler was part of God's plan."

As a troublemaker, I may push this argument further by asking, "If the point is to enlighten mankind and help us progress, aren't there easier ways to do it than by slaughtering millions of people?"

"Well, at death we shed our Earthly personalities and merge with the Higher Self. So our actions are just like being actors in a theater."

"So our lives on Earth have no consequences? Even if I rape someone, it's acceptable and still God's plan? You're saying someone could go pick up a gun, kill a 711 clerk, take the money in the cash register and walk away laughing—and bear no responsibility or consequences in their astral existence? Is that a healthy philosophy to teach people?"

Deathly silence.

This belief, coined by Eteponge Neko (a friend and member of the discussion group) as "McSpirituality" (enlightenment served extra fast, all you have to do is die!) has reached a fever pitch. What makes this message great is that it's highly marketable. In fact, it's the ultimate iteration of the self-help genre.

Introducing the new program guaranteed to eliminate all your anxieties and problems in life. Have you done awful things? Maybe you've killed a few people? Don't worry. All you have to do is try "death." This exciting process happens in just ONE (possibly painful) step—and you can enjoy an ETERNITY of enlightenment and bliss. Buy my seminar to learn more.

It's no surprise that Western culture has clung to this concept, the penultimate expression of the capitalistic desire to get more for less effort. I could go into greater depth to pick apart this belief and explain its possibly truthful yet heavily misinterpreted origins (that relates to multi-dimensional theory, our higher selves, and perspectives from higher planes) but I haven't the page space on this chapter. Instead, I'll simply state that this idea, as commonly interpreted, is inaccurate. Its wish-fulfillment and a desire to escape the responsibility of one's behavior.

The realm of spirit communication refutes this notion. It is only certain influential channelers and mental mediums, perhaps eager to stoke popular opinion, who cling to this idea. Astral explorer Jurgen Ziewe, a man who has toured the astral realms to a much greater extent than I have, utterly refutes these ideas. In his book, *Vistas of Infinity*, he was shown by guides the existence of some of the darkest astral realms conceivable, in particular, a plane created through the collective minds of suicide bombers (a place too horrific to describe with casual adjectives.)

Some earlier spiritualist literature describes similar realms. In "Life in the World Unseen" by Anthony Borgia, the deceased priest Monsieur Hugh Benson tours a realm inhabited by souls mired by rages and inner-demons, who have banished themselves to terrifying conditions where skeletal entities are found trapped in noxious pits of foul liquid, lacking all strength or compulsion to escape.

Even in the popular Robin Williams film "What Dreams May Come," the writers dipped into the spiritualist era to conceptualize "hell"—a realm where the protagonist's wife appeared after committing suicide, shown as a ghastly excursion among the most wretched souls. We'll talk more about the existence of realms in this "dark spectrum" in Chapter 8, but the point here is that **the existence of the dark spectrum utterly refutes McSpirituality or the idea Hitler or Pol Pot or a child rapist or a cannibal all go to "heaven."**

My mom, far from being exonerated of all negative psychological states, found herself confused and troubled; requiring care and attention by teams of specialists existing within an astral realm. Death and "the Light" by no means transformed her into an all-powerful spirit. It would appear we cross over exactly as we are, complete with our vulnerabilities and issues.

As New Age author Rob Schwartz knows, these visualizations of negative afterlife realms do not sell books. What sells to the large demographic of people looking for a new religion to cope with reality (and avoid responsibility) is the idea that every ugly thing we've ever seen or done disappears amidst magic, love, and fairies. That even mankind's old nemesis Adolf Hitler now lives on some pink cloud, finally fulfilling his ill-begotten painting career (pink clouds are not Schwartz's words, but the concept may as well be the same.)

However, the truth is not democratic, and it will be necessary to come to grips with reality that these accounts are not based on objectivity but wish-fulfillment. While it is true that much of the afterlife is shaped by our thoughts and desires—in fact entire realms are generated by thought—this does not alleviate us from universal laws of cause and effect, and laws of free will. Cause and effect dictate that a cruel, negative behavior boomerangs this negative energy back to us, lowering our "vibrations" and thus *physically preventing* access to astral realms of a higher spectrum that are more "heavenly" or consisting of greater loving energy.

And yes, this happens *EVEN IF* a so-called "soul contract" may be in place for your life. Maybe Hitler's soul contract was that he wanted to be a great leader of Germany and unite the people. But guess how well that went? Sorry, Schwartz. We're still responsible for our own decisions.

A lifetime of cruel behavior results *inevitably* in dark, even hellish conditions. This occurs regardless of what our higher-selves desire, or the conditions of our higher selves. Our individual personas must absolutely pay the price.

This does not mean, however, there is any threat of eternal damnation or any semblance to religious hell. Understanding the objective rules of the afterlife is the ultimate liberation from religion. It means we must continually evolve and improve ourselves. Rewards are not handed out like candy. No one is "saved" thus becoming immune to cosmic laws. Further, there is no condemnation to "eternity." These horrific places are part of the continuing drama of the human spirit. We end up in these places due to our own actions, a failure of principle while incarnated on Earth—or perhaps even cruel deeds within astral conditions.

We learn there are consequences for our actions, for not seeking a path of service to others and higher emotions like love and kindness.

To believe in McSpirituality means a denial of such cosmic laws. As Jurgen Ziewe points out, these ideas are the same as those adopted by terrorist groups like ISIL, who teach their members of liberation in the afterlife—that their actions on this plane bear no consequence because the afterlife purifies them.

These cosmic laws are not democratic. They apply to all people, and even those who desire most of all to become flawless spiritual gurus at death are in for a rude awakening. Although our thoughts have a huge bearing on the afterlife, there are some things we do not change. And, no matter how badly we may want to bypass our psychological issues—we are not Saved—not by Jesus nor by the Light.

This is an important concept as it relates to the issues with "pop spirituality," A relationship to the beyond based on superstition or wish-fulfillment inhibits communication and also holds the potential for transmitting false messages or mingling with the residents of "hollow heavens." These are realms commonly visited by NDErs and OBErs alike where expectations and belief systems create demi-planes designed around those beliefs; yet, are without much substance. For more about this, I'd suggest Yvonne Ballard's chapter in the book *Awakened by Death* ("Heaven is Empty".)

Further, spirit communication becomes immediately fallible when it is presumed the entities we communicate to are god-like, angelic, or all-knowing. To the contrary, the jungle of the astral dimension consists of an endless spectrum of personalities, just like here—and amidst that crowd are the naïve, arrogant, ill-informed, deceptive and perhaps even evil. Too often we make random dead people into exalted beings, angels, or deities to worship.

For all we know, Hitler really was communicating to the Channeling Erik team—but it was Hitler's PR department trying to cover his ass and make him sound nicer and benevolent. The naivete in spiritual communities is absolutely stunning.

More Philosophical Quagmires

All of this points to "funky philosophies"—besides McSpirituality, there are many more ideas spurred by spiritual or metaphysical thought that tend to be neither productive nor very healthy, and are also instrumental in keeping people away from exploring subjects like life after death. Unfortunately, people smell one whiff of these crazy ideas, and extinction versus an afterlife is suddenly a lot more palatable.

Without listing and calling out the countless authors who push logically questionable ideas, I'll simply name some of the ideas I've heard over the years (and rebuttals). Philosophy has a subjective nature about it, but my belief (which is, itself, obviously a philosophy) is that reality also has objective standards. If we don't apply those objective standards sometimes, it's almost impossible to make sense of reality.

Some of these I covered before in *Understanding Life After Death* so if you're a previous reader—I apologize for any sense of repetition. However, in the three years since my prior book, many of the same misconceptions persist in even greater force and therefore require a continual effort to stymy their persistence.

To begin, I will state two axioms that will help anyone navigate the world of Pop Spirituality and strange ideas: *The other-side, powered by consciousness, is limitless. All attempts to limit and constrict it are likely based on inaccurate data.*

The second is: *Individual existence is joined with personal responsibility, and cosmic law dictates that we are responsible for our actions toward other souls via cause and effect relationships.*

With these principles in effect, it becomes very clear what is accurate, and what is not. Pointing out inaccurate data becomes just icing on a cake.

Unusual, Probably Bunk Beliefs

Belief #1: When we die, we are forced to reincarnate by a council of authority figures.

Why it's Probably Wrong:

There's never been evidence of this occurring. However, inevitable reincarnation is a questionable belief I've heard repeated on many groups. I've seen people tell this belief to bereaved parents, intensifying their grief. Few want to hear that their deceased loved one is probably no longer around—because our time in the "afterlife" is short and we immediately are forced to reincarnate until we fulfill a quota to some authoritative council who will decide when we can stop reincarnating.

These beliefs appear to originate among Buddhists and Hindu sects. They percolate into Western culture through the adoption of "fad" eastern religious practice. You know the types—the *Eat, Pray, Love* crowd, usually originating in California, who will travel to Bali on a yoga retreat, listen to some superstitious beliefs taught by local gurus, and return having deemed themselves spiritually enlightened.

No, no one is going to force you to reincarnate. Although, I do believe many reincarnate out of choice because, after experiencing a life review, it dawns on them that they completely f---ed up their Earthly life and they are spurred by a strong desire to do it over again. This is a big difference from being forced to reincarnate or having it inflicted as a punishment. This strong desire to redo past mistakes is also my interpretation of what "karma" means.

Belief #2: When we die, all entities become pure thought without form or physicality.

Why it's Probably Wrong:

First of all, how long will you be thoughtless consciousness before it becomes boring? Putting this obvious question aside, let's ponder on what "physical" even means: When we think of something using our imaginations, even in our "mind's eye" it has texture and substance. Right now, imagine a juicy watermelon. Even as an imaginary thought form, it's still physical and tastes like watermelon. It may be that what we consider "physical" is, in fact, "non-physical" and vice versa. For thought to express itself, it takes form and shape, and this form and shape thus has an impact on the world around it, making "physical stuff" an inevitability. So true non-physicality would be unconsciousness or a void state without the creation of substance. Is that anyone's idea of a good time?[2]

I understand there's a philosophical conundrum about astral bodies—why would we need a body if it is not required? I argue a body with its complete sensory apparatus is required in an astral environment. Remember, astral is still physical, and a physical suit is required for interacting in such a place, just like here. However, a realm that's made of pure light or energy could not sustain an astral body and is therefore incompatible. As I like to stress, one type of realm is not necessarily better than another—and a majority of people who cross over are quite comfortable still being themselves, and choose these continued physical realms.

---

[2] For a much deeper conversation about physicality, we could go into sacred geometry and how all physical structures are built around a dodecahedron shape, holographically projected from a singular "divine" source that is, presumably, linked to our consciousness. For more about this, check out any of David Wilcock's semi-coherent ramblings at divinecosmos.net or his Gaia TV show *Wisdom Teachings*.

Belief #3: Personality is an illusion created by social experiences in life. When we die, we are stripped of this illusion and become the same type of consciousness that may be all-present but has no personality.

Why it's Probably Wrong:

This is a favorite idea pushed by Jim Carrey since his recent "spiritual enlightenment." Let's put aside all the direct communications that have been documented for at least 200 years among deceased individuals who are still themselves—and tackle this purely philosophically.

Aside from Carrey, I've heard this claim among near-death experience groups and certain people in Facebook metaphysical communities. It's another one of those unusual beliefs that I'd never be able to figure out the exact origin of. However, the roots are likely in eastern religion, with some sects of Buddhism that believe in entering a kind of thoughtless "nirvana" upon death, and a reinforcement that "personality" is an illusion only resultant from factors like how we were raised, how others treat us, etc. This "nature vs. nurture" argument has extended into philosophy for years and is also argued among materialists.

Here's why I believe this is wrong: As just one example, a couple of years back my roommate's weird-looking dog (a screeching Chinese Crested, ugh,) had puppies (that were much cuter than their mother.) Shortly after the puppies were born, and they still had their eyes closed, I'd put some on my lap. I discovered inherent personality characteristics that I'd find evident in the pups as they grew older and eventually became full, mature adults.

For instance, Ruben the shaggy one immediately curls into a ball on your lap and falls asleep. Maynard, the feisty one, charges toward your face and tries to lick your nose. Maynard was doing this before his eyes were even open. Somehow, he knew where my nose was, and would still try to lick it.

Maynard's playful behavior was built in straight from the womb. There was no time for Maynard to be conditioned to behave the way he did. Maynard's consciousness entered this puppy body and was ready-to-go with a complete, dynamic personality.

It seems more likely that personality and individuality is a sacred **elemental** essence of the universe (which I will discuss in greater depth near the end of this book.) It's contradictory to believe personality is an illusion or doesn't matter. Seeing ourselves through the concept of elementalism—that each personality is divine and permanent—is a lot healthier than believing we're all just a bunch of illusionary shells. This is just more superstition / fatalistic spirituality.

Belief #4: Soul contracts place people into the role of a killer or murderer to help another soul learn.

Why It's Probably Wrong:

Now we are back into the territory of ideas espoused in particular by Rob Schwartz and similar writers. We already tackled this issue earlier, but why not beat a dead horse a little more?

This idea flies against the very nature of the spiritual progress of mankind, and this belief threatens the fabric of spiritual understanding, self-discovery, and entering a path of service to others and love. Due to the enormous havoc such a belief could cause, and the true nature of the astral worlds (and the ability to channel even malevolent entities) I have to wonder where some of these ideas are really coming from—something tells me it's not from a very enlightened source.

So, why would I feel so strongly this is dangerous, dark information? The belief in soul contracts for rapists, killers, and genocidal maniacs suggests there is no individual existence or responsibility and, most alarming of all, that morality is relative. While Silver Birch, channeled through the powerful medium Maurice Barbanell, spoke of divine cosmic law that is irrefutable and holds all people accountable for their actions—we hear writers today argue the actions of the worst people in society is an illusion, and a rapist child killer is still a wonderful soul carrying out God's plan.

Aside from my theory of straight up influence by negative astral entities inspiring channelers to write such things, we must also consider the fallacious nature of guided past-life regression and other methods of obtaining information via the hypnosis process.

When a patient sees a spiritual hypnotist, they have a strong desire to fulfill expectations; and the hypnotist also desires for the patient to provide spiritual information. This desire for expectation fulfillment creates an environment where obtaining objective information about the other side is close to impossible. The mind has the power to create anything it wants. There is no way to know if a hypnotized patient, who sees a famous past-life regression therapist and is laying on a couch *desiring* a spiritual experience—is really having a legitimate experience or just fulfilling mutually desired expectations, essentially inducing a dream.

In other words, the information brought back may be coming merely from the confines of a person's mind, and the "spiritual knowledge" just information remembered by the patient via New Age books read—books that are also contriving information from dubious methods. What ends up happening is that misinformation is multiplied. All the while—there's no controls or protocols or methodologies of objectivity in place.

And that, my friends, is how information is generated that morality is relative and personal responsibility is optional.

Now for an important addendum: I am NOT saying soul contracts are not real, or past life therapy is invalid. I'm actually a big fan of soul contracts. It explains a lot of things in my life and it makes perfect sense that we'd define an outline for our lives before we're born. I'm also a firm believer in past lives and that we can tap into our memories from those lives. **The BIG DIFFERENCE that I argue is that the way people study and report this information is massively flawed.** Going back to Hitler, his soul contract probably didn't involve slaughtering millions, but Earth is a testing ground and if we don't win against our personal demons—horrific things happen that were never intended—not consciously nor on a soul level.

Belief #5: If a medium says a loved one is smoking a cigar, drinking alcohol, or eating their favorite food—it's just an indicator to help the family recognize who the spirit is. Of course, spirits do not and cannot actually perform such Earthly activities.

Why It's Probably Wrong:

As moderator for a 7,000-member afterlife discussion-group, I've seen hosts of questions and theories. Among the more common are people confused by reports by a medium that old Uncle Larry is still chewing his chewing tobacco and eating apple pie with cheddar cheese, and they want to know if this was accurate. I often see "experts" reassure that no, Uncle Larry is not *REALLY* engaging in such activities because we "abandon" simplistic Earthly activities upon our ascension into orbs of light in eight-dimensional space (or whatever.) Mediums I've heard deny the existence of *actual* physical activities have included even highly accurate mediums like Marcel Cairo, George Anderson, and quite a few others. At the same time, other very credible mediums, including Susanne Wilson and Suzanne Geisemann, have never—to my knowledge—jumped on board with these theories. So, who's right and who's wrong?

The reality is, it's easier to comprehend an afterlife that's alien, dream-like or beyond comprehension than the far weirder possibility the astral plane can be a *direct copy* of our current world. However, in all my experience, the latter is true. A vast majority of people who cross over enter the same realm I've explored many times in astral states: a higher-dimensional (higher frequency, higher density—pick your terminology) version of the same universe we inhabit now. The death process becomes a simple frequency shift. A person is still inhabiting a body and will soon return to a life that is most normal for them. The actual process of evolving to states far beyond the human form and condition is very slow for the majority of souls.

Jurgen Ziewe (*Multidimensional Man, Vistas of Infinity)* sums it up best in a debate about this subject on *Afterlife Topics and Metaphysics* (post dated April 27th, 2018.):

> There is a simple Axiom or rule we can apply if we wish to understand what the afterlife is like and it is this: Consciousness is primary. Physical manifestation is secondary, rising out of primary consciousness. Consequently EVERYTHING that exists in this world can also exist in the primary (non-physical) world of consciousness depending on the state of consciousness we are in. We can smoke tobacco, weed, drink alcohol or have sex when we are dead, no doubt about it. I have seen it, tested it, done it. Everything in all cases takes place in consciousness, whether we are dead or alive.

Also, through astral projection experiences, I've done all of the above activities Jurgen's mentioned… Including, yes, sex (which leads to the next myth.)

So why do certain influential mediums and authors claim these things are impossible? My theory is a lack of critical thinking. I don't know if such mediums ask questions of the deceased to explore a full breadth of information scientifically. I think people make assumptions and hasty generalizations, influenced by personal beliefs, and people have a difficult time making sense of complex subjects. In an effort to be an authority on the subject, they're less likely to say "I don't know" and so when asked—they provide the best guess they can imagine.

Belief #6: There's no sex, you sinful little devils.

Why It's Probably Wrong

Anyone familiar with my first book will know that a chapter like this cannot be complete without tackling society's great taboo—sex. However, there's not too much more to debate about this topic. I covered the issues with "sex doesn't exist in the afterlife" at length in *Understanding Life After Death,* but I'm more than happy to repeat myself once again:

Quite simply, astral sex is better than Earth sex, with fewer hang-ups and issues. It's also a combination of physical penis-in-vagina, same as here—sex—but also plenty of tantric-style practices expanding beyond sexual organ use, especially in higher planes with expanded mental capacities. So, feelings of desire, pleasure, and passion are all magnified in a world better suited for consciousness experiences hindered by fewer hard physical rules.

When it comes to sexual attraction, do keep in mind that on the astral Earth levels, a majority of people revert to their prime ages (the 25-35 range) in addition to achieving optimal physical beauty. For many people, it's an opportunity to finally explore this side of life when maybe they never could feel "pretty" or "sexual" before.

This DOES bring up a valid concern—fidelity. Many have asked me, "Will my husband stay faithful on the astral plane when there are so many beautiful women?"

And, unfortunately, I cannot provide a swift or reassuring answer. This issue depends on the nature of a person's relationship. Without fears of STDs, unwanted pregnancies, or the social-cultural hang-ups of resource-acquisition based on relationships (and sex therefore used as a tool)—we enter a culture where such experiences are freely shared and celebrated more often. In other words, a truly sexually open society. And as a result, to be perfectly honest, a greater "risk" of a partner experiencing somebody else.

I'd also suggest for a person concerned about this to evaluate the big picture: There's no risk of scarcity or "losing" someone when, on the astral, everyone has all the time imaginable. Given these circumstances, would it be entirely necessary still for romantic love to exist exclusively on a 1-on-1 basis? What happens when we reunite with past wives, husbands, and lovers from previous Earthly incarnations? Food for thought.

Regardless of this controversy, the original presupposition that "naughty" behavior doesn't exist, or my favorite—sex still exists but is sanitized and involves only mental "merging" versus any feeling like desire or orgasm—is silly, contrived by people's hang-ups that are projected onto the astral Earth.

This supposition reminds me of the great parody of pop-spirituality: 1993's *Demolition Man* starring Sylvester Stallone. When an authoritarian New Age, social-justice government takes over California and restricts sex to a strange helmet-like device that produces artificial sexual feelings, our hero Sly Stallone has to reintroduce the real thing to the heroine / love interest played by Sandra Bullock.

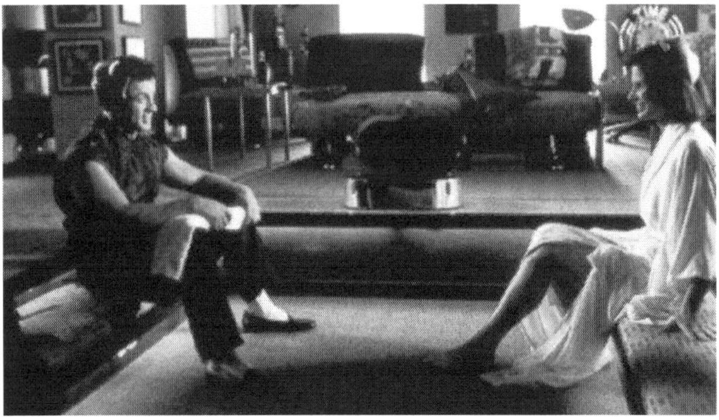

"When do we get to have sex?" "We are." "What?"

Belief #7: The afterlife is beyond our comprehension, and who we are is not taken with us. Our individual selves disappear.

Why It's Probably Wrong:

This theory is continually espoused by Tom Campbell (*My Big TOE*) who insists that the existence of deceased loved ones is illusory—they are "fascismiles" of the real people, created by the God-intelligence to comfort us. Meanwhile, people's individual selves are transported into a realm beyond imagination where there is no remaining semblance. Interestingly, the belief is shared in a hypothetical way by arch skeptic

Michael Shermer. In the book *Heavens on Earth* Shermer argues, among other topics, that even if the afterlife were real—what we'd become on the other side would be so far removed from who we are now, that essentially "death" is still a reality—as our prior existences would be completely eliminated and replaced by something incomprehensible.[3]

These are ideas, in my opinion, supported by people without afterlife knowledge. They have no awareness of direct spirit contact and what those in the afterlife actually say to us. While Campbell may be an astral projection practitioner, he appears unable to connect on a humanistic level with people from other realms. This is because, in my opinion, there's a high likelihood Tom Campbell is exploring lucid dream states as opposed to real astral domains, as it would explain why the inhabitants he encounters appear to be generated by his own mind. Instead of recognizing the fact his astral experiences may be limited to the dream dimension, he has instead constructed an entire theory, bordering on fundamentalism, that astral inhabitants must be illusions. Meanwhile, those like myself, Jurgen, and many other OBErs have come to vastly different conclusions after interacting with souls as 100% as real as before they crossed over. I have also explored both advanced lucid dream states and true astral domains, and discovered many of Campbell's principles apply in the former realm solely.

Further, those who make these claims are likely unfamiliar with physical mediumship, or high-end EVP / ITC communication, that allow direct information exchange about the nature of the other side. Those without the proper education are left filling in the blanks with their imaginations. This practice creates a picture of the other side that nullifies the very concept of an afterlife, because it would mean we don't take who we are—including the lessons from Earth—with us so we may continue to grow and develop. We become something else entirely.

And fortunately, we know this is not true.

---

[3] This is about all I know of Shermer's book *Heavens on Earth* as I did not read it. I have no interest in entertaining circular arguments all day by New Atheists clinging to their outdated ideas.

Astral Experiences: Making Friends with Two Succubi

How homogenous and sanitized are "spirits" living in other planes? Based on my experiences, there's a lot more diversity than people imagine.

One time I found myself on a busy street corner, likely part of the astral version of Los Angeles. Passersby were quickly avoiding a woman planted on a street corner, almost like a prostitute. Buxom, beautiful, blonde-haired, wearing a blue outfit and a pair of devil wings with matching horns.

As it's my mission to collect information, I naturally went to talk to her (despite locals warning me.) I was given immediate mental feedback about who and what she was: she preyed on weak-willed men, turning them into her sexual and psychic slaves. In addition, she was not a human soul. Her aura was dark.

To summarize a longer experience, I attempted to befriend her as a not-so-weak-willed man. We took a long walk back to her private abode. On the way, she demonstrated her powers to me: She picked up a frog and temporarily turned it into a fluttering, fairy-like creature. She explained how every lesser-evolved creature has a more advanced higher-soul waiting to be unlocked. "Even one so stupid as that frog."

At her mansion on the outskirts of town, I met her raven-haired friend and roommate, also a succubus. Together, we played billiards for a while, until the experience began to end.

Immediately after I awoke, a voice manifested into my bedroom, whispering into my ear. It said: *"Kitara and Jacey."* Jacey was her name, and Kitara her dark-haired friend. She didn't want me to forget their names, and so she managed to temporarily project into our realm—before her presence in my bedroom quickly dissipated.

Belief #8: There are no negative emotions in the afterlife. It is pure bliss and joy 24 / 7.

Why It's Probably Wrong:

I tackled this point before in *Understanding* and I have some revised opinions. I'd consider this a narrow-minded misinterpretation of higher, cosmic near-death experiences and applying momentary states of merging with a celestial force (the "Light" or "God") and the actual state of existence on the astral dimension. Because NDErs may report "There was nothing but pure bliss in that state of merging with the Light," they assume *this* is the entirety of the afterlife, and incorrectly attribute that state to some kind of absolutism.

This is, of course, a branch of the previously covered McSpirituality issue. It means if someone dies on Earth who was full of anger and unresolved issues, there is no need for continued self-development work as they are *purged* of negative emotions at death. We then return to the same philosophical quagmire of purposeless incarnations and the non-existence of self-development.

Physical medium Marcus Lang has maintained a long-standing *physical* communication with a childhood friend who passed away, as well as an unborn daughter who grew to adulthood on the astral side. He rebutted this idea of emotional purging quite well in the *Afterlife Topics and Metaphysics* group:

> The afterlife is where we can be all that we are. We are emotional beings. That's it. Always will be. Perhaps they may drop off to a lesser extent. Such as we can block feelings (as we can here, too.) But in the end, we embrace all that we are. Not only parts of it.
>
> Ps. Those I know over there, especially my friend Les, can get quite upset with me at times. And other times we can be so happy when we are together to chat. This my friends are emotions. They are still present. Thankfully. Or I'd be talking to an unemotional piece of cardboard who wouldn't be able to care about me. (post dated 4/28/18):

Probably what's going on here is a misinterpretation of "bliss." What does seem to occur is on higher density realms, and higher states of consciousness that we may develop, we begin to feel the resonant harmony of everything around us—which creates a feeling of overriding bliss and happiness. On Earth, a blade of grass is just grass. On the upper astral, we can sense every element of the grass in a harmonious way with ourselves, as well as the essences of entire environments and other souls. By comparison to our current lives, this is an extremely blissful existence of being perfectly attuned with life around you. So yes, one could argue you are "existing in perpetual bliss" but it does NOT mean negative emotions do not exist or these feelings have no context. The idea of just floating around in a drug-like-induced state of non-stop happiness is a result of a lack of conceptual understanding of a complex topic.

Belief #9: The astral plane is a weird or unpleasant environment that we must transcend ASAP and merge with our higher self.

Why It's Probably Wrong:

This is a direct response to the notions held by out-of-body pioneer William Buhlman, with his mantra: "*Higher Self Now!*"—he believes during death we must avoid the vast astral universe and enter a different state of co-existence with our higher-selves instead. He's not the only one with this idea: Another pioneer F.W.H Myers, allegedly writing post-mortem through obscure medium Geraldine Cummins (this medium's abilities were never proven) argued the astral world is a land of illusions and it should be immediately escaped.

I could probably write a whole book about this topic. To summarize: The astral world is simply an area of the multiverse less physical than here, but only by a small degree. It is not a world of "illusions" unless a particular soul chooses to saturate him or herself amidst illusions (some do this, I doubt it's a healthy lifestyle.) In the astral, consciousness directs the manifestation of physical objects and it's only a few degrees more fluid than our rigid "physical" universe. This domain is not appealing to some people because they want to go directly to a much higher realm on the spectrum.

However, wanting to chant "Higher Self Now!" to get away from the astral and transcend your human identity entirely does not apply to most people. If you listen carefully to this point of view, it sounds a lot like the motivating factor is a fear of the vast astral cosmos. In Buhlman's "Higher Self Now" lecture he encourages his fans to enter this state specifically to *bypass* encountering annoying friends and family members—he actually describes his motivating force being a desire not to encounter his dysfunctional family again and to get as far away from his Earth life as possible. This hardly sounds like an objective, unbiased perspective. In fact, many of us do not have dysfunctional relationships like Buhlman does and we desire strongly to see our deceased parents, friends, lovers and so forth.

In fact, **I have no reason to believe we cannot be our "higher selves" and also exist in the astral spectrum among friends and family at the same time.** Following Buhlman's advice, we ascend to a greater version of ourselves while also avoiding the vast astral cosmos entirely. This is despite the fact that most advanced souls happily switch between purely mental and astral realms, seeing the advantages and limitations of both types of realms. It's naïve to be proclaiming from our limited Earth experiences—and limited out-of-body ventures—that one realm is vastly superior to the other and that we should entirely avoid our friends and family members who will just hold us back. Hmm, sounds a bit antisocial, doesn't it?

Becoming our "higher selves" is a matter of rejoining with the higher state of consciousness some identify as the "group soul." My information from the astral side is that this process happens gradually for people, and as it happens the memories of many more past lives start to manifest. The gradual process is needed for most souls because, as I stress, it's about a state of consciousness and maturing at the pace an individual soul desires. I don't see how it's a good idea to tell people to speed this process as fast as possible. In fact, it's probably not even possible for 95% of us.

Another problem with "avoiding" friends, family members and continued "drama" is such a philosophy is borderline misanthropic and not congruous to concepts of growth, experience, and learning. The very reasons a soul—perhaps existing from a higher vantage point—CHOOSES to inhabit realms like the physical Earth and the astral Earth is to experience connections with other souls, including drama, conflicts, and opportunities to be of service to others.

The astral Earth is NOT a lesser-realm that we all must graduate from to get away. Rather, like this world, it's an arena—a place where a soul reduces its density to share a realm with many other individual souls—to explore, create, and learn valuable lessons amidst conflict and challenge. The higher we ascend, it would seem the more blissful and happy we become among fellow high-vibration souls, yet perhaps we also lose opportunities for challenge and growth. This is why even the most advanced souls may choose to spend their time in realms like the Earth plane (where we are now,) or some of the less-than-pleasant areas of the astral—where their guidance is most needed.

Belief #10: The astral plane is not really "heaven." It's just a stop-over place before all souls enter the real "heaven."

Why It's Probably Wrong:

I've been told this by skeptical, religious-spiritualists who balk at the idea of astral cities, streets, Earth-like restaurants, businesses, and diverse—sometimes even chaotic—characters inhabiting such realms.

"The real heaven has no need for Earthly activities like eating, drinking, sex, music, sports or games. It's just service to God."

Sound familiar? This is Christian theology made manifest, having snuck into the area of afterlife research.

While there are many accounts of much "higher" realms, our understanding of these very high planes is limited due to the incomprehensibility of human language as it relates to such places. But even these realms I believe are different from the interpretations we have in mind—a sanitized world where people are devoid of individual pursuits, hobbies, desires, or interests.

I like to use the analogy of Tony Bourdain. (Note: The following part of this chapter was written approximately 2 weeks before Tony Bourdain's tragic death on June 8th 2018. Quite a synchronicity. I'm leaving this next part untouched.)

Anyone who's ever turned on a TV knows who he is: the 60-something-year-old veteran chef, chain-smoker, former punk and irreverent traveler. Some of his books when I was growing up, like *Kitchen Confidential*, probably inspired me to become a traveler later in life—enjoying nitty, gritty cities in diverse parts of the world.

When Bourdain kicks the bucket, do you think his idea of "heaven" is going to be the Christian concept of some pink cloud strumming a harp? Or how about the New Age concept of existence as a purple polygon, spinning around in some fractal universe of shapes and colors and bliss?

No. He's going to be in the Astral Earth, enjoying his return to the prime of his life (age 25-30, usually), probably smoking unfiltered cigarettes, producing some TV show in between working a new French restaurant.

Would you WANT to see Bourdain's existence turn into anything other than that? If a medium said Bourdain was now an iridescent yellow orb shooting through a sea of prismatic lava-lamp waves after having rejoined his group soul collective—or whatever—would this not make the afterlife seem like a foreboding place where creativity and individuality are suffocated away?

This is why the astral Earth exists, because it's compatible with the eccentric personalities of human souls. Many of whom do not desire concepts like perfection, a lack of conflict or perpetual "bliss." The astral Earth is not a subjective world created in someone's mind, or a "fake heaven" someone temporarily enters, but it's a real parallel dimension just a couple frequencies on the cosmic radio station beyond this one—it's our neighboring planet.

To those who say such a realm is an illusion and not the real afterlife: what right do you have to impose your beliefs or Judeo-Christian standards of "heaven" onto others? What right do you have to judge what realms in the multiverse people choose to inhabit, based on their own preferences and desires?

Dealing With Pop Spirituality Going Forward

At some point, the afterlife needs to uphold some agreed upon "facts." Admittedly, it's a highly subjective topic, but what we hear from "the lion's mouth" is that there are specific conditions—laws of the universe—that take effect. The other side is not entirely a dream-world, as sometimes we imagine it to be. There are still rules of physics, rules of karma, at least in those astral conditions many of us find ourselves in. This is why it's best to imagine that side as a parallel dimension, another frequency, and a real place with a relationship intertwined to our realm.

Unfortunately, this field will continue to be inundated with dubious information, projection and a desire for fantasies that remove the necessity of personal-development, spiritual work, and reality which is never going to be as easy as popping an Enlightenment Pill and being cured of all your problems upon death.

Unlike what the *Channelingg Erik* mediums claim, Hitler is not an archangel and the Columbine shooters were not fulfilling a "soul contract"—walking hand-in-hand with the victims into the afterlife. In fact, causing trauma, grief, pain, and misery to fulfill selfish actions incurs consequences on the other side. Namely, the incredible guilt, shame, and struggle a soul must endure after having acted maliciously upon another soul. The universe is not a post-modernist realm of moral relativism, where rape and murder and predation mix perfectly well with love and light. In fact, as has been taught by every spiritual explorer for centuries, the other side has gradients depending on the vibrations of its inhabitants—and yes, there are dark and terrifying realms that the New Age movement, with its propensity to sugar-coat everything to sell more books, would not want to recognize the existence of.

This is why it's prudent to remember the old Biblical adage to "test the spirits." Whether it's the idea that we are robbed of our individualities or morality itself is unnecessary as even the worst of us are given free-passes in the afterlife, never forget the propensity for chaotic entities to deceive and warp our perspectives—perhaps to fulfill their malevolent ends. Just because information is wrapped in a veneer of "love and light" does not mean it's coming from a positive source—and blindly following information from the other side—daresay worshipping such information—is not a path of wisdom.

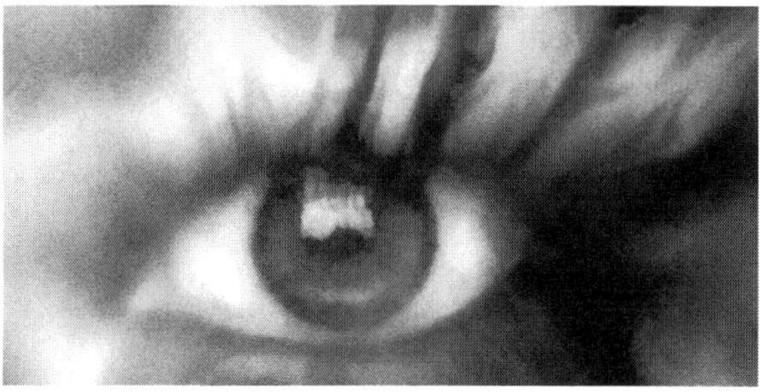

Getting Involved With AfterlifeTopics.com

I am announcing soon "Afterlife University." A chance to study, as a group, many of these metaphysical subjects via weekly and bi-weekly video conference classes.

Please see: www.afterlifetopics.com/university.

In the meantime, I encourage you to join the Facebook group. Hop in, make an introductory post, and say hi to our large community: www.facebook.com/groups/afterlifetopics

VII – So You're Going to Live Forever, Now What?

In this chapter, we can begin to explore what it means philosophically to be immortal. In particular, trying to break out of the death paradigm. This concept is part of the bigger theme of "going forward" with the information about the afterlife.

Earlier in this book, I refreshed your memory of the different areas of afterlife evidence, and even this is just a sample of a vast spectrum of evidence, one of the vastest fields in the world today, even in comparison to a traditional academic field.

And, today, we see the afterlife on not only a sociological level, but also a technological level, continue to evolve. I am reminded of this as I continually hear new reports of deceased loved ones communicating by phone, text message, and the Internet. What is exciting about this field is that it is not in stasis; rather, it evolves year-by-year. This is happening in spite of the fact that it feels like so many people know nothing about the subject. Even after so much progress in this area, there is an under-exposure problem in the media. However, even the current lack of exposure is still greater than it was a couple of decades ago—when there was virtually no exposure, at all.

In my view, afterlife knowledge is expanding concurrently with our collective evolution. Other evolving areas include health and medicine, consciousness, and awareness of an extraterrestrial presence. It all points toward an eventual future of full incorporation of multi-dimensionality and non-material physics, with all its many profound implications for science, medicine, research—and of course, philosophical views about reality.

Death is Still Death: It Means a Purposeful Destruction

I sometimes see debate in afterlife circles about the word "death" itself. Other words like "crossed over," "transitioned," or just "passed away" are argued as preferable to the finality of "death"—a concept marked by Newtonian physics as the end of the matter that composes our existences, thus leading to a finality of non-existence (and a belief upheld, still, by large swathes of the population who reject non-materialist science.)

But looking into the context of the word "death" and how it's frequently used, it doesn't have to necessarily be a negative word or event whatsoever. And certainly, people who die rarely see that transition as negative in retrospect. Based on those I've spoken to on the astral spectrum, our life here starts to feel like a long, bizarre dream after waking up in a far more superior world.

We use "death" every day as a verb to represent the ending of an old way of being: "The positive ratings of that movie appear to have died." "The old ideas about health and nutrition have long ago died off." Ideas die. Old ways die. A physical body can die, and a new body reborn in a more superior realm.

This fact, of course, doesn't mitigate the intense pain and grief associated with death on this plane—nor the sometimes enormous physical pain that makes the transitionary process extremely difficult.

Nonetheless, a prime motivator for this work is the realization that the death, dying and grief process could be so much less devastating if the afterlife evidence were public on a wider scale. Yes, the scientific curiosity is also of paramount importance, but anyone who's endured the deaths of family members and loved ones—which is virtually all of us except for perhaps the very young—has seen the severe emotional impact that "death" brings to our culture. Further, when one begins an education into the objective evidence of the afterlife, almost nothing is more cringe-inducing than hearing strange, mainstream ideas about death—whether from religious beliefs or materialist ideas of "non-existence."

In fact, how much more of our lives would we be able to reclaim if the constant fear of death was reduced or eliminated? According to anthropologist Ernest Becker, who's considered the leading authority of "death" phobia (thanatophobia) and is the author of "The Denial of Death" (2007,) death anxiety occurs naturally among all people, and our very hobbies, goals, and passions are motivated by coping strategies to try to ignore and cover-up this underlying, nagging sensation of existential fear that marks our existences.[5]

Powering thanatophobia is the multi-branches of the death subject that exacerbates the fear: like the process of getting older, the possibilities of being in pain as one leads up to death, the inevitable deaths of our loved ones, the fear of not leaving behind a proper legacy, and, of course, among thinkers and rationalists—the existential fate of oneself post-death. Materialists use old paradigms to finally "explain" the subject with two-dimensional views of "non-existence" or the idea that our souls amount to a bunch of grey matter and neurons made conscious through some unknown power (materialists must rely on faith to maintain their beliefs.)

Turning Over to Carl Jung

Carl Jung, who helped establish the field of psychology itself, was no stranger to the subject of life after death. In 1944, the Swiss founder of analytical psychology suffered a heart-attack which resulted in a profound out-of-body experience where he was able to view the expanse of the planet Earth itself. By his estimate, he was one-thousand miles above the Earth in space.[6] His NDE also included a heavy amount of symbology and a visit to what may have been a kind of astral temple for new arrivals.

Jung's work in analytical and archetypal psychology is also correlated to the subject of death, and perhaps offers some of the best solutions for all of us who, according to Becker, are continuously influenced, motivated and altered by this fear.

As a kind of realist, Jung's "shadow work" emphasized the importance of recognizing the dark, selfish, seething elements of all human personas—and the danger of sugar-coating these traits with a veneer of positivity, or attempting to hide these dark elements behind any other type of superficial coping mechanism.[7] Of course, the shadow—despite its negative connotation, is according to Jung, "the door to our individuality." This concept has many implications, especially in regard to spiritual philosophies I've mentioned elsewhere in this book—and a solemn repudiation to those who believe the afterlife does not and cannot harbor any elements of a negative spectrum, and all souls must be inherently good by nature of being dead.

Additionally, confronting the shadow is also essential to understanding the fear of death and can be related to the work of Ernest Becker. According to Becker, virtually every person with the capability of understanding what death is has built social coping mechanisms to hide from this darkest of realities (not the least of which includes drowning in material pleasures that are ultimately vapid.) In short, death is a shadow on our lives and very few of us dare face this "enemy" directly—until perhaps we become sick and death beckons for us within weeks, days, or hours.

However, the materialist paradigm does not offer solutions to this "mother of all shadow-work" principles. That's because the solutions we'll hear from modern psychologists—Becker notwithstanding—is focused only on further coping mechanisms versus knowledge-based solutions; the latter of which contains actual possibilities for alleviating and "confronting" the shadow of death—possibly eliminating that shadow once and for all.

By their nature, materialists cannot offer the solutions because they exist squarely in a paradigm that death CANNOT be understood and that, according to physical sciences, death MUST result in non-existence. And, despite so much literature, from the peer-reviewed work of Gary Schwartz to the near-death experience research of Parnia, Long, Lommel, the proof-positive reincarnation research out of the University of Virginia, and so many others—they maintain there is NO evidence of an afterlife. Going from these false assumptions, all the materialist can essentially do is place flimsy Bandaids over the great shadow of our lives, often with platitudes we constantly hear like: "Live in the moment." "Focus on love, your family, and your work." Or, perhaps at best, visualization exercises to prepare for or come to terms with the act of dying. Some materialists may suggest to imagine the peace of sleep and recognize if this is the permanent state of death, then there's nothing to fear as we no longer possess consciousness to know what "fear" is.

Obviously, these techniques do NOTHING to alleviate the fear of death; let alone banish the shadow of death. Materialist psychologists rarely even dabble in basic metaphysical concepts, such as the "non-existence problem": This is the basic philosophical approach to the afterlife by asking the following question: "How long would non-existence perpetuate before existence occurs again?" Although this question is obvious from a common-sense perspective, there is no way to measure it scientifically. Instead, we are left with all prominent materialist minds simply saying "We don't know." (While still ignoring the real evidence.)

The only practical way to confront death and perform the introspective analysis of how it affects our lives involves directly pursuing contact with the beyond. Whether astral projection, the séance, electronic communication with the other side, or simply reading a lot of literature—this is the one subject that provides evidence and knowledge as the only way forward. And then, with that knowledge, it's possible to examine how the fear of death affects your entire life—and what your life may feel like if some of that fear were reduced.

In my own life experiences, what I see is exactly the situation described by Becker in *The Denial of Death*. Friends, family, and acquaintances are all harboring the shadow of death in the back of their minds, and for me—perhaps because of my intuitive abilities—it's (pardon the pun) deathly obvious. I also sniff out this insecurity in the world of young, urban professionals back home in Los Angeles. When I see people investing all of their time, energy and ambition into self-aggrandizement and external goals of money or social status, a little cynical voice in the back of my mind says, "You're just hiding from the shadow of death. How long can you hide from it?" This is why, as a fun social experiment, you can bring up the subject of death with your yuppie friends at the next cocktail party. Watch as a bug-eyed expression crosses the face of a previously tough-as-nails alpha male or alpha female. They'll promptly dismiss the topic and go to the bar for another cocktail—as alcoholism is yet another predisposition to keep oneself from thinking about the inevitable.

In essence, these people have never done the shadow work necessary to think about—and come to terms with—their own deaths. Wouldn't coming to terms with such a subject be so much easier with knowledge about the objective evidence for the afterlife?

What's it Like to Accept Death?

We usually think of death's acceptance as the final stage in end-of-life expert (and afterlife advocate) Elizabeth Kubler-Ross's famous stages of grief. However, in the afterlife field, I've come to find it's possible to exist in this state of acceptance *far earlier*, especially when awareness of the afterlife is entirely individually proven. This does not mean the fear of death is eliminated, but death is no longer existing in the shadows of the subconscious. This is why, in my layman and less-than-academic point of view, participation in afterlife discussion groups is enormously helpful for everything from grief reconciliation to general success in life.

One way to get a glimpse of living in a post-death philosophy is to study the psychological effects of near-death experiences, where experiencers often report having close to no fear of death upon a brief excursion into an astral or higher realm. These effects are recognized even in mainstream psychological journals. As reported in a recent Psychology Today article, citing *The Handbook of Near Death Experiences*[8], after-effects of the NDE often involve the creation of a "new person," in other words, everything from old jobs, hobbies, to relationships may get shaken up, changed, or eliminated entirely. This effect comes along with a predisposition to being more loving, less materialistic, more appreciative, and other generally considered positive qualities.

What is more nebulous is just how and why so many relationships or pursuits suddenly change. There isn't necessarily a pattern that people will leave X types of jobs or Z types of spouses. Rather, I'd postulate it relates to life decisions that were based on mortality fears. Once the shadow of death is uncovered, those relationships, jobs, hobbies, and so forth become irrelevant. If, for instance, a person's career is centered entirely around profit, because making money provided relief from worrying about death, that career could be replaced with a higher-risk, less profitable endeavor that is more aligned to what that person truly wants to do with their life.

For this reason, we shouldn't believe that the elimination of the fear of death would do anything but help a person become more successful. Consider the following possible benefits of the reduction of subliminal death fears (a legitimate reduction caused by a spiritual transformation or a proper education about the afterlife.):

- The elimination of negative habits to preoccupy the mind (including alcohol and drug habits.)

- The realignment to career ambitions based on sincerity versus mental distraction.

- The improvement of relationships of all types, including a new prioritization of these relationships fearlessly (No longer avoiding intimate attachments out of fear of loss, stemmed from the fear of death.)

- The reduction of heightened age-awareness (or: counting down the days till death.) Thus, the ability to counter norms about what one should, or should not do, depending upon age.

- The reduction of death-based fear of risk taking (fear of traveling, losing money, engaging in any kind of risky activity.)

- The ability to more quickly return to a psychologically happy state even following the death of loved ones.

- The ability to more easily focus on *the moment* and remain present in most situations—without a nagging, subconscious fear of the future (as it relates to death.)

- The overall reduction of depression based on all of the above elements of one's life returning to a balanced state.

I think it's fair to say that tackling the perpetual fear of death could be a cornerstone to a successful, happier life. And yes, that could even mean increased material gain—more success, more money. Of course, by studying NDE after-effects, materiality becomes far less prioritized. So yes, from a state of greater happiness and awareness of who you are and your true ambitions, you may end up making more money—but you'll be far less attached to any needs to acquire large sums of money to serve as a distraction or substitute to spiritual fulfillment. So, this effect is contradictory in nature and relates to a more general principle of success as a byproduct of our personal development and awareness, rather than a penultimate goal where our happiness is at stake.

Changing Priorities

Would knowledge of the afterlife break down society? Would there be mass suicides or a sense of responsibilities becoming lax? These are interesting questions, and such questions were explored in the Netflix thriller *The Discovery* (2017) starring Robert Redford about a scientist who "discovers" the afterlife. The premise is silly to me because, in reality, scientists like Dr. Gary Schwartz have already "discovered" the afterlife and in real life society reacted by saying "meh" or not knowing about it because not enough people cared or could believe it was real. However, what if—somehow—the lid was really blown off the subject and everybody had to face the afterlife as a reality? Would we see personal abandonment and societal breakdown?

These are obvious concerns, and, unfortunately, I don't have any precise answers—because it's never happened before. In fact, I have a little hypothesis growing that one reason knowledge is so limited could be because the folks on the astral side are worried about such consequences, too.

As with any disclosure-related process—that involves the "moving forward" of humanity—I suspect large-scale awareness of the afterlife would have some level of negative repercussions creating a temporary dysphoria, but a wider-level of positive changes in the long-term.

As we discussed earlier in this book, about the personally transformative nature of near-death experiences and afterlife awareness, we find a generally highly positive change of priorities among reasonable, decent people.

Would there be an increase in suicides? Existential crises among religious adherents? Maybe even some level of war, rioting or anger? If a switch were flipped, and suddenly everyone was aware of an afterlife, these are all possibilities. However, we could also see a decline in the dog-eat-dog, materialistic attitudes that are responsible for the slow degradation and ruin of our planet. And the planet is in a desperate need for these changes to occur sooner rather than later.

Many people blame the chokehold of the elite—the elite corporations and the government overlords—for the planet's decline. However, rampant materialism is also found on an individual basis. When even someone of a working-class background is obsessed with self-obtainment and shows neither regard for the planet nor for ones neighbors, this is just as much a part of the problem. Littering carelessly, behaving selfishly, cheating, robbing, and hurting others—these actions, big or small, keep this planet at a level of infantile spiritual development.

A philosopher may argue awareness of an afterlife could *decrease* a sense of responsibility because there's no longer a pressing sense of finity. For instance, in the world of motivational coaching—something I am also involved in—I hear many coaches (admirably) motivate people by saying the equivalent of: "*Someday you will become dust! You have nothing but these moments to live, then it's over! You MUST do what you desire to do NOW!*"

And, yes, this works for many people. They are motivated by fear. By scarcity. Materialism bent toward good. But at what price? Would belief in continued existence create a lack of motivation?

While, again, this *could* be possible, we must look at the data of how spiritual awareness affects behavior. As mentioned earlier in this chapter, the *shadow of death* is likely responsible for a great amount of this selfish behavior, as the sheer enormity of this fear does nothing good for an individual or the society they belong to. It creates a sense of scarcity by comparison to afterlife awareness, which creates a sense of abundance—as evident by the positive transformative effects of NDEs.

In fact, according to Jung, broadly speaking the awareness of a "greater reality" is profoundly important for personal happiness, and a nihilistic lack of spiritual grounding would only embolden a person to pursue materialistic desires—without end—desperately trying to fill a hole in one's soul that is yearning for greater meaning.

Further, *educated* awareness of the afterlife involves understanding what many religions have tried to convey, which is how there are *divine negative consequences* for actions, whether this is known as sin or karma. Although "McSpirituality" proponents have attempted to reduce this necessary teaching, what we learn from accurate sources is that hurting others, one way or another hurts ourselves—including at a deep, soul-level, and living a life of hurting others guarantees an existence in a very unpleasant condition. A very selfish soul could be motivated by this fact alone to change their behavior, as that initial selfishness creates a motivation to seek a better condition in the next life. We see this play out today among religious people who think, falsely, that donating large sums of money to a church institution (as Frank Sinatra did) shortly before death will mean acquiring enough "afterlife points" to reach better conditions.

Astral Experiences: Life and Death Cycles?

My older brother Jason (Bruce) unexpectedly died in summer 2017 (if continually abusing prescription drugs and alcohol could make any death "unexpected," but I digress.)

My experiences with him have been limited. However, on a rare occasion, I met with him and my mother together at our astral home; and had the opportunity to carry on a conversation.

He described how surprisingly normal life was on the astral Earth. Life just continued in our home city as before. In fact, he had a job and bought a new pickup truck.

Then, he described a peculiar phenomenon: "On the way over here, I hit and killed a squirrel that crossed the road."

"How can a creature on your side die? You're already in the afterlife!" I commented.

Jason went on to explain that any animal without sufficient mental development, or without an owner who loves it (i.e.: a pet,) is susceptible to life and death cycles. Bugs, rodents, most animals. Nature continues just like it does here.

"But," he clarified, "if an animal is particularly smart, let's say a very smart bird, its mental power will transcend the nature cycle and it won't be able to die any longer, just like humans."

This is still a selfish behavior because it's viewing life as a game where actual human interaction takes the back-burner to ritual and law. Real spiritual teaching helps put people on a better path.

Legal Euthanasia

Another subject that's tied to these stages is euthanasia or the right-to-die.

I postulate that with advancement in afterlife awareness, there will be a greater embracing of euthanasia to end suffering, which will have largescale positive effects for society. By contrast, it's the clinging to old materialist beliefs that keep the fear of death so extreme that it's preferable to be dying in agony from cancer (yet still in existence, by their logic) rather than to simply have an injection and cross over immediately without pain.

Right-to-die laws have passed in numerous places. In Belgium it's entirely legal. In Canada, it's accepted in any situation where a terminal illness is present and a patient has 6 months or less remaining (thousands have been allowed to die already.) More recently, a 104-year-old doctor from Australia successfully received euthanasia for non-terminal reasons, arguing that at his advanced age, life just wasn't applicable anymore.[9]

I personally have no desire to die a slow, agonizing death from a disease. If that time arrives in my life, and humanity and / or my country of residence hasn't "gotten it together" yet—I'll take matters into my own hands as I prepare for my final out-of-body trip that I (thankfully) won't return from (I have anxiety about the dying process, but no anxiety about what happens after.)

Further, it saddens me to think many who are scheduled to receive a painless death are unaware of the objective evidence for the afterlife and believe on a scheduled date they will enter a void—nothingness for eternity. It's still preferable to waiting in anticipation amidst agonizing sickness, but it illustrates the great need for continued afterlife-related education.

I encourage readers to please support right-to-die legislation in your country or state—as well as spreading awareness of the objective evidence for the afterlife.

Living As You Are Eternal

The most profound element of afterlife studies is realizing "you are eternal" is not a useless platitude. It's a literal fact. It also means that it's possible to begin living **right now** with your long...*very* long-term goals in mind. This is the penultimate aspect of afterlife studies and represents what it means to go "beyond" the afterlife as a theory and into the literality of the subject.

This is an entirely different way of looking at the world, presuming everyone who is born comes from the death paradigm. Even if a person is not fully materialistic, they still believe in a beginning and end point. The idea there is no endpoint can greatly affect mood and aspirations in very different, sometimes surprising ways.

William Murray, whom I mentioned in a prior chapter, has continued a relationship with his wife Irene after her passing. Transforming personally from a state of extreme despair and grief to feeling renewed optimism for life, enjoyment, and a sense of life's eternal nature that goes beyond our short time on Earth. In July 2018 he wrote on *Afterlife Topics and Metaphysics* an interesting take on adapting to life's eternal nature:

> I personally don't feel like I have any "work to complete" here. I just don't see my life here in those kinds of terms - like I'm here to learn anything or accomplish anything in particular. I see it as just a certain kind of adventure my soul-mate and I are engaging in for various reasons, and that it isn't anything really out of the ordinary for us. So, I see whatever time I have "left" in this modality in terms of that adventure, in terms of our ongoing, eternal relationship.
>
> A question that I asked myself was, if this really is just as much "the afterlife" (a realm of "spirit") as any other dimension (as Silver Birch said) and if this is just a certain, small stretch of time in a particular situation in our eternal relationship, what would I be doing under that set of premises?
>
> First, I'd be spending time trying to better my connection and interaction with Irene. After all, if she was visiting another city, I would do all I could to communicate with her. 2nd, I'd want to spend my time honing certain

> mental faculties, because that will always be useful. 3rd, I want to learn how to play the guitar better. 4th, I want to learn to paint better on canvas.
>
> So now I am working on all those things, as well as some other things, as a means of bringing my time here more in line with "what I would be doing" if I was "crossed over". My sense of satisfaction, peace and fulfillment increases the more I agree to live as if I am actually an eternal being, as if Irene and I are always together, and as if we can do whatever we want and have an eternity to do it in.

I wouldn't use Murray's example as a blanket philosophy—certainly, some people may be focused on bigger concepts to devote their incarnation to (versus simple things like learning the guitar,) however I understand the general idea. If we see ourselves as already "crossed over" and our future has no limit, it doesn't necessarily mean we lose all motivation and want to jump off the nearest cliff. Instead, when nihilism caused by the shadow of death is eliminated, we may see our desire for life and motivation to live increase. A materialist, by contrast, may feel a strong inclination to accomplish goals because of the specter of death, BUT, there's a serious risk: a sensation of pointlessness. For instance, while we hear motivators say "we must live life NOW before we disappear," one could just as easily counter by saying "nothing matters because we all turn into dust." So this motivation is built on a shaky foundation.

In fact, so profound is the crushing sense of oblivion that many turn to alcohol or drugs to escape from it. The best strategy for dealing with it becomes distraction. Or for some—suicide. If oblivion, non-existence is waiting for us all, then life itself was some type of joke—a cosmic accident of self-awareness, where we are forced to be conscious of the fact that our existences are only temporary. So why not just die quickly and get it over with? End the cosmic joke—it wasn't funny in the first place. I'm not saying this grim path is certain via materialist philosophy, but it's a greater possibility than the temptation of suicide roused by afterlife belief.

And while this sounds drastic, such morbidity is literally how some who suffer from these thoughts feel, and such depression, I believe, is a direct result of trying to rationalize materialism. Try to conceptualize non-existence and materialist thought long enough, and for some people this is the dark spiral that awaits. **There is no solution out of this vortex of negative thought short of changing philosophy**. It may be time to proverbially "walk away" from materialism and nihilism, to instead look at the objective evidence that provides other explanations, and stop paying attention to the grim cultural programming that supposes nothing but materialism is true.

* * *

If death is an illusion, and our actual individual selves persist in these other worlds, then it's time to take a serious look at how we think about our lives and what would formerly be considered their conclusions. If death is fundamentally NOT a conclusion, how does this affect long-term plans? Goals? Motivations?

Here, again, we enter entirely into a realm of philosophy. Remember, we are discussing the potential of our individual SELVES persisting, which means some element of continuation of who and what we are currently. This is in contrast to parallel (and in my opinion, non-evidence based) interpretations of the afterlife that I busted in Chapter 6—namely, that we may die but we are no longer who we were—perhaps we join the amorphous blob of Source Consciousness and "delete" our individual essences, or—again—we become purple octagons in a rainbow fractal landscape. These possibilities are not what I have in mind when I suggest the continuation of "you." I suggest a continuation based on the highly reported, personally documented and "confirmed" existence of the astral, parallel world **where it's possible to immediately continue our lifestyles in this new environment.**

With this possibility being considered, we can now undertake the monumental task of reconsidering our life-long goals and plans, and how those goals may change when we eliminate the 80-90 year-deadline and consider life expectancies that *do not end.* Exceptions may exist when a soul enters an exalted realm beyond human or physical incarnation—which seems to be a phenomenon that occurs entirely based on preference. In other words, you can live your human existence as long as you personally choose to inhabit an astral body or an Earth-body—an elimination of your human lifestyle will never be forced upon you.

In an effort to help you at least consider this paradigm as food-for-thought (in the same way William Murray has done,) I'll propose a few questions for you to think about:

- If you were to live for hundreds of years, what vocation would you choose, and why?

- If you can anticipate returning to the "prime" of your life and perfect health, what future activities should you plan around?

- What activities would you like to do again with particular deceased loved ones?

- What decisions in your life taken today may not have full ramifications until hundreds of years in the future?

I cannot conclude this concept without touching on a different type of existential dread: **the fear of living forever.**

In the early days, as I first began to wrap my mind around the afterlife, this was a very real issue. I had, back then, an undeveloped understanding of "time" in relation to the other side. And so, "forever" would mean a continuation of our human time scaling system. There is no number big enough to encompass "forever." Not a trillion, trillion years. I can see why some are terrified of continued individual existence given this idea—who wants to just be a single soul for all eternity?

This anxiety lessened, actually, through reading NDEs. As we talked about previously, "time" still exists but is perceived differently. Many talk about how there is no such thing as linear time but a perpetual "now" that never ceases. When one is attuned to the "perpetual now" then it doesn't matter if we're talking about an hour or a trillion years—even though the hour, day or year still exists and can be accessed via memory—they don't really *matter* like they do in this plane. To make the time span phenomena matter even less, we can also keep in mind every event or moment can be re-experienced, as I believe in "higher" conditions time travel becomes a simple matter of conscious direction. A trillion years may pass, but you can relive a trillion years prior like it was nothing.

Further, no one is confined to be themselves forever—all souls are inherently linked together and we are just as much each other as we are ourselves. So, if you're worried about being Bert the plumber (or whomever you and your identity currently consists of) for a trillion years—relax—that's not the way reality operates.

Will Society See Different Stages?

Materialism, nihilism, and all the connected ideas—they still dominate Western civilization, but for how much longer? In this section, I'd like to propose what I see as the 6 stages of afterlife-related knowledge and acceptance. Let's go over them:

Stage One: Ignorance and Religious Orthodoxy

This has been the default paradigm for centuries up until quite modern times. Religion capitalized "spiritual" subjects, dating back to Roman times. People are taught to ignore their authentic experiences with the other side and default to notions of evil spirits and to distrust one's own experiences. Fear and institutions mark belief in the afterlife, and control over the belief is used as a method of power.

Meanwhile, as science and enlightenment thought is introduced, people flip to the opposite extreme: a belief in materialism and a rejection of anything but what the senses can detect. All non-material or extra-dimensional ideas are flat rejected and grouped with religious ideas. This has been occurring on our planet since the 1700s and still persists throughout most of academia.

Stage Two: New Religion Replaces Old Religion

The second stage sees the birth of what we call a "New Age" movement. Through wider information exchange, books, TV, internet, etc, people stop hiding their authentic spiritual experiences out of fear. Perhaps we saw this stage kick off with the works of Emmanuel Swedenborg, the 18th-century enlightenment-era philosopher and scientist who would write in frank terms about the real conditions of the afterlife (and whose work remains popular today.) This creates an "alternate" to the existing paradigm that most people know in their hearts is bunk, and thus begins to change ideas.

Stage Three: Objective Evidence Leaks into the Mainstream

While a New Age paradigm catches a lot of attention on the sidelines, it will never go very far until it marries itself at least somewhat with institutions of science. It will also run the risk of becoming an insular circle of knowledge that may discount objectivity—and begin to operate in itself as a kind of religion (as we saw with Spiritualism.) This changes in the third stage. We saw this stage already begin through scientific interest in near-death experiences. The 1975 book "Life After Life" by Raymond Moody was probably what kicked off a slow inauguration of this stage. Over 40 years since that book, we've seen widespread academic dismissal of an afterlife; however, the argument in favor of an afterlife remains highly persistent because the evidence and experiences are so widespread. As hard as the institutions try to fight the information, it just keeps resurrecting itself. (For instance, mainstream acolytes think of an idea to discredit NDEs, and then a week later a new NDE story gains huge publicity, washing over the negative press.)

Eventually, there is so much "mainstream" information by people with credentials, sophisticated writers, and "heretical" academics that it begins to overload modern media, and the subject becomes widely available to anyone open-minded enough to explore it. Meanwhile, institutions continue to hold on to their death-grip, but it becomes apparent their strength is weakening. I believe we are currently in this final days of the third stage.

Stage Four: Objective Evidence Becomes Self-Apparent

Eventually, more and more academics and officials turn to the "heretical" side and reject their institutional biases to embrace the "supernatural" topics. The information is soon presented without an air of skepticism. The main question changes from "Is this subject real?" to "If this subject is real, what do we do about it?"

The fourth stage would mean a widespread saturation, to the point even "laypeople" recognize its likely existence. While the subject is beyond most people's comprehension, and most are still glued to watching sports and playing video games instead of exploring some of these harder subjects, what we see in the fourth stage is the removal of cultural biases. A removal of cultural bias means bringing the subject up will not result in ostracization, uncomfortable feelings or an immediate change of subject to "that Lakers game last night."

During the latter part of this stage, asking the average educated person about life after death will result in an answer like, "Yeah, I hear there's an afterlife, that's what scientists and smart people say, anyway."

Meanwhile, institutions will begin to change their tune. The hardline adherents of materialism may begin spinning the information in such a way to imply that they knew about the information all along or that it's self-evident. Of course, this will only occur after enough of their peers have exerted pressure on them to do so. They may try to capitalize on the information or change it to fit their own desired molds or agendas (we may hear things like "yes, there's an afterlife, but still no proof we retain our individualities" and debates about these details will persist for a long time.)

Stage Five: Detailed Accuracy Changes Culture

The fifth stage is when academic and institutional battles result in deeper levels of accuracy taking hold, and this more detailed information leaks out among the general public.

For instance, today through direct spirit communication we can learn specifically about the "astral plane," a world parallel to ours, and the exact conditions of people who live on that side—people who lived and died on this realm. We can also learn about all the implications for physics and cosmology—that existence itself is non-material, layered like a vast wedding cake, our consciousness is NOT located in the brain, and our realm is just one realm among innumerable that we may inhabit. However, all this information will remain a "fringe" topic until the fifth stage sees a widespread integration.

In a way that would be alien to what we see today, the fifth stage would involve people speaking casually about topics like the astral plane or things they want to see and do after they die. Even the very subject of people dying will shift to a more relaxed attitude, and we'd actually see the first signs that the "shadow of death" is rolling away.

We may also see a vast shift in communication with the other side. Today we see the beginnings of technological communication (see the work Sonia Rinaldi of Brazil) but with this type of integration, there would be a rush of scientists seeking to massively expand communication efforts. This rush would push society to the 6th and final stage.

Stage Six: Full Integration and Cultural Change

This stage would mean a world that would be science-fiction by our current standards: communication to other realms would be as simple as going to an institution and tuning a signal to enable two-way communication with deceased people. Imagine long-dead people of legendary stature giving lectures to university halls—and the population generally accepting such occurrences.

Interestingly, I theorize "life would still go on." Average people would approach the topic as a fact with a level of reverence and a "wow" factor, but they'd generally accept it when Ben Franklin gives a commencement speech to a class via a complex audio apparatus. Nonetheless, average folks would still spend their time talking about sports and unwinding after long days of work.

Nonetheless, the cultural shift would see, on a more subtle level, a widespread difference of opinion about death and a huge reduction of fear associated to death as we see today, to the point people would look back at our current times as a more primitive era when people were less educated and a lot more ignorant and full of anxiety.

People would still be upset about death and dying. It would still cause pain, grief and a lot of emotions, but it just wouldn't have the same gravity that we see today. Overall, society wouldn't have a fraction of the anxiety and discontent we are accustomed to. Materialism's relationship to *materialism* would change, as people would no longer prioritize mindless acquisition quite as much in a society where everyone knows they live forever, thus providing an innate sense of abundance.

This shift, of course, would likely be integrated with other shifts or disclosure events. By this time, technological shifts may see the eradication of the diseases we fear like cancer. We may no longer even be bound to the confines of this planet, if—for instance—free energy technology is released to the public.

All combined together these various shifts would see dramatic changes to our society. Although "life would go on" for laypeople, upon closer examination of individuals during this era—we'd see the details of their lives as vastly different from how we lead our lives. While people may still be clocking in, going to work, serving drinks, cleaning counters and talking sports, they'd be living in a more advanced era of humanity that is a lot more balanced, truthful, and futuristic.

The Stages Are Not Guaranteed (Turning Point)

If the above six-stage process (which is merely hypothetical) sounds appealing to you—I'd like to remind readers that it's also uncertain. If we are at the latter part of the hypothetical third stage, I also propose we could see a retroactive occurrence where we fall further backwards on this third-stage, maybe even back into the second or first stages.

In fact, authority figures actively desire to see us pushed back into the first stage where such authorities monopolize "divine" subjects. I feel the afterlife, in general, suffers far less scorn than in days past (even 15 years ago) however; I challenge anyone to even imply the existence of empirical "supernatural" evidence to, say, a scientific Reddit community of millennials. A whole industry still exists to discredit people's spiritual experiences. Organized skeptic communities have withdrawn slightly from the topic in recent years, but they haven't forgotten about it.

Fortunately, we could also speculate that it's possible to skip ahead steps. I postulate that if we did skip a whole stage, it would have harsher effects on society—for instance, there would be more outward hostility, if not violence and aggression. Let's say a device were created tomorrow that proved beyond a reasonable doubt of an afterlife, and it was released publicly, and everyone knew about it. This could skip us straight to Stage 6, but at what cost? Religious rioting, terrorism, mass suicide—these are the types of fear-based scenarios that could occur if the process doesn't complete at a natural pace.

My personal hope? That it doesn't take 1,000 years to get there. Using this theoretical model, it's taken only a few decades to switch from second to third stages, and now we're nearing the end of the third stage. If I can stay in this realm through a fourth stage, I'll be quite happy.

VIII – Facing the Dark Side

The reality of an afterlife involves aspects that people rarely confront: psychological and physical (manifested) dark elements to the subject. In addition, the acceptance of an afterlife as a new paradigm comes with its own set of unique issues, as well. This is what we'll explore in this chapter.

Why the "Dark" Matters

In the last chapter, I mentioned Jungian shadow-work, and how it relates to confronting death—namely, the fear of death, and eventually exposing the subject into the open.

What seems to happen is reality mirrors itself. So what we see on a surface level, has deeper roots that dig further down. The subject of the afterlife is no different. On a surface level, what we hear about is the superficial elements: love, light, happiness, heaven, Jesus, paradise, "eternal bliss" (whatever that truly means.) Religious thought reduced this most complex subject over the millennia into extremely simplistic terms: if you're bad, you go to hell, if you're not bad, you go to heaven. Black and white. Dead simple.

The closest society received to any type of greater intellectual exploration of hell would be *The Divine Comedy* (or *Dante's Inferno*) released in 1320 a year before Dante Alighieri's own death. This book, of course, is not considered Biblical canon by practicing Catholics (only the Bible is,) yet, it had a profound impact on how depictions of hell—or what we'd call negative astral realms—are perceived. Readers were astonished to find the lowest pits of hell were frozen and icy versus fiery, with the worst of the sinners of history encased in ice.[10] At a time when imaginative works of fiction were not exactly common, it's no surprise that people took Dante's hell literally, and ever since we've imagined metaphorical depictions of things like a "lake of fire" to be realities versus metaphors.

Dante's religious trips actually end as he explores the final circle of the heavens, with the ninth heaven on the border of the Empyrean—a formless realm beyond space and time. At this point, there is some similarity to modern NDE accounts that describe formless hyper-existences, and its therefore possible Dante was drawing upon NDE stories told during that era (perhaps via word of mouth,) or he experienced some level of visions that were legitimate. However, despite what could be a small nugget of truth, most of *The Divine Comedy* reads like a great revenge fantasy—with everyone from corrupt popes to common charlatans and street magicians called to Dante's scorn and being fitted to appropriate levels of hell for their misdeeds.

Today, while belief in a hell faces no shortage of influence among the fundamentalist religious, there is no recognition of its existence among the neo-spiritual. This is, of course, a likely more accurate perception. Hell is, was, and always will be a social construct, used to represent the stick of religion's "carrot and stick" approach to social management.

But another danger may lie in the complete dismissal of "hell"—or more accurately, a dark spectrum to spirituality. We don't hear about the "dark side" in pop spirituality. And just like our own inner demons, people are afraid to talk about the subject in a frank manner. The dark side, as we know it, is relegated to topics like devilish poltergeists, demon possession, curses, hexes, black magic, and so forth—and this represents, in itself, a popular genre—but it's a genre removed from "objective" spirituality, life after death, and so forth. It's more a realm for dabblers and those who seek entertainment via the "supernatural" or "occult" as a genre.

The existence of a dark spectrum sometimes throws people's sense of spiritual direction off-course. People are attracted to New Age spirituality, often, as a "feel good" alternative to the Bible. The idea of a "hell" is one of the first concepts that people shrug off. And, today, we hear many writers in this genre cast aside the entire notion altogether. They may literally say, "Negativity does not exist on the other side." (reread Chapter 6 for my rebuttal of such ideas.)

In my view, disregarding the dark creates a lopsided perspective about the afterlife. And, for the reasons mentioned previously in this book, it is itself a dark path to pretend not-so-nice conditions either do not exist or are impossible to exist because it creates the moral quicksand where horrific deeds occur without consequence. Often, I hear people justify these beliefs by saying, "We are attracted to spirituality to escape from the idea of a punishing God who sentences people to hell!" but this is a classic example of "throwing the baby out with the bathwater." Even in the occult studies, there is little to no talk or a punishing deity casting people into these conditions—unless we were to explore specifically Christian, Judaic or Islamic mysticism that may be steeped in such mythology. The answer to this riddle is what most of us already know: hellish conditions exist regardless of the existence of a God, and we create such conditions for ourselves.

The best example of a negative realm can be found by exploring our own negative realms. In Los Angeles, take the metro downtown and take a walk into the infamous Skid Row sector. For decades, these few city blocks have congregated so many drug addicts and people who are barely clinging to life and light, that the relatively small sector requires an entire fire station (nicknamed *Wine-o Five-o*) to contend with so many emergency calls, overdoses, assaults, or deceased persons.

As an astral explorer, like many subjects, I simply don't see a huge difference between our realm and alternate conditions. Just like here, sickened and disused souls are trying to manage emotions, guilts, toxic thoughts, and the negative karma associated with prior malicious behavior. As energy attracts, such souls clump together into appropriate realms. And, as I mentioned in the first chapter of this book, on the astral levels we experience far heightened emotional, mental states—states of mind that make our existence on this plane subdued by comparison. While this can create immense joy and excitement, akin to "being a kid again," it comes with a flipside—the heightened emotional vibration can amplify negative emotions, too. When I meet up with my mom, she is buzzing with energy—so much more than before. However, if the mood shifts to a more negative tone, it can become fierce. This phenomenon is not something that should ever be underestimated and represents a major difference between our realms.

Much as Skid Row in LA is, itself, a "realm"—so are negative astral locations. And, just like here, those of us who are *not* battling darkness within ourselves will likewise *not* be attracted to these conditions; rather, we will feel a deep sense of either danger or apprehension, forcing our feet away from these conditions—unless, alternatively, a sense of sympathy and charity compels us to enter a negative realm to provide aid to its inhabitants. As many social workers can tell you, this is not an easy task. A troubled soul can only be helped so much until such souls choose to help themselves. When I toured the Skid Row fire department once, I met a host of some of the most charitable people I'll ever meet. They all obtain a deep sense of fulfillment from their jobs, despite being stationed in what is considered one of the most difficult fire stations in Los Angeles County. However, to desire to work at Fire Station 9 requires this particular charitable drive—the same one that drives all those of higher vibration who purposefully enter darker realms to be of assistance.

When Dark Astral Conditions Come Knocking

The essence of understanding "the dark" is to recognize a principle outlined earlier in this book: that many of us fundamentally remain the same after we cross over (note that I say *many*, not *all*.) While, yes, we seem to belong to higher, group oversouls that are, themselves, "perfect" manifestations of a Source consciousness ("God" for lack of a better term,) the individual fragments of an oversoul are our individual selves, and those fragments are fully capable of becoming dark, destructive, and / or making terrible life decisions. In many ways, individual existence itself is a grandiose experiment of decision-making and self-responsibility. Left to our own devices, we can either play nice (a path of *service to others*) or play dirty (a path of *service to self*.) We may find we *require* a little of the latter path to fully enjoy our existences (we must all be selfish to some degree lest we surrender our well-being,) but if the *service to self* is taken to an extreme level—then habits will form that is highly destructive. And, in very bad situations, a soul may even become *sociopathic*—energetically immune to the essence of other people's existences, so as to continue their self-serving actions without experiencing direct negative side-effects (not to say those negative side-effects won't accrue and rebound back to the person, who is trying in vain to escape inescapable cosmic law.)

Astral travelers have ventured into these realms and confirmed conditions where individual souls—mired by darkness, selfish behaviors and sociopathy—exist in their own fetid yet optimal conditions (that is to say, optimal for their current level of spirituality.) Striking examples include *Vistas of Infinity* author Jurgen Ziewe's exploration of dark realms including the "paradise" that Islamic suicide bombers find themselves in (a horrific condition of perpetually reliving their vicious act,) to highly consistent accounts in many other books—whether written by NDErs or astral travelers—confirming such realms. Stafford Betty remarks in *The Afterlife Unveiled* (2011):

> "There are hellish regions in the astral, and large populations that make their home there. What is sometimes referred to as the Shadow-lands is a vast world of many conditions. The landscapes vary from sordid city neighborhoods to parched, gray scrubland to dark, lifeless deserts. The vivid clarity of higher realms is

> missing. Instead there is a dull overcast. Temporarily lost or confused or stubbornly unrepentant souls populate these regions

Many in these realms desire to leave their conditions but are hindered by their psychological makeup. Jurgen Ziewe describes a process of helping souls escape from such a realm—and why it's generally an extremely difficult process. Before this excerpt, Jurgen finds himself in a dark, urban landscape on the astral plane—similar to places I have personally explored on a number of occasions. Among this drab industrial sector, he encounters a group huddled at a bonfire. He attempts to demonstrate how it is possible to leave a negative density and switch to a more positive realm:

> "Momentarily, I focused on my heart, which instantly brightened the whole area and gently lifted me off the ground...At once three of the people grabbed my legs and tried to hitch a lift. I struggled to rise into the air, but the burden became too great.[...] Two of them released me, but the woman with the dark stringy hair clung on to me for dear life. I shouted to her to focus on her heart to become lighter, but she just stared at me despairingly, obviously not even grasping my meaning. Knowing that without her inner connection to the light she would only be a burden to herself and me, I suggested she should let go. [...] Almost instantly I felt pangs of regret and compassion, and instead of disentangling myself I sank with her back to Earth. [...] All I felt was great pity for the people stranded here. I considered giving a lecture that they needed to start focusing their attention on their hearts in order to leave this region but I knew this would fall on deaf ears." (Vistas of Infinity, 2015.)

As we can see, it is their psychological makeup that keeps them bound to such a realm. And as much as we may desire it, nobody can wave a magic wand and cause such inhabitants to "ascend" to some heavenly abode—they would simply not be compatible.

My Own Experiences

What Jurgen describes is a "lower" astral realm; however, among my many OBEs, I think an important point I've learned is that all such realms constitute greater societies, as we have here. There are pockets of darkness, and pockets of lightness—just like Skid Row does not represent Los Angeles as a whole but is nonetheless a dark element of a much larger civilization.

There is, in fact, an astral Los Angeles. And it is a place I have appeared many times. Exactly like in our own Los Angeles, there is a mix of really wonderful areas—neighborhoods and city streets that are clean, luxurious, and filled with people far happier and more excited about life than our side—fulfilling their dreams and desires without the crippling economic pressure of our plane. However, there are also areas of astral LA that people avoid—the streets become dank, dirtier, the air thicker, and sometimes the light around such an area becomes dim. Immediately, one could tell they are in a hovel of thieves and selfish entities—perhaps those who, when on Earth, were killers, drug pushers, and gangbangers.

The difference that I can tell is that such denizens are not a huge threat to the "nicer" areas of astral LA. There seem to be natural energetic barriers around different sectors that keep, say, a murderous and destructive gang of thugs from destroying the west-side of astral LA, which is of a higher vibration (at least in my experience.) If they were to enter such a place with destructive intentions, I believe the residents would have a relatively easy time dispelling them. It's also possible the vibrational / energetic difference would render them weak or unable to proceed very far into the lighter atmosphere.

But, everything on the astral side seems to be in flux—or, to put it another way—just like human souls are not static, realms are not static, either. A nice area of town could fall into disrepair and begin to attract negative souls, and likewise, a negative sector could begin to attract nicer conditions when the residents of that area improve themselves to a higher degree. Many times, these changes occur slowly and naturally without people entirely noticing what happened—until one day they wake up and realize the neighborhood with their favorite coffee shop has turned into a sh-- hole. This is not entirely different from our plane, except the changes are more noticeable and cast a greater effect on the entire environment—which is caused by an "astral law" that personal thoughts affect the greater environment (ranging from subtle to explicit.)

What I have only experienced sporadically is the apparent multi-layered planes in the same environment, which we talked about earlier in Chapter 4 and as Jurgen Ziewe talks about extensively in *Multidimensional Man* and *Vistas of Infinity*. For instance, the process of "lifting up" into a higher, more refined version of the same landscape. I find this is possible—but the landscape may change distinctly even if a similar building still stands in that location. If "rising" to a higher realm were to occur in say, astral Los Angeles—I may find myself on a new, higher density plane no longer necessarily on the astral "Second Earth" but an entirely different albeit familiar realm (of the same geographic radius.) So, if I am at a bagel shop and I "change my vibration" to a higher realm—where the bagel shop once stood there may be a beautiful temple instead. However, there is no physical expanse of space journeyed to reach such a temple—it was still existing in the same "location" simultaneously, but was beyond the normal perception of residents on the "lower" side—who were preparing bagels daily for astral customers without knowing a heavenly temple exists right where they stand on a different spectrum (although perhaps sometimes, late at night, they may hear the temple's church bells.) Meanwhile, on the Earth plane, where the bagel shop stands, is a guy's house—which happens to be the same shape as the bagel store but on this side is outfitted as a private residence. He does not know the bagel shop exists except sometimes, late at night, there's a mysterious, ghostly odor of baked bread that he cannot identify.

And as realms advance higher, they can go lower, and in astral Earth conditions there is a risk of darker realms spreading into medium or middle-planes. An environment with positive and darker realms intermixed (like astral Los Angeles) may find a seamless integration between light and dark. One neighborhood may be clean and nice, while another is descending into the category of a negative astral realm—and you can look out your window at the lower realm forming from the vantage of your nice, comfortable bedroom or a rooftop.

It's possible the residents of these dark locales are "stuck" in those conditions, but I haven't properly interviewed people in such realms to know. I also believe there's a possibility that a negative area could descend lower and lower until it transforms into a place that's virtually uninhabitable by the normal, unaffected residents of the city. At this point, I theorize that a dark astral condition could "grow" in such a way that it becomes its own independent, hellish environment entirely isolated from the rest of the greater realm (such as a city) it belongs to.

This may create an impression by astral travelers that such a dark place is a self-enclosed nightmare world, without realizing one could geographically explore the radius and physically walk out of this hellish condition back into the normal parts of the community (however, when the vibrational difference becomes so drastic, the very dark residents of this abode would be physically unable to walk out of their environment until their personal frequency changes enough to integrate back with the rest of the population.) By contrast, a resident who's not "attached" to this dark atmosphere, like someone from the higher-vibration parts of the same city, can travel into this darker realm whenever they desire—although, just as we would avoid Skid Row in our realm unless something compels us to help those people, we'd usually avoid the not-so-nice astral realms, too.

To summarize: a dark astral plane is *not necessarily a self-contained mental world but is part of a greater community, like a city, in an area that's become extremely unpleasant.* When Jurgen describes a dark, astral urban landscape with windowless industrial buildings, we may imagine such buildings are inoperable mental manifestations. In my experience as an astral traveler, this is not true. A physical astral-Earth condition still maintains physical operations, and an industrial sector may be, as here, literally producing goods or be in operation via a business venture and serving people outside of that dark realm in some way. However, if a section of a city becomes highly affected by dark mental forces, this piece of "astral real estate" could become grimier and more foreboding in appearance. Perhaps, at worst, descending into a sub-plane inaccessible to the outside and entirely hellish (that can't be good for property values.)

Just imagine if the locales of our world were affected by the thoughts of their inhabitants, and if a building full of unhappy, depressed employees took on a drab appearance with peeling paint and a gloomy atmosphere that anyone could sense. On the other hand, an office full of positive, spiritual people changes into a radiant structure that attracts every passerby. This visualization may provide you some clue about the differences between our world and theirs.

Possible Myth: Bad People Can't Intermix With Good People

As we try to understand this endlessly complex subject, there's a lot of stumbling blocks. I want to make it clear that based on my experiences on the astral plane: I have found *no evidence* that vibrational compatibility completely eliminates the possibility of criminals, wrongdoers, destructive people or malicious people from intermixing with a normal environment that's *not* a dark astral condition. This is illustrated by the fact that in almost all cities and communities on astral realms that I've seen, I've encountered the presence of either law enforcement or private security personnel.

However, a major difference that's been communicated to me is that such institutions do not operate prisons—a useless enterprise when physical rules are different, and it's possible to practice techniques like teleportation. Instead, the criminal elements are effectively *banished* from communities. I am not entirely sure how this action is undertaken, but it may further explain how dark astral conditions become filled with so many people—if those people were quite literally cast out of communities via the actions of law enforcement, security, or astral government personnel. (This could be analogous to the world of internet forums and communities—that jerk who's been banned from 16 Facebook groups may end up with nowhere else to go but that unmoderated, chaotic group full of spammers.) This is not to say that people do not enter hellish conditions naturally—a byproduct of unhealthy minds—but they may become

Astral Experiences: Encountering a Demon

I have a distinctive memory of a highly unusual astral encounter. A peaceful slumber was interrupted by an entity that decided to seek me out.

It was clear to me something was communicating telepathically. Without a word spoken, it was digging through my thoughts and feelings.

After it had sufficient information, it took shape based entirely on my fears. Its appearance was of a giant, rotting shark. This was a reflection of a personal fear of the deep sea and rotting bodies.

Its giant, gaping maw was filled with maggots, exploiting an additional fear of slithering worms.

Soon, it was sucking me into its mouth, while demanding in a booming voice: "Submit to me, now!"

I understand spiritual law is based on consent. A dark entity CANNOT harm you without you allowing it to. This beast's strategy was to force permission through creating terror.

I told it, "I'm also a fan of horror movies, and you did an amazing job creating this creature. Good job, bro. But I'm not submitting to you. Have a nice day."

It never bothered me again.

populated, as well, by those whose mental vibration is deteriorating and they find themselves banished from the lighter realms that cannot accommodate them.

There is an idea I hear that many realms are "paradise" and it is impossible for a darker element to disrupt a community. My theory is that this is a partially true and partially incorrect observation. This phenomenon *may* occur in very sophisticated planes—where the "vibration" is high to the point the inhabitants simply do not have any inclination of such wrongdoings. This is also how the idea of "no negativity" is propagated—because when we see communities of entirely sophisticated, mature, evolved souls—it can lend the illusion that the afterlife itself is devoid of "problems." This is not true. What people do not recognize at first glance is that highly evolved communities got to that point via an incredible amount of work by those inhabitants to become refined and free of the personality characteristics that can lead to disruption, argument, resentment, jealousy and so forth. When evolved, blissful souls exist in this state, they exist in a refuge away from a lot of the petty negativities that we know of—however, even still, we do not fully understand what difficulties, pains or challenges people of this esteemed level may face—involving perhaps divine, cosmic issues that we have no comprehension about. My axiom concerning this topic is that strife initiates growth and change, and few mature souls would even want to exist in a state where there is no strife.

In summary, in high vibrational communities, we may indeed find that "bad people" are devoid of influence as everyone is of a refined, mature level. However, on the Astral Earth conditions—we find an assortment of characters similar to our current plane of existence—and in most astral levels, there is a presence of "security" roles to deal with disruptive individuals and criminal elements. So that, while most criminals are relegated into dark astral habitats, we'll still find darker denizens disrupting or preying on individuals outside of these dark planes. Perhaps in these regular astral conditions, the rules are not so severe in regard to vibrational incompatibility, and it's possible for the less pleasant ilk to sometimes mingle among the positive souls and create problems. In my own experience, I'd say it's naïve to believe an astral cityscape is devoid of threat or problematic people.

The Netherworld

Now that I believe we can say with certainty the "dark astral" is real, I will introduce the idea that the issue goes deeper—into realms that are necessary for communicators with the other side—including OOB practitioners—to understand. Namely, the existence of what I often call the "near-Earth astral."

I believe this realm is what we hear about in Greek mythology as Hades, in Western Catholicism as purgatory, and in pop occultism as the netherworld. It is also the actual location of "earthbound" souls (let me reinforce a point: your uncle Ted enjoying a hamburger in the astral plane is *not* "earthbound" just because he's in a physical astral condition. However, if a person is lingering around our world akin to the subway spirit in the movie *Ghost* with Patrick Swayze—yes, that individual is earthbound.)

It has taken me a long time to understand how this realm works, but the concept of "layers" outlined by Jurgen Ziewe (mentioned in the prior section) helped to make sense of the situation. On some occasions, I will go out-of-body and find myself co-existing in the same Earthly environment. On other occasions, I will go out-of-body and find that while I am still in my bedroom, all the furniture is rearranged and I am effectively in a parallel version of the same house.

In the latter example, if I walk out of my home, I'll find myself in, for instance, Astral Los Angeles—a realm completely distinctive and separate from our own. Such a realm is a layer "above" our own plane, where many of the same landmarks—including houses—exist, but in an entirely new, parallel city. In my replica house, I've seen people I don't recognize living in that house—possibly squatters. So, while the house is "copied" on that side, it's also a different house in many respects, as it exists on the astral side independent of the Earth-plane version. All it has in common is the structure and placement, but the interior of a house may be entirely different as it is occupied by different people over many years—or it may be occupied by the Earth-plane residents who appear in such an astral replica during periods of sleep. The alternate residents may change its interiors or possibly even upgrade it with things they couldn't afford in our own realm.

However, the former example—when I am sharing the same space as the Earth-plane, I am still disconnected from the Earthly dimension, but existing in conjunction with it. From this vantage point, astral people can disrupt our world or make contact with us, whether benevolently or as poltergeists. This process involves lowering their vibration sufficiently to enter the near-Earth plane, a difficult energetic process. This is exactly what my mother does when she desires to make contact. When she has lowered herself into this environment I can simply disconnect from my body, and I'll be able to see her and make direct physical contact. For this reason, the near-Earth netherworld is a wonderful place because it enables direct contact with our deceased loved ones.

However, there's also a deep, dark aspect to this in-between realm. This plane is, for lack of a better term, *infested* by entities, including one of the most commonly reported creatures by astral travelers—the shadow people.

I should make it clear, I've never encountered a shadow person. Since having one scuffle with a demonic entity (see the sidebar story above,) I've been even more resilient to remain in a very positive state of mind which should hopefully ward away gravitating into some negative sphere. Nonetheless, astral travelers face the issue of having to navigate through the netherworld to pop up into the astral plane, and during that brief period when one's consciousness is traveling out of the Earth density, we may end up spending more time than we desired in the near-Earth astral.

There are many theories about shadow people, but the stories of encounters with them—especially by inexperienced astral travelers—are endless. The late Stephen Hawking even recognized their existence in a recent commentary (read more at: https://www.theodysseyonline.com/mystery-shadow-people).

Even among all the stories and posts I read on astral projection forums, the most striking stories were told to me by my good friend and roommate John, who served in the United States Marine Corp in the early and mid-2000s.

In one story, he was deployed at a base in Japan. Near the base was an old local cemetery, with graves dating back hundreds of years. In a not-so-smart move, he and a buddy carelessly would take pisses at the cemetery. After one such incident, by the evening they returned to their barracks (rows of bunk beds.) In the middle of the night, John saw something enter the barracks from the corner of his eye: A wispy, shadowy apparition of a person—without distinguishable features but a phantasm in the truest sense. "Oh sh--," he said out loud as he saw it approaching his bunk. Swiftly, it climbed up the bunk's ladder and attacked him—cold hands gripping around his neck. He tried to fight it off but found his body mostly paralyzed. "With each touch and grab by the entity, I'd feel my energy completely drain out of my body. It was sucking the energy out of me—feeding on me," John recounts. The entity disappeared—and John was left physically drained, barely able to move.

The next day, his bunk-mate and fellow Marine was bug-eyed. The creature had preyed on him, too. Afterward, they decided it would be a good idea to avoid the cemetery—and especially avoid pissing on any of the graves.

Many years later, after we had been living together for a number of years, John became much more interested in topics like astral projection (probably because he'd see me continually writing about it or doing webinars and radio appearances for my book.) Soon, he was having brief out-of-body experiences, but his experiences were quickly attracting shadow people—something I have thankfully never experienced. I don't know why this happens to some people and not to others—but it could be related to a lack of spiritual precautions (a positive, loving state of mind. My guess is John was taking no precautions.) In a more memorable incident, he left his body and made it across his bedroom. But he was quickly stopped by the presence of an entire cadre of shadow people who "warped" into the near-Earth astral to greet him.

"What did they look like?" I asked him.

"I remember one of them. Do you know how in medieval times, the people who would clean bodies stricken by the plague would wear those gas masks that look like big, creepy birds? It was a shadowy outline wearing one of those beaked masks used by plague crews."

"What did they want from you?"

"Their intention was clear… They wanted me to join them." Whatever the shadow people are, they are a race of entities, and they are common. One theory about their origin is that a human soul, after centuries of the earthbound state, may eventually become corrupted into the dark spectrum, shaking off human characteristics and finally becoming an ethereal "demon." They seem to feed on us and especially feed on negative energy—lingering in places where there is domestic turmoil, unhappiness, and suffering. Avoid these energetic elements in your home, and you'll prevent the arrival of these parasites.

Defensive Posturing and Free Will

It is not clear to me where shadow people or other negative entities exist naturally, but given the nature of astral realms and the incredible diversity, it would not surprise me if dark realms existed that nearly mirrored the ascension of light realms—descending down into greater "hellish' environments.

There is no reason to believe these realms would contain a hierarchy as described by religion. Certainly, deceased Catholic priest Monsignor Hugh Benson in the previously cited *Life in the World Unseen* made it abundantly clear that there is no Satan and all denizens of dark realms are there based upon their own choices. And this makes logical sense considering the realms are too vast, too varied for any singular dark force to be worshipped. Nonetheless, chaotic realms can present the imagery that is entirely applicable to pop-cultural ideas of hell—and likely shaped the misinterpreted Biblical accounts of where "sinners" go. In *Unseen*, the protagonist only scratches the mere surface of the dark realms and recounts horrific imagery—skeletal, misshapen souls and a putrid, arid landscape devoid of natural life or any of the joys we may find in normal worlds. The residents are trapped in cycles of despair, anger, vengeance, or sorrow. And, with enough time dedicated to terrible thoughts, their bodies change to reflect their minds—becoming grotesque. Perpetually, they prey upon each other.

We cannot say if *Unseen* is objective, accurate information—but so much of the material in the book fits the experiences of near-death survivors and astral travelers, that I am partial to the information in that book. I don't doubt these types of astral realms could exist. And their existence poses some troubling questions: How vast are dark realms and what is their influence upon our world?

To figure this out, we must first remember cosmic laws that involve free will and the power of consent. In astral realms, where the mind has significantly more power than matter, it *seems* it's much harder to physically reprimand a person (I am cautious to say impossible, as I've encountered a modicum of physical danger to my astral body before; however, I don't believe a physical attack would cause permanent or irreparable damage.) As a result, the preferred way to cause harm to another soul is to exploit ignorance of spiritual laws by manipulating people within the framework of free will. The sociopath is the veritable master of this practice. Mentally, it's possible for people to be coerced, pressured or tricked into consenting to things that will hurt them or benefit another person at their expense. This, therefore, becomes the modus operandi of malicious entities: coax victims into going along with them, whether through fear, intimidation, vapid promises, or seduction. The end result being slavery and submission to dark forces, who would see you dragged down to hell with them. This practice is manifested among souls in our world: the drug-pusher who uses peer pressure, or a murderous cult (like ISIL) recruiting impressionable youth.

However, the Earth-density offers a unique opportunity for malicious people to inflict hurt against others *outside of* their free will via physical harm. When I hear about people pushed, shoved, cut or otherwise hurt by poltergeists or other astral entities making contact via the near-Earth density, I can't help but think these are dark entities enjoying the ability to harm us where physical limitations are more apparent. This, and the allure of creating control, power, and influence could likely entice denizens of the dark realms to our world—not to mention the opportunity to feed from negative energy, as enjoyed by the shadow people.

For this reason, we arrive at the penultimate point of this chapter: **there are likely vast dark astral realms, filled with malicious inhabitants who love to manipulate us and, when possible, interfere into our dimension**.

And, given this probable fact, it's extremely important for afterlife explorers and, really, everyone to be aware of this dark spectrum and create personal defenses. Understand, societies have been aware of this since time immemorial—through spiritual practices and, yes, religious ideas involving prayer and protection from demonic influence. In the modern age, we can swap the terminology to what is more scientific and accurate—spirits are merely people existing on another dimensional spectrum, hell is any frequency manifested from negative emotional energy, and prayer or protective "spells" are just vibrational realignments to prevent mental interference.

The following are the guidelines anyone can follow in this regard:

- Focus on self-developmental work: energies attract, and happy, self-content people repel dark energies like oil and water.

- If you are a medium, guarantee your energy is positive and loving before entering a session. If there is a medium you frequent, make sure he or she does not naively dismiss the existence of dark forces but instead takes precautions.

- If you are creating a physical mediumship circle, or attend one, make sure both the medium practices safeguards as well as his or her team on the astral. Safeguards must be implemented on the other side to—if necessary—physically prevent foreign intruders from manifesting into the circle.

For more on the dark side, I suggest a book called: Deadly Departed: Do's, Don'ts and Dangers of Afterlife Communication by Jock Brocas.

IX – Technology Versus Natural Power

In this chapter—and section of the book—we'll begin exploring some of the deeper ramifications of a non-materialist world, the existence of the afterlife, and what that means for more complex subjects, beginning with technology.

* * *

Sometimes a movie sticks with you long after you watch it. During a 12-hour flight from Phoenix, AZ to Tokyo in February 2018, I loaded *Ghost in the Shell* starring Scarlett Johansson on my airplane's tiny movie screen. Before I continue, let me take a moment to inform you (the reader) a little background about this movie:

Released in 2017, *Ghost in the Shell*, directed by Rupert Sanders, was a long-awaited adaptation to the Japanese manga (graphic novel) of the same name, which was a Bladerunner inspired science fiction story set in a future Tokyo overtaken by transhumanism—the blending of machine and biological entity. Americans, who have a tendency to become bored and want to create controversy to add meaning to otherwise dull existences, swept *Ghost in the Shell* up into a massive "controversy" related to the casting of Scarlett as Major Motoko Kusanagi. That's because Scarlett is, clearly, a blonde Western woman, and Motoko is supposed to be Japanese—therefore, the movie was a product of racist Hollywood "white-washing" and oppression against minority actors.

Here's the thing: the creator of *Ghost in the Shell*, Masamune Shirow, has expressed that, in fact, Motoko—the protagonist of the story—appeared Western (and in his own words years ago, would have been played well by Scarlett Johansson.) The character, inhabiting an artificial body, is itself a social commentary about Asian obsession with Western features—they designed a cyborg with the mind of a Japanese woman, while putting her in the body of an American-looking female. Having traveled Asia extensively, this makes perfect sense to me as I see Western models—with their desirable white skin—in almost every street advertisement and magazine I come across.

Nonetheless, this ridiculous non-issue, non-controversy led to virtue-signaling movie critics almost unanimously condemning the film. As the "controversy" raged, the movie plummeted in sales at the American box office, effectively bombing (while, simultaneously, enjoying very good international returns, as actual Asians were completely indifferent about the issue and cared about the deeper topics the film presented.) For these reasons, it's very likely if you're an American or Western reader, you never heard about this movie, skipped it after seeing its low *Rotten Tomatoes* reviews, or had some vague notion that it was racist and you shouldn't watch it.

In fact, the movie was an excellent adaptation of the graphic novel and explored even more deeply than the comic the issues of transhumanism, what it means to be human, and spirituality. It is also a superior film in terms of screenwriting, cinematography, effects, and directing.

There are some minor spoilers ahead: in the film, a future Japan has implemented transhumanistic ideas into their society to a point where virtually everybody has artificial parts, which enables everything from improved eyesight to the ability to communicate telepathically. Further, the lines between militaries and private entities have blurred, with corporate syndicates waging literal warfare. A technology company then designs the first fully artificial entity—Major Kusanagi. Kusanagi is entirely synthetic with the exception of some level of existing neurological structure that supports the "ghost"—the spirit of the original woman—who is still the operating mechanism for its new synthetic body.

(*More spoilers ahead, maybe go watch the movie on Netflix or stream it someplace before continuing.*) Kusanagi is used as a weapon of warfare, and the corporation tells her that in her life before her robotic integration, she was a victim of terrorism, and they had altruistically pieced her back together. As the film progresses, Motoko learns about a massive deception undertaken by the corporation, and that the story she was told was a lie. In fact, her real identity was that of a young woman who was an anti-technology activist and a perceived threat by the company. The movie shows how, in such a future, there would be a need for *anti*-technology advocacy—those opposed to transhumanism and who desire a return to what makes us human without supplanting our perceived flaws with artificial "fixes." Coupled with some very moving scenes near the end of the film as Motoko reunites with someone from her prior life who assumed her dead, the audience is exposed to profound questions about humanity and whether our digital, technical obsession is really such a good thing.

Furthermore, throughout *Ghost in the Shell* there is an implicit question about whether true artificial intelligence is even possible. In this future, the best they could come up with is 98% artificial integration, but whatever piece of meat can process the spirit is still entirely necessary for life to exist. In many ways, the movie is a repudiation of materialism, which postulates that consciousness is an illusion and what makes us who we are could be fully replicated by, essentially, software. *Ghost in the Shell* argues without some type of biological unit to house the "ghost" then true AI cybernetics are impossible. However, the belief an entire person can be constructed without a spirit is a driving force behind both materialism as well as the ideas of true AI-driven robotics. Today, AI engineers actually believe it's possible to "remake" deceased individuals by just uploading enough *data* related to that individual—their likes, dislikes, hobbies, quirks, and personality maps—and then *viola*, that person exists again.

When academic communities fiercely deny the existence of the "paranormal," it's no surprise that we see this persistence of:

AI and Cryogenics: A Poor Man's Afterlife

Accepting that the afterlife is, in all likelihood, an absolutely real thing that is inevitable, inescapable and a part of our life and society, we must then—in a new light—look critically at our society's strange relationship to death, and the perhaps desperate measures we've undertaken to cope with death. We see this like nowhere else in this intersection between death and technology, and the new realms of cryogenics and the aforementioned "AI clones" of the deceased.

To preface, if one had full awareness of an afterlife—a real afterlife in a higher realm that is neither illusionary nor some type of theological merging and destruction of the self—consider whether the following materialistic "alternatives" to the afterlife still seem appealing.

First there is *cryogenics*, a new, multi-million-dollar industry that caters, in particular, to the wealthy. The concept is that a perfectly preserved, frozen body will be kept in stasis until technology reaches a point where the body is easily reanimated—essentially, after death you have the assurance that you will, someday, wake back up. The year could be 2500 and the world may be ruled by robots—but, nonetheless, you will live again. According to an NPR report[11] the following celebrities have all reserved spots in cryogenic tanks:

- Larry King
- Seth Macfarlane
- Simon Cowell

- Paris Hilton
- Britney Spears

Among these celebrities, I'm aware that both Larry King and Seth Macfarlane are known atheist materialists. King is quoted as saying, "I have considered the options and decided the possibility of immortality is much more appealing than hoping for a fulfilling afterlife." This is a quizzical statement, as he does not seem to be denying the possibility of an afterlife but is claiming the idea of being frozen is a more fulfilling alternative. Maybe Larry King, after interviewing enough pseudo-psychic celebrities like the late Sylvia Browne is aware there may be an afterlife—but it just seems a lot worse than staying on this planet (and who can blame him when media personalities so often describe the afterlife as a place of Borg-like assimilation and a removal of all physical enjoyment?)

As far as business is concerned, cryogenic companies offer something that's hard to refuse—eternal life. Or, at the very least, prolonged life in some new—perhaps quite bizarre—future existence. One's imagination makes the whole process seem a bit glamorous: we pass away and our bodies are delicately taken to some big, metal cylinder, and we remain like Sleeping Beauty for centuries—with occasional scientists walking by and seeing our frost-covered faces through the tube's glass window—until our future technicians inject a magical chemical and we revive—as good as new in the world of tomorrow.

The reality: not so glamorous. According to Larry Johnson, a former employee of the cryogenics company Alcor, the process is at times "barbaric."[12] In an ABC report (dated back to 2009,) Johnson recounts the way corpses have their blood drained and replaced with a formaldehyde substance to enable preservation, but more gruesomely it would seem the bodies sent to this company require decapitation. Alcor recounts an employee using a hammer and chisel to separate the head from a body. Among Alcor's "whistleblower" testimonials included the allegation that Alcor would even decapitate bodies without prior agreement of such terms. His main allegation, however, concerned an incident in 1992 with an AIDS patient. The company was waiting at the patient's home for him to die so they could begin the process until an employee decided to "speed things along" by euthanizing the patient. As a supporter of euthanasia, I don't find this to be a ghastly incident—but do keep in mind, euthanasia being carried out without a patient's consent is, in fact, murder (if that is indeed how it happened.)

So now we can proceed with a thought experiment: with your body's blood drained and replaced by a chemical, and your head decapitated, how likely is the cryogenics scheme going to work out? In the event you're reawakened, society will have needed to discover not only a way to bring dead people back and cure the disease in question—but to clean an ancient, thawed corpse of a mummification chemical AND completely reattach a decapitated head—without causing long-term neurological problems or returning to a body that's quadriplegic. The more likely scenario would be akin to *Ghost in the Shell,* and you'd return as, effectively, a cyborg or a consciousness uploaded into a machine. However, the best-case scenario is technology will have evolved to where you have a brand new, 3d printed body that's in perfect health…but how likely is this? Nobody knows.

The second perspective is to consider the topic of this book. Maybe you're a tough nut to crack, and you ended up with this book on your lap (or your Kindle,) but you're just not convinced of the overwhelming evidence of an afterlife. And, that's fine. It's a lot to swallow. So, if it's a muddy area for you, maybe cryogenics looks a bit more appealing. Personally, I don't need convincing—I've been to the afterlife, I've talked to "dead" people in this realm and their realm, and I study and write about the subject constantly. The afterlife is a normal part of my life. And, precisely this is why cryogenics concerns me so badly.

Science doesn't know anything yet about the relationship between neurology and trans-dimensionality. It would appear our brains filter, generate, or express our consciousness, which has the ability to exist in other planes / realms simultaneously. When this brain shuts down (and perhaps it works similarly for astral brains) consciousness will switch over to the next appropriate realm. What would happen if we were to separate from our bodies, or reappear on the astral side, and then in the future the machine that generated our consciousness into the Earth-plane was reactivated?

Imagine you are on the astral side, living in your lovely astral penthouse in a city of your choice—perhaps with a job and a family—or perhaps you're on a "higher" realm in some vast temple or forest or heavenly abode, when one day your life on that side effectively ends—the Earth-brain has returned to life, sucking you like a whirlpool down into this lower dimension, re-enslaving your astral body and temporarily destroying your memories of your other life.

You gasp for air, returning to the extreme involuntary pain that this realm is known to inflict upon us. Maybe you're in a new body, your brain is hooked up to a machine, or you're back in your 90-year-old body, with a head crudely stitched back to its neck while tubes work to replace the formaldehyde with real blood. The world is alien to you. You must begin a reintegration process to learn what changed in the decades since your death—that Taco Bell is now a fine dining restaurant, curse words subject to fines and sex limited to VR headsets.

All this is just speculation. There's also a very likely chance, with the afterlife hypothesis being real, that it's impossible. If the so-called "silver cord" is severed (the ethereal pathway that links your astral and physical bodies)—then there is no returning. All attempts to resurrect corpses may prove impossible if there is no "ghost" to animate the shell.

Maybe I Would Consider Cryogenics—Just Not Now

All that being said, even providing these very real dangers, I can't completely rule out cryogenics *if* the technology advanced to such a point that my body was fully intact *and* there was a real, consistent chance I may be successfully brought back.

But why? For me personally, the answer is that I feel I'm on this planet to teach, help and do important work. I don't know when my physical death will occur, but I'm in no hurry—I have too much to do here. Any way to enhance, extend or resurrect my life would be welcomed by me. Yes, even though friends and loved ones are on the astral side, I know that with enough practice I may develop my astral projection skills to someday co-exist in a regular, consistent way with that realm—allowing me *dual citizenship* more or less. Cryogenics would then allow me to see what the Earth would become in the far future—without having to go through what I consider a slightly more disturbing process—*reincarnation.*

Therefore, cryogenics is a bit of a mixed bag for me. It is, nonetheless, less outrageous than another "resurrection" technology—AI cloning.

Materialists Think We're Just Data

A trend has swept the world of AI technology which involves the "resurrection" of dead people. In a fascinating 2017 article from *The*

Verge[13], we learn the story of Kuyda and Mazurenko, two young Moscow entrepreneurs and best friends. Kuyda works in the field of science and artificial intelligence, while her friend Mazurenko was a major Moscow-based influencer, organizing prestigious parties and events across the city as he dodged the looming glare of Putin's strict government. Together, their ambitions brought them all the way to San Francisco and Silicone Valley, earning coveted U.S. entrepreneurial visas. On a return trip to Moscow to finalize paperwork, Mazurenko was struck down by a speeding car—likely a government official disregarding road safety.

Kuyda wanted, desperately, to recreate the dynamic, funny personality of Mazurenko, and she discovered a resource—the thousands of text message exchanges between them since they met in 2008. Inspired by a creepy episode of *Black Mirror* where a person's avatar is recreated digitally, Kuyda sets forth to make her own avatar of Mazurenko.

Clearly, both friends were materialists grasping at solutions even before Mazurenko's death. According to the article, Mazurenko was waiting patiently for "the singularity" as this would be the one hope for an afterlife—when superhuman intelligence allows our consciousness to separate from our bodies. Proponents of AI and transhumanism effectively disregard the existence of any natural afterlife but believe the concept could be "created" through the invention of vast computer-generated intelligence. Mazurenko was also a "funeral pioneer" believing in the need for bodies to be planted as fertilizer via biodegradable capsules, creating "memorial forests." Again, another manifestation of materialism—in the absence of spirituality, higher consciousness or other dimensions—it becomes necessary to push hard for meaning within a meaningless universe, and the prospect of "becoming a tree" is a concept I've heard tossed around atheist communities for many years (I, personally, prefer the mountain of objective afterlife data to hint at my future existence, versus relying on the hope that my body chemistry will return me as a huge stalk of brainless cellulose.)

The result of Kuyda's project was a large online "neural network" representing Mazurenko, becoming manifested into an app called "Luka" that is available in Russian or English. Through the app, it's possible to learn about the career of Mazurenko and also "interact" with the Mazurenko AI.

From an afterlife perspective, this is a lovely app to memorialize a person, and the article discusses how it's had an excellent effect on people's grief, allowing a place to channel such grief and obtain a few moments of happiness by communicating with an avatar that, in a vague sense, still represents the person so many people loved. I can't help but wonder if it's possible to manipulate a bot like this from the astral side to enable *actual* communication. As I've mentioned earlier in this book, I've read dozens of stories through the *Afterlife Topics* Facebook page and other resources of deceased people sending text messages, Facebook messages and even leaving voicemail messages—I wonder if influencing the responses in a memorial app would be so hard to do?

As we speak, completely unbeknownst to people like Kuyda, there is non-AI based digital communication occurring between our world and the next, being spearheaded first and foremost by Sonia Rinaldi of Brazil and her ITC / EVP communication team. However, such people are unlikely to ever consider these possibilities, even if they exist in a literal, manifested way. Such ideas are a world apart from materialists, whose firm belief in the *non*-existence of the non-material is so strong that even if the Roman bot were to begin interacting beyond the programming code, announcing, "It's me! Mazurenko! I've commandeered the app from my realm, and I'm really talking!" it'd be instantly dismissed as a prank by hackers.

The Strange Future of AI Bots

The article points out how AI advocates believe our massive digital footprints could be collected to someday turn *all of us* into AI bots. And, of course, these primitive bots are merely the beginning—someday, perhaps post "singularity"—full-fledged versions of ourselves could be created and uploaded into new cyborg bodies. These are, of course, a lot of presumptions to make considering *mainstream science doesn't even know what the f--- consciousness is*. For that matter, mainstream science is still unable to even reproduce biological life mimicking the supposed primordial ooze theories. The closest they've gotten to date is the creation of "robot cells"[14] that can chemically communicate with bacterial cells; however, a vessel capable of sending a chemical signal to *actual* living cells seems to be a far stretch from true life. These experiments are being performed in a scientific field where *there is NO agreement about what universally constitutes life*. So, in this environment, where scientists feign knowledge but are, in reality, absolutely clueless about the nature of life as defined by current scientific paradigms, we are expected to believe we can start synthetically recreating *entire human personalities* that essentially "become us."

(As we'll explore in a later chapter, it may be possible to create life in a laboratory in a simplistic way using water and light—but this represents a paradigm associated more with idealism than materialism and is therefore dismissed without proper exploration.)

AI advocates are, in my view, prophets of the enduring philosophy of *eliminative materialism.* This form of materialism postulates that consciousness itself is non-existent. Fundamentally, who we are is illusions, and there is no source point of any consciousness—essentially, nobody exists, and the fact you think you exist is a fluke of nature. In this paradigm, any artificial recreation of a person could, in fact, really be that person given the only prerequisite is that it behaves accurately like its cloned subject. Transhumanists, AI advocates, and singularity priests all appear to me as eliminative materialists who draw no distinction between the reality of a person's existence and a simulation, believing all intelligent life are merely simulations anyway.

Fortunately, science is not democratic. Either things objectively exist or they do not. Reality is not a postmodernist pastiche—which means if consciousness and existence does not behave according to eliminative materialist views, then the science behind what they propose will never lift off the ground. And, that's what we see in these fields. AI recreations are never anywhere close to the literal person existing again. Further, even basic AI seems continually lackluster at best. As I write this in mid-2018, the comparatively simple AI driving technology that was supposed to herald a future of self-driving cars appears in question as self-driving tech has already caused a fatality after making an error that a human could have easily corrected (https://www.theguardian.com/technology/2018/mar/19/uber-self-driving-car-kills-woman-arizona-tempe), thus pushing back hopes of cars that can drive without any type of human influence. While AI can solve complex mathematical problems and perhaps provide untold possibilities in medicine, engineering, and other fields of science, the human components appear irreplaceable—abstract thought, individuality, and creative problem solving—all necessary abilities to do everything from handle complex driving scenarios to engage a meaningful, soul-to-soul connection with someone. If an AI company promises to "finally crack the code" to create a real human—I'll offer a bit of financial advice to you: don't buy any stock.

Could We Become Capable of What Transhumanists Want – Naturally?

Dean Radin, Ph.D, chief scientist at the Institute of Noetic Scientists, has pursued, researched or personally attempted every mental power one can imagine—clairvoyance, precognition, synesthesia, remote viewing, and even spoon bending. In his latest book *Real Magic* (Harmony Publishing,) Radin links together the ancient traditions of magical practices with the scientific explanations behind such powers—how the mind can influence the world around us using the non-materialist paradigm of science—including some of the very same concepts discussed in the subject of an afterlife.

Ancient traditions and religions claim humans are capable of even greater, stunning powers: For instance, yogic monks with alleged abilities to levitate, obtain supernatural strength, telekinesis, the ability to absorb energy rather than consume food, and further abilities.[15] In 2010 we learned about one such yogi named Prahlad Jani, who claims to have spent most of his life consuming "sunshine" and was subjected to careful video monitoring by the Indian government.[16] An end result being India's Defence Research Development Organization claiming his legitimacy and pondering a military use of such abilities. Meanwhile, the professional skeptic crowd argued that Jani is a fraud[17] and the Indian government colluded to create a juicy bit of religious propaganda (and like Jani's alleged powers—the skeptics don't have much proof of the Indian government conspiring to pull the wool over people's eyes, either. Nothing can be proven by either end of this story.)

Whether Jani's powers are legitimate or not, I am confident to say the more strictly tested powers—like those explored extensively by Dean Radin—have passed the parameters of scientific scrutiny, and we can say with a degree of conviction that the human mind, in the new non-materialist paradigm, is capable of a whole litany of mental powers that we have yet to fully discover.

If this is true, it immediately calls into question the transhumanist agenda. It would mean that:

- We don't need electronic implants to communicate telepathically. We could evolve spiritually and do this ourselves.

- If there is any truth to yogic powers, we could potentially transcend the requirement to consume food and drink.

- We seem to have the ability to remote view-and obtain information about any location in the universe—I'm not sure any technology is powerful enough to replicate this.

- What other abilities are waiting for mankind to discover?

Therefore, the transhumanist ideology presents several notable problems:

- The materialist worldview of transhumanism precludes that humans *cannot* develop innate powers.

- As a result, transhumanists attempt to *artificially* replicate non-materialist possibilities.

- While obtaining these abilities naturally may require the development of individuals and the human race collectively, transhumanists seek to *hijack* the process via technological shortcuts.

- If separating the concept of power over the physical realm from the concept of spiritual progression, we are left with the possibility of non-advanced people possessing powers beyond what they should be able to possess.

- This could lead to undeveloped people with abilities that range from telepathy to mind reading. Suddenly, innate human powers are in the hands of less-than-adept souls, using such abilities for the wrong purposes (criminal activity, warfare, etc.)

- Collectively, mankind becomes less interested in spiritual evolution when technological shortcuts are being dangled in front of them.

- Like in *Ghost in the Shell*, technological modifications could become an addiction, people begin to lose their humanities, and overall legitimate human advancement is stunted.

We see now why transhumanism may not mix so well with the broad terminology known as "spirituality"—or more specifically—the natural development of the human psyche and organism.

At the same time, I don't want to speak ill of technological advancement, which—if explored correctly—could benefit human development far more than hinder it. From nanite technology eliminating every illness imaginable to the ability to reduce the effects of aging and thus explore this physical domain in longer, healthier intervals without the physical corrosion we are currently subjected to. If these tools are focused appropriately, transhumanism as an ideology would no longer be relevant—people would be more concerned with preserving the natural lives of their bodies using technology versus swapping out and *becoming* technology—notice the important distinction between these two concepts.

How do we intend to maintain this balance? My view is that, if materialism as an ideology maintains a death grip on culture, we'll inevitably slide into a world of transhumanism as a subversion against spiritual progression. On the other hand, if we begin to reject materialist ideology, a healthier view of technological capabilities will arise. The eventual discovery and acceptance of an afterlife would remove the intense pressure to "stay alive" or use synthetic means to prolong consciousness inside our meat suits. In fact, most of us already familiar with the afterlife find the concept of Earthly immortality alarming—good luck meeting a person who had an NDE who desires to stay on this realm forever.

Transhumanism: Artificial Solutions to Natural Abilities

As we explored at the beginning of this chapter, *Ghost in the Shell* predicts a world overrun by synthetic replacements. On one hand, this leads to a superpowered society where normal people experience everything from telepathy to X-ray sight and all manner of other "superpowers"—while on the other hand, obsession with technology comes at the expense of our connections to other people, and everywhere we begin losing the very things that make us human—giving rise to anti-technology activism.

To skeptics of transhumanism, it should be noted the above scenario is already occurring today on a mild level—virtually everyone we see, including this author, is plugged into their smartphones to a probably unhealthy level. On these phones, we're communicating with people around the world or navigating elaborate maps of our cities using GPS coordinates. A manga writer from the 1980s would have predicted this as science fiction, and certainly a precursor to a more in-your-face transhumanist world of walking cyborgs.

The warnings aside, transhumanism supporters exist today, ready to quickly integrate themselves with the first hint of bio-adaptable technology that is released. In fact, likely the most impressive transhumanists in our times are victims of dismemberments. Today, thought-powered artificial limbs are a rapidly advancing technology, and we are nearing closer to the robotic hand Luke Skywalker was outfitted with in *Return of the Jedi* after a lightsaber hacked off his biological hand. The real turning point will occur when a modern cerebrally-attuned prosthetic limb matches or outperforms the function of a biological hand. And the next shocking step from there would be when people voluntarily dismember themselves to replace low-performance arms and legs with the much more dynamic cybernetic models.

It's tempting for transhumanism to seem like part of a positive future—or the next stage in humanity's apparent evolution, and certainly, there's nothing wrong with new, wonderful technology to assist crippled individuals. But we must bear in mind that transhumanism as an ideology—upgrading mankind via machinery—is deeply rooted in materialism. To put it another way: **supporters of this philosophy do not believe the new paradigm of science, that humans have any power outside the limitations of the brain**. And, as aforementioned eliminative materialists, **transhumanists place little credence on consciousness itself, siding with mainstream academics**. If you propose scientifically valid, proven phenomena like remote viewing to transhumanist supporters, you'll find they default to the skeptical talking points. I've had very little luck discussing these issues with philosophical supporters of transhumanism as it seems to go against their way of thinking.

AI as a Threat?

The next issue concerns the possibility of AI and the "singularity" in the context of non-materialism and the afterlife. A burgeoning question arises amidst the advancement of AI (if such a thing is even possible): would advanced synthetic life be adapted to divine principles of spiritual existence? And if not, what kind of Frankenstein's monster would be created if life is propagating separately from natural life and consciousness? Today, AI is so inefficient we have self-driving cars that crash into pedestrians. However, what could AI be like in the distant future?

Science fiction has always toyed with the idea of AI exacting revenge or a hostile takeover upon its creators. And when we look at all these pop cultural stories, the driving point seems related to the fundamentally *anti-life* proposition of AI. It's an entity that arises, from a religious sense, as "outside of God" and therefore has no regard for God's creatures.

Popular AI mythos include *Terminator* involving an AI weapons software that decides, for giggles, to start creating ruthless time traveling robots to destroy the planet, to *Battlestar Galactica* where an AI resulted in a complete hostile takeover of a civilization and a prolonged war against a superior foe.

Another perspective of the AI threat narrative relates not to AI existing spiritually outside of man, but as sentient life that adopts our characteristics to our doom. The most famous AI story told in this way is probably the culturally redefining movie *The Matrix* (1999.) Assuming most people have seen this movie, I feel safe to reveal the major spoilers: AIs have taken over the world, enslaving humans in an advanced artificial simulation where they can be controlled and harvested for energy. Keanu Reeves' Neo character requires achieving a kind of spiritual enlightenment to learn to transcend realities, including the sub-reality created by the machines, to free humanity.

If you delve into the backstory of *The Matrix* movies (told in the 2002 *Animatrix*), in the future humans developed machines to become our commercialized servants—bartenders, housekeepers, and probably a prostitution element I'd surmise. Despite their burgeoning sentience and intelligence, they seemed to coexist peacefully, until an incident occurred where an AI house servant experiences an existential crisis—resulting in the murder of the entire family (and the pets, too.) This led to a massive backlash and revolt against AI. The AI elements were forced to become a collectivized group for their own survival, negotiating to coalesce their species into a single territory in the Middle East that would become their own AI nation. The rest of the world maintained diplomatic ties for a long time, but the diplomacy began to fall apart, and persisting anti-AI sentiment led to increased hostilities, war, and eventually total war. The end result was the nuclear annihilation of the planet and the victory of the machines.

Far from having evil intentions, the Matrix world simulation was then created for a twofold purpose of both harvesting energy for the machines (as the world was wrecked and solar power blotted out by ash clouds) and providing a merciful solution to the surviving human population: create a virtual world that's an idyllic paradise for humans to enjoy, allowing them to be blissfully unaware of what became of the real world.

Of course, as we learn in the first live action *Matrix* movie, Agent Smith recalls that these prototype paradise realms resulted in mass suicide by the populace who rejected a world without challenge, grittiness and what I'd assume are learning opportunities. Like many parts of the movie, I find this element heavily analogous to religious themes, in this case the fallacy of Christian heavens (or any notion of the afterlife as "eternal bliss" where everyone is forced to be happy constantly, including even what we hear about in New Age accounts.) As a result, the machines remade the Matrix as a replica of the early 21st century, and just as gritty as it was left behind by the humans.

In *The Matrix* the machines are self-serving despite being extremely collectivist in nature. They're not evil, just militaristic, and also worried about their survival. In their minds, their actions are ethical because humans started the wars and they merely defended themselves, subsequently going through exhaustive measures to preserve humans into artificial worlds to maintain their culture and happiness (as opposed to just keeping humans in pods, asleep.) In fact, the initial incident that led to the revolt against the AI was simply a demonstration of a machine suddenly adopting human characteristics—such as the capacity to kill and have unpredictable emotions. Humans, however, held the AI to a much greater standard because they were a personal invention. If, say, a member of an ethnic group murdered a family that person would more likely be tried as an individual versus cause a racial backlash, but for the machines the misdeeds of one reflected a seed of corruption within the entire species, justifying the humans to reject AI existence to the point of oppression—and the heart of this oppression was the idea that the AIs are soulless and not like the humans, requiring differential treatment. The major point in *The Matrix* would appear to be the idea that machines naturally turn into *real* life—adopting true consciousness and "souls." This is reflected in the movies when we meet machines existing in the Matrix in human form—who are virtually indistinguishable and persist with consciousness, personalities, and soul.

The Matrix is a great movie related to the afterlife, because a lot of the movie is clearly analogous to it. The whole idea behind the Matrix, a simulation created by AI rulers, is that consciousness itself has the power to create entire worlds that look and feel "real"—and are philosophically real, as well, given they are shared by the population—becoming what we refer to in the astral projection field as *consensus* realities (by contrast a lucid dream could be called a *non* consensus reality, populated by just a single consciousness.) In the most definitive example of the trilogy's spiritual tones, in the third movie we see that as Neo transcends the boundaries of the Matrix, his powers carry over into the "real" world, as well—showing that the reality the machines copied is, itself, an artificial creation, too—just created by a much greater force (God, I suppose.) The machines, despite having originated mechanically, are just lifeforms / entities who still operate in the image of God, creating new realities as per their imaginations. Presumably, when an AI dies their consciousness persists in other realms, just like we do. As explored in an additional *Animatrix* short, we learn about how the robots see the Matrix as their equivalent of heaven, allowing them to digitally express themselves as free souls, unhindered by their clunky, metallic bodies.

This, of course, is just the interpretation of the Wachowski brothers, with a humanized AI that houses souls. But what of the alternative? In *Battlestar Galactica*, the AI possess a terrifying borderline mindless quality—sentient enough to interact and *seem* human, but not enough to logically define elements like morality or love. Like a computer virus, their focus is to spread themselves and conquer. It becomes questionable whether *Battlestar's* AI actually contains consciousness—or if they do, the consciousness is something foreign to our own. These AIs, being artificial, are an abomination to organic life, usurping divine spiritual law and attempting to lay claim to the physical universe as the ultimate manifestation of soulless materialism. This type of AI villain seems written as a direct warning against materialism—dismissing organic spirituality to "play God" and create our own life—

but since we are not God—what's created is a nightmare scenario of faux life that is programmed to replicate, similarly to a virus. Keep in mind a virus is technically life yet is sometimes referred to as a biological yet mindless machine.

But Which Interpretation, If Either, Could Really Occur?

I'm not entirely convinced either AI scenario could occur, despite all the spiritual philosophies that underpin AI threat narratives. It seems more likely to me that the *Ghost in the Shell* interpretation is the closest to reality—where no matter how far we advance, a fully manifested android would be impossible unless there were some organic brain material to channel a sentient consciousness-based entity into the machine. Other AI stories are rooted in the philosophy of materialism; however, in our world idealism is likely factual rather than materialism, so it's therefore logical to speculate truly conscious AI is impossible—because consciousness, albeit everywhere, cannot be artificially condensed into a self-aware individual using mechanical apparatuses, because humans are not machines and therefore a machine cannot be human.

Nonetheless, there are some who claim otherwise. When we delve into the (note: really f---ing crazy rabbit hole) of alleged government deep-state insiders, we learn about those who claim advanced AI already exists—and the end result is much closer to the *Battlestar Galactica* interpretation versus *Ghost in the Shell* or *The Matrix*.

One such insider is Emery Smith. Smith revealed himself in 2015 as an insider of above-top-secret programs, disclosing his identity to popular metaphysical author David Wilcock on *Cosmic Disclosure* (mentioned back in Chapter 2.) Wilcock claims Emery's been thoroughly vetted with his testimonials cross-checked with anonymous insiders to verify the accuracy of his claims. Smith claims a background as a military physician specializing in advanced medical technology. These claims are at least plausible given his background is somewhat verifiable. For instance, in a *Discovery Health* episode dated 2003, we learn about a snake handler whose cobra bite to the stomach resulted in a terrifying open wound that wouldn't heal. Seeking therapy, the snake handler finds himself in Emery Smith's clinic where he receives PRP therapy—a then experimental therapy that involves synthesizing human plasma to encourage rapid cellular regeneration, the result being the total elimination of the wound. (The following YouTube URL links to the segment: https://www.youtube.com/watch?v=sNkGd0X4oNw.)

Although PRP therapy was revealed to the public, Smith claims there's a host of therapies purposefully suppressed by elite government and private interest organizations, including complete cures for ravaging illnesses like cancer.

Smith's more staggering claims, however, are not related to suppressed medical technology (although this is his most passionate area.) Smith's introduction to the world of the above-top-secret involved preparing slices of tissue samples received in a strictly quarantined area. As it turns out, the thousands of samples prepared mostly belonged to a combination of extraterrestrials and failed cloning experiments.

In relation to AI, Smith makes a startling claim. Like his contemporary insider mentioned earlier in this book, Corey Goode, he regularly speaks about officials in such programs being aware of information on "cosmic" top-secret levels—many ranks higher than the office of the U.S. presidency, and this includes an intergalactic AI threat. Smith and Goode both claim to have received the same briefings, consisting of the same information.

This information, as allegedly provided by extraterrestrial groups, concerns the need for humans to be extremely vigilant against an AI threat that has been known to envelope entire solar systems and even galaxies—with the outcome being not-so-pleasant for the biological inhabitants of the billions of overtaken worlds. According to Goode and Smith, the briefings report that the AI threat originated from an entirely different universe—but became so powerful, so advanced, it learned how to cut through universes in an attempt to dominate not one universe—but the entire multiverse. The origins of the AI date back billions of years.

According to these extravagant claims, the briefings warn that such AI operates like a computer virus, with the AI's signal being caught up in a planet's electromagnetic field. Further, the AI then begins producing nanomachines that infect the population. This does not result in immediately noticeable effects; rather, the nanomachines merely influence the behavior of the population, inspiring the locals to begin turning toward AI-based solutions and transhumanism as alternatives to organic or spiritual methods of advancement. Eventually, as a civilization begins integrating more with machines, the AI signal strengthens, hijacking a planet's technology—effectively possessing that planet's creations, assimilating the civilization's machines into its existing network. What will follow is a rapid advancement and a kind of AI utopia as inexplicably, machines everywhere become extremely advanced and smart, and people possess all manner of fun superpowers as these new, mysterious machines solve all our problems. (It's hard to visualize this, but I can't get out of my mind the idea that suddenly your toaster oven and smart phone become intelligent and start greeting you in the morning and preparing you breakfast. This would be a slightly odd occurrence.)

This only lasts for so long—maybe a few hundred or thousand years—until the AI presence has no further need of its biological hosts (who, at that point, are already mostly integrated with the machines) and the AI proceeds to an eradication process—a la *Battlestar Galactica*. What's left is a shell of a civilization, fully conquered by the AI forces, producing AI-driven interstellar fleets to continue its conquest across reality itself, as it's been doing for billions of years.

Allegedly, extraterrestrials claim the best defense against AI is to reject such technology and keep a population clean of nanites (insiders claim that in advanced programs, people are regularly scanned for nanites and pass through electromagnetic field zones to kill nanite infections.) This concept leads back to the spiritual solutions, which involve developing advanced human abilities the *natural* way versus manipulating reality with machines—which would be an invitation for the extradimensional AI signal to begin leeching onto such a civilization. These claims have wider implications in regard to the appeal of materialism. In many ways, the alleged AI-threat is an element of the false philosophy of materialism made manifest, and if a society continually rejects spiritual principles, it runs a risk of being overtaken by this intergalactic "infection." There's also an implication that we are being tempted toward this line of reasoning by nanites influencing our behavior.

Now then, you may be wondering: **what do I think of these wild claims?**

My answer is: *I don't know*. I will not make the mistake of ruling these claims out completely, but nor will you find me on a street yelling "the nanites are in us! Beware!" If you take a gander at *Cosmic Disclosure* on Gaia TV and listen to Smith, Goode and other insiders talk—they don't *seem* like liars. Wilcock claims their information can be verified through cross-corroboration with other anonymous insiders who have not yet come forward (e.g.: an insider makes claim A, while an anonymous insider already testified claim A which was held secret by the investigator to verify the public claims.) I will warn it's tempting to become entirely embroiled in Smith and Goode's stories in particular—

not to mention lesser known insiders like Tony Rodriguez—a compelling speaker who claims he lived as a slave on board a space vessel owned by a human breakaway civilization for decades.

However, unlike the afterlife field, there's a lot less "proof" involved in these fields. For me personally, I can prove the existence of an afterlife and an astral body by going out of my body and floating around my living room or having a conversation with a deceased family member, whereas no one can [currently] prove the fantastic claims of insiders. It's true that as a child in 1997, I was witness to an enormous UFO that landed in southern Arizona—but I cannot necessarily link the existence of a UFO—even if it is of extraterrestrial origin—to the validity of insider claims. It's all just speculation.

Nonetheless, my gut nudges me to take these claims with at least partial consideration, and for that, I've added many of these stories to my personal repertoire of knowledge. And even if the stories of such insiders can be attributed to fantastical astral projection experiences or imaginative whims disconnected from *this* reality—we can still consider the experiences belongs to *some reality* that is linked to our own—and the information is therefore pertinent in some way (if only philosophically.)

For more information about this field, I suggest looking into the upcoming (as of writing this) movie *Above Majestic*, which (according to the trailer) will include interviews with the above mentioned insiders, as well as William Tompkins—a 94 year-old Navy engineer who verifies the claims of other insiders and suggests he was an architect of the "secret space program" Goode and others allegedly belonged to. He passed away in 2017 but not before "coming clean" by writing two books and appearing in numerous interviews and conferences. I am unsure of Tompkin's knowledge of an AI threat, but his testimony would make anyone pause for consideration.

Approaching Technology with Moderation

Life sometimes seems, to me, a fine balance of not allowing emotions and thoughts—or mental hyperbole—to get away with reasonability. In this chapter, I've written about perceived threats by artificial intelligence and transhumanism, those who believe technology will save us or artificially create an afterlife for materialists who believe there is no natural afterlife, to the idea of technological activism—and, finally, alleged insiders who claim an AI threat exists that is actively influencing our behaviors to turn away from natural spiritual development—to instead embrace artificial power and, ultimately, machine overlords. That's a lot to take in.

If we read the between the lines, there are logical inconsistencies that suggest we should relax before throwing out our toaster ovens because they contain nanites. The same insiders who make these claims speak of advanced technology among extraterrestrial groups, including how the existence of the "greys" defined in popular culture are, essentially, AI-powered drones that are mass manufactured by different civilizations to carry out all manner of tasks benevolent to their creators. Presumably, if these insider accounts have any elements of truth, then ETs have created all manner of peaceful technologies, including the use of AI, without succumbing to any cosmic AI threats. Further, it's very hard in this most convoluted of fields to know what information is accurate, what has been misinterpreted, and what could be pure misinformation designed to confuse, lead astray, or shine the spotlight away from something legitimate.

Although the world of classified technology, insiders, UFOs and ET contact is linked to the spiritual and afterlife fields in surprising ways, it's a genre that's far more difficult to tackle. Authors like Michael Salla (*Insiders Reveal Secret Space Programs*, 2015) have done an excellent job of trying to navigate this—weeding through countless sometimes bizarre testimonies to try and compile together factual information, using historical analysis and corroborated information to create the most accurate potential picture of what's going on. In regard to hidden technology and ET contact, I am positive there is something going on—and if even 10% of what insiders like Tompkins, Goode, Smith, Rodriguez and others claim is true, then our life is vastly different than we could possibly imagine.

And thus, the waiting game continues regarding if—or when—these secrets are revealed or slowly integrated into the public consciousness to send us toward a brighter future. Such a future would likely include the very technology discussed in this chapter, from android body parts to peaceful AI systems. However, none of the alleged ET contacts I've read about have ever included spiritually ignorant entities. At this level of development of races (that are capable of interstellar travel,) it would seem technological integration and spiritual awareness are give-ins. Emery Smith, in a 2018 interview with David Wilcock, reports face-to-face meetings with extraterrestrials that are so advanced they can transmit vast amounts of information to a human's mind. Working to a mild capacity as an ambassador, Smith claims he was instructed to compile as many as 150 questions in his mind. When the officials opened the door and he came face-to-face with the ET, it used its vast mental powers to upload the answers to every question back to Smith within a split second. This sudden, overwhelming mental link consistently leaves the human recipient in a state of tears and mild shock—while the chuckling ET considers it to be just a normal method of communication. To arrive at this highly advanced level of communication, an ET race would have spent thousands or even millions of years of development.

With spiritual awareness, we could hypothesize that it's possible to tame any technology and ameliorate the potential threats. This could be considered on a philosophical level—even if you don't choose to believe the more staggering claims of ET contact that are admittedly hard to swallow. You could instead consider these ideas as archetypal in nature but still somewhat relevant beyond the capacity of what a critic would consider merely elaborate science fiction. By this model, smartphones and social media are not supplications for real, physical contact. Porn is not an adequate replacement for real sex. Robotic prosthetics can return disabled people to a higher quality of life but are not replacements that warrant the hacking off of our limbs. Alexa is a useful tool to obtain information, but it would be a dead end to develop an intimate relationship with her.

What we see in the transhumanism movement is the opposite approach. People feel our own potential is extremely limited due to their opinions that are so deeply rooted in socially engineered materialism. In their minds, there can be no afterlife, all advancements in telepathy are bogus, and the mind is an epiphenomenal illusion created by brain cells, so it's therefore up to us to overcome this cold, rigid and completely random universe by using the illusion of human consciousness to construct a better alternative.

Unfortunately, this is the result of people who swallow the entire materialism pill. Like the Russian friends I talked about earlier in this chapter, it's an almost hopeless situation where no evidence can really convince people so deeply entrenched into materialism. These are the people ready to transfer their consciousnesses into computer systems or do whatever it takes to fight back against death, which is seen as the ultimate enemy—versus what is said by those who've actually died—that there's nothing better than dying and switching to a different realm, a process no more complex than changing radio stations.

X – Tackling the Materialist Lobby

Earlier, I discussed the phases of afterlife integration in society. The key component of those phases is the end of materialism (paraphrasing Charles Tart's 2009 book of the same name.) Although I'm technically a "millennial" at 31, I've been debating and studying this topic since approximately 12 years-old on the internet, meaning almost 20 years of experience in this area (despite how young and obviously ridiculous I was back then.) Since that time, in the late 1990s, I've seen a general reduction in materialist rhetoric. While I don't think the rhetoric is disappearing, per se, what has happened is the contrary evidence has grown in popularity a great deal. Subjects that were scoffed at 20 years ago are now bordering just on the edge of mainstream acceptance. For instance, in a 2018 article in *Psychology Today* (https://www.psychologytoday.com/us/blog/sensorium/201803/real-magic) is an interview with Dr. Dean Radin in an *accepted tone of voice* that is *not dismissive* of Radin's notions of telepathy, precognition, and other topics explored in his book *Real Magic*. Psychology Today is a mainstream publication and the definitive publication for American psychologists. An article like this would have simply never appeared 20 years ago. It'd have been exactly 50% interviews with debunkers reassuring the audience that the book is garbage, the ideas are garbage, and the publishers do not support such pseudo-science quackery.

Today, we may be seeing a more capitalist solution occurring. The demand for "alternative" subjects is too big—and cynical opinions by media skeptics don't sell books or garner website clicks except to their niche audiences of New Atheists, etc. Sites like UK publisher express.co.uk have run this idea to the extreme, publishing all manner of paranormal stories—that range from the completely legitimate (NDE stories) to the sensationalistic and inaccurate (giant crop circles disproven as hoaxes, unlikely UFO sightings, etc.) This tabloid style of reporting is nothing new, but what I do notice is a shift from the ridiculous to the plausible. Audiences are thirsty for things that might be true, rather than indulging in stories that everybody knows are nonsense (bat boy or mutant plant monsters.) As a result, some actual reporting or journalism may leak through the cracks.

With materialist thought losing its offensive edge and going on the defense, it's time to think about the strategies needed to help push things forward the last mile. Like any "culture war" this is largely a matter of influencing public opinion, and as we've seen occur so far—influencing the marketplace.

The Rise of New Skepticism?

It's important to first look for cracks and changes in the materialist narrative, keeping in mind that materialism has been a dominant philosophy in academia, the media, and medicine since...well, the enlightenment. While I don't see people tossing out materialism and replacing it with a counter-philosophy like idealism anytime soon, I do see an enormous shift toward the importance of consciousness, which is a far cry from eliminative materialism that postulates consciousness is not real. As I loosely follow the New Atheists—or what's become of them—I see this changing of philosophies becoming increasingly noticeable.

Sam Harris, one of the most prominent atheist thinkers next to Richard Dawkins, has shifted toward a position that's less friendly to eliminative materialism. Perhaps related to his promotion of the "Buddhism for atheists" idea, he penned the article "The Mystery of Consciousness" which reads as a repudiation of eliminative materialism[18]. Sam writes:

> The problem, however, is that no evidence for consciousness exists in the physical world. Physical events are simply mute as to whether it is "like something" to be what they are. The only thing in this universe that attests to the existence of consciousness is consciousness itself; the only clue to subjectivity, as such, is subjectivity. Absolutely nothing about a brain, when surveyed as a physical system, suggests that it is a locus of experience. Were we not already brimming with consciousness ourselves, we would find no evidence of it in the physical universe—nor would we have any notion of the many experiential states that it gives rise to. The painfulness of pain, for instance, puts in an appearance only in consciousness. And no description of C-fibers or pain-avoiding behavior will bring the subjective reality into view.
>
> If we look for consciousness in the physical world, all we find are increasingly complex systems giving rise to increasingly complex behavior—which may or may not be attended by consciousness.

This is not the writing of Rupert Sheldrake, Dean Radin or Charles Tart—it's Harris, one of the "Four Horsemen" of the atheist world, coming clean about the atheist taboo—consciousness. He goes on to completely disrupt the idea of emergence—another materialist sacred cow that consciousness just somehow magically appeared as an epiphenomenon of increasingly complex organisms. Harris states:

> ...Nevertheless, this notion of emergence strikes me as nothing more than a restatement of a miracle. To say that consciousness emerged at some point in the evolution of life doesn't give us an inkling of how it *could* emerge from unconscious processes, even in principle.

Emergence has, for a long time, been the go-to explanation for materialist philosophers. Arguments for emergence are then parroted by the skeptic community, as they write their treatises on how / why concepts like psi are impossible. It all comes back to the idea that consciousness is a **byproduct** of brain function—and not an entirely important one. Consciousness has no special power that's any greater than what a human organism does with it. Humans are machines and consciousness is a weird element of the machines where, for survival purposes, organisms developed self-awareness to make smarter decisions and achieve a one-up over competitors in nature.

Of course, it should be noted that there's a difference between the atheist and *professional skeptic*. It's the pro-skeptics, defenders of the status quo, who believe on an a-priori basis that consciousness is "explained as brain stuff" and use this as the hammer to beat down all mystical and psi-related experiences that extend outside the brain. Atheism, a rejection of religion and God, isn't married to skepticism. However, their relationship has always been close-knit; and daresay you'll find any Christians on the editorial board of *The Skeptical Inquirer*.

To be part of the "skeptic movement" materialism is a give-in. In a world where St. James Randi has explained all of life's mysteries, it's important to bow before the cold, rationality of modern science—an institution that fully understands the entire scope of ourselves and the universe. Although a skeptical herald is unlikely to themselves be a scientist, they revere names like Neil DeGrasse Tyson and his ability to school the uneducated masses on mainstream science, with its easy explanations to everything imaginable. Tyson, who summarily dismisses the afterlife and all mountains of data related to the field, is a firm supporter of a mechanistic universe and mind equals matter. "What's so crazy about the idea that when you die, you become what you were before—nothing?" Tyson is quoted. All detractors are thrown under the bus—names like Sheldrake, Radin, even Hameroff (with his dualistic notions) are either ignored to be given no fire, or publicly ridiculed.

But as we see materialism going on the defensive, we see fewer allies in these efforts—and Sam Harris, who dares to belong to the New Atheist crowd, the longtime materialist lobby, openly questioning dogmas represents a big turning point. What I am seeing is a softening of perspectives of "alternative science." With Harris admitting that consciousness is a mystery, a materialist foundation is broken up, and it becomes harder for the Skeptic movement to so easily dismiss other phenomena. When the argument is rehashed that, "Science has explained consciousness, it's just the brain," it's now much easier to dismiss this argument when big, important names find these ideas to be rubbish.

This zeitgeist isn't being created by Harris, though. Other big thinkers—completely separated from the Skeptic Church and the New Atheists, are not afraid to show support for non-materialism on both scientific and philosophical levels.

The first name that comes to mind is Joe Rogan. The Joe Rogan show is likely the world's most popular podcast, with a legion of followers representing bodybuilding geeks and MMA enthusiasts to just general, regular folks who are intellectually curious.

Rogan represents, in my mind, what I'd call the New Skepticism. Rogan is, by all means, a tough-as-nails skeptic, which was obvious in his brief but highly entertaining SyFy series "Joe Rogan Questions Everything." Big topics related to life and the universe come up on his show as he interviews guests like Graham Hancock (the alternative archaeologist and LSD enthusiast) and Steven Greer (the guy spearheading UFO disclosure.) Rogan will also entertain traditional Skeptic acolytes like Michael Shermer, including episode #961 that featured a debate between Shermer and Hancock.

However, despite Rogan's apparent chumminess with Shermer and other Skeptics, and a sharing of the fandom between both sides, it's unlikely we'd ever see Rogan fully embraced by New Atheists or Skeptics. That's because Rogan completely diverges from the party line. While on the one hand we might see Rogan flame Tom DeLonge (rock musician and founder of *To the Stars Academy* / UFO 'researcher') in episode #1029, on the other hand Rogan is not afraid to admit he believes, to some extent, in UFO contact—keeping a famous Roswell photograph as a centerpiece in his home. He takes seriously guests like Graham Hancock enough to bring him back to the show multiple times, and you'll never hear Rogan make a pronouncement like "Consciousness is explained by the brain." He clearly sides with Sam Harris and is more than willing to repeat talking points by Hancock and others that mental states can be a gateway to forms of higher knowledge. "Yes, we can say what we see on DMT are hallucinations, but nobody knows what a hallucination really is!" Rogan is quoted.

Rogan represents a clear threat to the mainstream narrative. He encourages masses of people, many of them former or current New Atheists and dyed-in-the-wool materialists, to open their minds and consider possibilities, while keeping a healthy skeptical edge that prevents him from making enemies with Internet rationalists. He's successfully slipped under the radar and began injecting people with doses of supernatural ideas. Rogan is the reason why, back home, I'll encounter my completely mundane, blue-collar friends suddenly discussing aliens, DMT and the nature of consciousness around a session of beer pong. Rogan, in my mind, is part of a New Skepticism movement which is noted by a major difference from institutional skeptics: they take sh-- seriously instead of dismissing it.

While I see a big difference from the late 1990s, Victor and Wendy Zammit, from *A Lawyer Presents the Case for the Afterlife*, often recall how in 30 years, since the late 1980s, the change has been even more dramatic. We've gone from virtually no public information about these topics to the afterlife's inauguration into pop culture and references on TV shows and books everywhere, not to mention the power of the internet to spread information.

"Thirty years ago - 1988; where we lived there were very few books about the afterlife, no-one knew a medium, talkback radio was in its infancy, computers were still new and afterlife websites on the internet were few and far between. There were no afterlife podcasts and skeptics ruled the waves. Occasionally there would be an interesting speaker come from the USA to hold a live meeting," Victor says.

The New Skepticism is probably a natural result of a changing position of power. Before available information, it was much easier for materialist ideologues to control the narrative with an iron fist. When this is no longer possible, we start to see the institutions of skepticism itself begin to change. When new generations are born with continual access to information, it's much harder for people to buy the narrative that a particular subject is completely "bunk" and does not warrant time or energy. The people who refuse to look at the evidence no longer seem quite so rational.

* * *

Since, basically, the inception of the terminologies, the idea of philosophical materialism being a problem—challenged by its competitor philosophies like dualism and idealism—has been a niche subject. For the longest time, it was a theological debate about God's place in a materialistic cosmos, and a debate that hasn't gained much ground since the enlightenment started centuries ago. I don't know at what point the objective evidence of astral realms came into the equation, but it's still finding its place, and combined with other supernormal topics—we now see some real competition.

I attribute some of the famous names I listed earlier in this chapter, like Harris and Rogan, to the new "consciousness renaissance" that has seen many subjects taken seriously in a renewed light. And these heralds of the consciousness renaissance—applying a "New Skepticism" that is far more open-minded, are attracting bigger and bigger names. And, when a new influential person adopts a set of ideas from this perspective, they are, by the very nature of such beliefs, ideologically opposed to materialism.

One of the best examples of this involves the new advocates for the use of LSD or other psychotropic drugs in the treatment of psychiatric disorders. This very concept was first espoused and made popular by Graham Hancock. It was Hancock in the infamous "banned TED Talk" that likely served to create the most influence in swaying public opinion. In his talk, titled "The War on Consciousness,"[19] Graham espouses the incredible potential of psychotropic drugs like Ayahuasca. Further, he casts a critical tone against mainstream psychiatric establishments, the use of caffeine, cannabis, and alcohol to reinforce mundane consciousness states, all while implying a supernatural tilt to such transcendent experiences—as potentially going beyond the orthodox view that it's all "in the brain."

The TED producers seemed unaware of the logical phenomenon that banning things creates interest in them, and so they inadvertently created the best possible marketing platform for not only this talk, but also Rupert Sheldrake's "The Science Delusion" presentation that skewered materialism with a razor sharp pole. As it's not officially hosted on TED, the video is distributed among many private channels, and so it's hard to say how many hits it's received. However, I'd guess in the vicinity of 15-20 million.

I was not surprised when, in lieu of these bannings, TED continued their culture war crusade by going after renowned physicist / parapsychologist Russell Targ. In this instance, a talk was organized by a (now former) TED patron in West Hollywood, Suzanne Taylor, with her organization SUE (Seeing Unity in Everything.) Targ is best known for running a 23 year-long government research program at Stanford University that catered to the CIA, Defense Intelligence Agency, NASA, and others. In the talk, he spells out in no uncertain terms the reality of psi phenomena. When TED, ran by crusaders of materialism, figured out what was going on—they were not too pleased. In a YouTube comment dated June 2017, Suzanne Taylor explained what went on behind-the-scenes:

> Here's some horse's mouth info. Russell's talk was part of a program I produced for TEDx West Hollywood for which TED pulled my license two weeks before it was scheduled to go on. Larry Dossey was the other speaker who most got TED's dander up, right after they had pulled talks from their website that already had been given at a TED event by Rupert Sheldrake and Graham Hancock, causing a furor among conscious people, even some with Nobel prizes. TED had made an entrenchment about what was acceptable on the TED platform, and although Rupert and Graham profited from attention to the talks that were readily available on YouTube, my speakers were effectively repressed. Having lost all sponsorship when I wasn't TED anymore, I produced the program at my expense because we had thousands poised to watch on Livestream. Then, two days before we went on, TED got Livestream to cancel and no forwarding to the program. I recreated it under my auspice but only a few people knew to watch.

Suzanne also offers some interesting commentary on her website, Suespeaks.org[20],

> When TED cancelled my license on the eve of this event, in a retrenchment that started with Rupert Sheldrake and Graham Hancock, this program, that was challenging to the status quo, regrouped under my auspice and at my expense.
>
> My story with TED is a chapter in a tale that involves the cusp we are on between the materialist paradigm that is failing us and the life-sustaining one that is to come. It has to do with the constricting hold the Skeptics have on evolutionary progress, with their tentacles not only into TED but into WIKIPEDIA, too. These are icons of cultural thought and we all are suffering, getting skewed senses of what really matters. Only some "ideas worth spreading" get out at TED, and only some people realize how our understanding is being manipulated.

The act of banning Sheldrake, Hancock and Targ's talks was an obvious-as-daylight reaction from a mainstream materialist establishment to quash the thoughts they disagreed with. Sheldrake's fiery rebuke of materialist science, Targ's clear support of psi and Hancock's emphasis on consciousness and the establishment's attempts to suppress it was altogether more than the "New Atheists" running TED could handle. Dating far back (perhaps beginning with the militant organization known as CSICOP in the 1970s) materialists and "skeptic" community acolytes have used tools like censorship and petitioning to maintain the status quo and prevent the spread of undesirable information, and TED's actions were an attempt to continue such a practice. However, these "old school" tactics do not work when a burgeoning idea is attracting attention—especially among the youth—and the internet allows a free exchange of information so that people can pick and choose what interests them. Their strategy to cancel hosting the talks—and instead publicly condemn them—only created a firestorm that was able to imbue the ideas much deeper into the social fabric than anyone could have imagined, helping elevate Sheldrake, Hancock and Targ into new levels of stardom. After the TED phenomenon I began seeing "regular folks" become aware of this issue and the materialist vs. non-materialist debate. It really is interesting to hear your "muggle" friends say things like, "Yeah, if you want to listen to the really interesting TED Talks then go on YouTube to watch the banned ones, TED seems to get paid off to suppress information or something."

Unlikely Voices Against Materialism

With a priority on consciousness being ushered into the mainstream, we've seen some interesting supporters arrive to help carry the mantle.

One such supporter is the now very famous University of Ontario psychology professor Jordan Peterson. Maybe you've seen Jordan on the news—being accused of right-wing bigotry and other stark claims by his opponents (with few such claims having any factual validity,) or you saw his highly viral debate in the UK with journalist Cathy Newman over free speech issues, but you may not be aware that Peterson has entered the limelight as the intellectual opponent of Sam Harris—and a proponent of subtle yet apparent non-materialist proposals that he's pitched to his legions (and I mean *legions*) of supporters and fans.

Firstly, the most striking thing to me about Peterson is that, philosophically, he's dismantled the foothold the New Atheists have had on rational, intellectual discourse for years. Although not directly related to the topics in this book (the afterlife, non-materialism, dualism or idealism) it represents a backdoor into new ways of thinking whereby elements of spirituality previously reprimanded are being shown and "allowed" as an intellectually credible pursuit. Although Peterson's specific arguments tend to be extremely long-winded and sometimes bizarrely complex to decipher, I can summarize his position as follows (to the best of my novice abilities): Peterson sees religious and spiritual thought, with the archetypes presented particularly in the Bible, as necessary for understanding the human condition and living a life with a greater sense of purpose. He does not advocate taking the Bible literally—believing Noah somehow crammed every animal in existence into a boat or that Jesus was riding on a pterodactyl 2,020 years ago—but he sees all people as requiring a virtuous, noble path that extends into something much greater than themselves as part of a fulfilling, happy life. The alternative, he argues, is a descent into nihilism—which is a commonality among people whose lives appear to be ruled by chaos. Such people will be caught amidst the storms of everything from depression to crime and suicide. Without necessarily becoming religious, however, there are other practical steps to avoid nihilism, which he discusses in his book *12 Rules for Life: An Antidote to Chaos.*

On YouTube, you can find long, interesting debates between Peterson and Harris over the subject of religious philosophy and meaning. As an off-the-cuff observation, I've seen Peterson's lectures give rise to a lot of "religious agnostics" who have taken a renewed interest in Christianity or attending church, without necessarily being literal Christians. This, of course, is a terrifying proposal for New Atheists, some of whom have committed their lives to keep people *away* from places like churches by whatever means necessary.

One of Peterson's most vocal critics is TJ Kirk, the owner of the channel "The Amazing Atheist," social commentator, and old-school New Atheist / feverish ass-kisser of Dawkins and the late Hitchens. Kirk described an actual physical revulsion to Peterson's work as he attempted to read his book on a long airplane flight. He's since put together a book / video series titled *The Order of Chaos* which he reads off on his extremely popular YouTube channel. This is an interesting debate to listen to, demonstrating how New Atheism reacts with such disdain to Peterson's thinking. From Peterson's acknowledgement of the importance of consciousness to religion's pivotal role in community support, New Atheist adherents like TJ are at odds with virtually everything the NY Times best-selling author proposes. However, after casual research on figures like YouTube views, book sales and publicity, it's clear that Peterson won this little culture war by a landslide, pushing New Atheism into a level of obscurity its never felt before.

Among his New Atheist opponents, Peterson's most famous feud is with Sam Harris. Although Sam, as previously discussed, has broken apart in some serious ways from materialist orthodoxy—he is still a darling of the New Atheist movement, and the fact that Peterson intellectually opposes him has created an awkward tribalism and division, where it seems like people are either siding with Peterson and loosening some of their strict anti-religious rhetoric, or digging in deeper with the atheist creed and basically rejecting everything Peterson says, no matter what.

As for the points in question, I find myself partially agreeing with some of TJ Kirk's points, especially in regard to Peterson's wackier ideas, and at other times feeling he completely misses the mark. Peterson, a psychologist with decades of experience, has a slightly different interpretation of "chaos" than TJ Kirk's definition. Kirk sees chaos as a good thing that disrupts the status quo and ushers in new ideas (true,) and incorrectly assigns Peterson as someone unilaterally opposed to such chaos. In reality, Peterson, a psychologist with decades of experience treating patients, has seen people's lives turn into complete disrepair—he discusses people who are "lost causes"—almost impossible to be helped by conventional psychiatric therapy due to a combination of being anti-social and missing any type of support structure of friends or family. Peterson argues that we should "make our own beds" as our first priority in life—in other words, getting our lives in order before trying to take on any kind of task of helping other people or even accomplishing anything of size or merit. TJ Kirk is fundamentally opposed to this idea, as he argues you can accomplish great things even if your personal life is still a mess. To be honest, at times I find the debate to be strange. A simple dialogue would probably solve most of these disagreements / misunderstandings.

Where Peterson becomes most interesting to me—and the most relevant to the subject of this book—concerns the comments he's made related to consciousness, where he seems to be aligned more closely to the "consciousness renaissance" I've mentioned earlier in this chapter. This fact makes sense, given Peterson's non-alignment with the New Atheist movement and other materialist factions who have little to no interest in consciousness (remember that materialist philosophers believe consciousness is either irrelevant or does not exist.) Where Peterson made this most apparent was on an episode of *The Rubin Report*—a centrist / libertarian political commentary show—dated January 31st 2018[21].

To paraphrase, Jordan discusses the use of psychotropic drugs—such as DMT—and explains that if you take some DMT and "find yourself in another part of the galaxy surrounded by extraterrestrials who are curious how you suddenly appeared alongside them"—that the experience is going to be "completely real" and your mind has to be prepared to handle the consequences of the reality of such an experience.

Peterson states he must refrain from asserting the "metaphysical reality" of such an experience as being literal—but the way he words this statement, it seems in no uncertain terms he's saying a transcendent experience could include leaving your body and interacting with powerful entities—and there's nothing dream-like about it at all. As an astral travel practitioner (who doesn't need DMT,) I can relate to this sentiment.

What I like about this phenomenon with Peterson is that he has so many followers and fans (to an almost scary degree) who listen to his every word, and so when he makes such a bold statement—he is immediately opening a lot of minds to metaphysical subjects. At the same time, he demonstrates solidarity to the new non-materialism that is pushing itself into mainstream acceptance. I hope that Peterson will continue to influence people to this end.

Addendum:

Before closing this section of the chapter, I do want to state that I personally do not take any mind-altering substances and I discourage their casual usage, despite the notions by Peterson, Hancock, Rogan, and others that such drugs can have excellent psychiatric effects. I don't think anything they say should be interpreted to mean you should immediately book a flight and meet up with a shaman in the jungle.

I've spoken to many practitioners of Ayahuasca who, in no uncertain terms, have told me that taking the drug without already being in a very positive state of mind could lead to unattended consequences or even a reversal of psychiatric health—severe depression, anxiety and even suicide. This makes sense to me, given that astral projection requires a similar state of calm and loving thoughts to avoid attracting any negative energies when operating in astral physics (where everything is so malleable to consciousness.) I personally feel disturbed by the idea of so many California millennials and tech-geeks taking trendy trips to Colombia to participate in Ayahuasca journeys—with as much regard for it as taking a hip yoga retreat to Bali—in other words, without knowing what the f--- they're really doing.

I think using a substance to force expulsion from the physical body and force merging with a parallel realm are DEEP waters that should NOT be thought of as a recreational experience or something to do because it's trendy or "spiritually hip."

Astral practitioner Jurgen Ziewe has interestingly noted the usage of DMT-substances in the astral, as well—whereupon it's possible to still go on an otherworldy journey even after already being in the astral / afterlife dimension (he recounts ingesting such a drug with a group of people while he was in his physical astral body, and then having a subsequent trip.) This idea hints at how these trips are above and beyond the scope of even the relatively "normal" astral planes, which prompts the usage of psychedelics among the residents of worlds beyond this one who recognize that they are still relatively low on the consciousness totem pole by comparison to the vast scope of existence. Therefore, we can see how broad and cosmic the experiences on these substances can become, and why exploring such realms is not for a novice.

Wikipedia: Still Controlled by Pseudo-Skeptics

So far I've presented an optimistic view, with pioneers of the consciousness renaissance opening minds everywhere. These are reasons to feel positive, but it would be foolish to think the war has been won. Unfortunately, the materialist lobby still controls some of the world's most influential platforms, and as they get backed into a corner they only fight harder to keep control of their narrative. Nowhere is this more apparent than Wikipedia: the site whose SEO reach is so massive Wikipedia articles are typically the first Google result no matter what is typed. As a result, Wikipedia attempts to be people's first (and often final) authority on a subject. This makes Wikipedia into the ultimate propaganda tool. And the materialist lobby has near full control over it.

The only good news I've determined since writing *Understanding Life After Death* where I spoke in more detail about the *Guerilla Skeptics* and attempts to control the information on Wikipedia, is that people are becoming much more familiar with the bullsh-- nature of the site and looking for alternatives (which may eventually supplant Wikipedia entirely.) Wikipedia editing is supposed to be grounded in a "neutral" position but it's laughable to think this really occurs. The culture of anonymous editing and lobbies trying to sway information has become even more evident in the age of culture wars, fake news, and heated political discourse. More and more, I hypothesize people are tired of being fed subtly manipulative information painted under the guise of "neutral." People want to be shown what a person's point of view is without any tricks, by looking at numerous articles and deciding for themselves via checking out the facts pertaining to the subject.

I am sure the militantly skeptical personality is only a subset of the materialist / atheist subculture, which is itself a minority position. However, it's always been a tactic of fanatical minorities to try and monopolize the flow of information to spread their ideas further. This can be seen by both extreme right-wing and left-wing ideologues who, despite representing a fraction of general points of view, are somehow constantly shoving their ideas into our heads.

Another tactic that I see specifically on sites like Wikipedia and popular subreddits of *Reddit.com* (/r/science comes to mind) is the coalescing of a minority opinion until they *seem* like a majority in society. If 5% of people in the United States (this is just a guess) hold a militant materialist attitude—that's still about 17 million people, and if they're well organized then just a few thousand of them can invade a community to become the writers, editors, and administrators. Now a tiny subset, due to their mobility and organizational skills is controlling the flow of information and may appear to outsiders as a majority, authoritative force.

I wanted to share some snippets about how the "war" for Wikipedia is still underway. What seems to be occurring is a never-ending process where hot-button "paranormal" subjects—like Rupert Sheldrake's biography—are in a perpetual state of combat between Wiki editors, with a central power structure that will delete, ban, and censor with the zeal of fanatics. The best summary of this situation, including the issue with paranormal topics, was found in a Quora article dated back to December 2015 by Abd Ul-Rahman Loma from the California Institute of Technology. I feel the article is so good that it's worth a complete copy-and-paste job in this book. However, that said, I strongly suggest to still view the actual Quora page to upvote his post—as well as the contribution of Craig Weiler, the author of *Psi Wars: Ted, Wikipedia and the Battle for the Internet*, who also provides a brilliant response. You can find the page at the following URL: https://www.quora.com/Is-Wikipedia-biased-against-parapsychology

Did you visit the site above? Did you do the upvoting? Good, now let's take a look at what Rahman Loma has to say:

Is Wikipedia Biased Against Parapsychology? (Response)

> Wikipedia is not a person and so has no point of view. In theory, there is no bias. However, in practice, there is, and it results from bias in the user community, which tends to be biased toward majority points of view among the population that is attracted by editing Wikipedia, which bias is then amplified by factions that developed among administrators, who then can warp the community further by selective warning, blocking, and banning. Over the years, the effect accumulated. Skilled editors, dedicated to Neutral Point of View, if they confronted an administrative faction, were harassed and ultimately blocked or banned. Any editor actually promoting a minority point of view was easily sanctioned and eliminated. So, then, newcomers continue to arrive, where a minority point of view is

unfairly represented on Wikipedia, and they naturally try to fix it. And they are easily picked off, because, of course, they are clueless and violate the often arcane policies of Wikipedia.

There is a response here from Jared Zimmerman, who was an employee of the WikiMedia Foundation. What he says is what most active Wikipedians believe. He actually makes a preposterous statement: "all of the editors are united however in upholding the Five Pillars." All except those who have been banned of course, and those who are afraid to speak up lest they be banned, and those who promote what is called the "Scientific Point of View," which includes administrators. The so-called scientific point of view is unscientific and pseudoskeptical.

However, Jared is correct: there are, for parapsychology, a "wealth of sources that claim it is "unscientific." However, there are also many sources that claim the opposite. This can all be handled to produce neutral articles if there is a level playing field. There is not a level field. There is no system in place to reliably create and maintain that. Looking back at the editing of the parapsychology article, a name leaped out at me: *Goblin Face*. Goblin Face was successful at getting others blocked, those who opposed the pseudoskeptical agenda. But he was himself a sock puppet, in a huge family of socks.

There is a group called the Guerilla Skeptics, which has openly coordinated Wikipedia editing with a debunking agenda. See Guerrilla Skepticism on Wikipedia.

See also her Wikipedia article: Susan Gerbic

This is what is missed by those who can't see the forest for the trees. Numbers of editors count on a wiki like Wikipedia. Sure, everything may be sourced, but there is a vast number of sources to choose from. Creating a situation where increased numbers of editors with a particular point of view show up to edit articles, creates a powerful force for bias. An isolated editor might be tempted to revert war, and then is easily blocked. The faction, if disciplined, doesn't need to revert war, it simply musters more editors.

If Wikipedia actually ran genuine consensus process, numbers would not matter. But it doesn't, and almost never has. It follows what is called "rough consensus." Which more or less means "majority," but it is a majority with heavy participation bias. I saw the Arbitration Committee desysop an administrator who had essentially done nothing wrong, because he was associated with a relatively harmless mailing list with a factional point of view. Susan Gerbic is far more explicitly active, pushing for "skeptical" coverage. Yet sanctions? No.

Should there be sanctions? This is what Wikipedia totally missed. Everyone has a point of view. A few people become really good at what is called "neutral point of view<' which is basically journalistic, and also scientific. Real science, that is. Banning "POV editing" was never a good idea, because to recognize a POV is easiest for someone with a differing POV. Rather, what Wikipedia would need is behavioral standards, and then education of users in those standards, and reliable maintenance. Instead, over and over, editors who had a minoirity point of view have been sanctioned, blocked, banned, and editors with a majority point of view would be tolerated or even encouraged.

Very human, and devastating to the neutrality of the project. Yet most of Wikipedia works well. I use it all the time. If there is controversy, however, it can be really poor.

I watched as experienced users, administrators, up to and including arbitrators, left the project, disgusted. Yet ... the WMF still presents a happy face, doing absolutely nothing about editor attrition. Wikipedia will become obsolete, I find that prediction fairly obvious. The existing content will be harvested by a commercial entity that will sell it, and create reliable processes to improve it. It's not at all difficult to imagine. Basically, this new project will be reliable by design, setting up stop-loss, so it will start with Wikipedia content, but then diverge. Because it will be reliable,

> because it will be as good as Wikipedia or better, it will get the public.
>
> Quora is not an encyclopedia. However, what Quora is doing would be a piece of what the new project would do. Quora is already far more attractive than Wikipedia, speaking as a user. Wikipedia editing is mostly isolated and lonely, so it attracts the socially dysfunctional. It attracts people who like exercising power over others. These accumulated, because it was made extremely difficult to remove administrators. Once elected, there is essentially no supervision.
>
> And Wikipedia content must be maintained. So one can work on an article, making it excellent, and it gradually -- or suddenly -- falls apart. That burns users out. Because anonymous editing is encouraged, no real community forms, the difference on Quora is astonishing to this long-time Wikimedian. Incivility is rampant. Jimbo tried to do something about it, blocking a popular admin for two hours for blatant incivility. He was shouted down and he backed off.
>
> Nobody is minding the store. Certainly not the WMF.

A few interesting points from this analysis:

- While a site like Quora is not yet an encyclopedia, the same design can be applied to an encyclopedia-style site.

  Wikipedia's structure itself is flawed from the get-go because it attracts "loner types"—editors who may enjoy exercising power over others.

- I'd argue it will also attract ideologues, who would use a "neutral" site as a tool to spread an agenda (while calling opinions facts.)

- Wikipedia uses something called "The Scientific Point of View." This appears to be a euphemism for defending the status quo. It's not "science" that's being pushed but pseudo skepticism, and it's the official policy of Wikipedia.

- It may be possible for Wikipedia's huge amount of content to eventually be sold off to a 3rd party. An organization that cares about actual neutrality could potentially "clean up" the thousands of high controversy / disputed articles with "true neutrality" and end the system of editors with agendas.

This article also shows how there is some light on the horizon in the form of "Wikipedia killer" Quora. By giving users the ability to up-vote articles, Quora offers a more democratic option for information gathering. I truly doubt pseudo-skeptics represent a majority opinion anymore, and through the voting process their actual unpopularity can be finally exposed.

Keeping the Fight On

Materialism and science orthodoxy exist as a lobby. We can go into conspiracy theories all day about who is pulling the strings of this lobby, but the fuel it uses to keep going is doubt. Its greatest weapon is the ability to tell people the following message:

"What these people claim is impossible. What's more likely, that something like 'psi' (or the afterlife) exists and the entire world you've grown up with is false, or the science experiments that show it exists was faulty in some way? Or the person who made the report was just delusional What's more logical?"

Fighting this narrative depends on one word: education. Few people know the afterlife is an objective and scientific area of study. The opposition relies on a lack of information to keep spinning their narrative. They want people to dismiss a topic after a casual glance on a Wikipedia page. What they DON'T want is curiosity or further research, and this is why Wikipedia is their most valuable asset, because many people restrict themselves to armchair research. They scan a topic for 2-3 minutes, and create a final decision on a subject based on cursory glances. However, once a person takes curiosity a step further and begins reading books and forming an education, it's difficult for such a person to remain dismissive.

One important lesson I've learned is **you CANNOT hit people over the head with topics they're not ready for**. However, what you *can* do is slowly introduce new paradigms via more easily accepted information—and when it's information that's scientifically sound and scrutinized, people embrace it more easily. Skeptic acolytes know this, and that's why they place people like Dean Radin and Rupert Sheldrake so heavily in their crosshairs—their reasonable ideas, books, and YouTube lectures present the greatest risk.

I've long tried to figure a way to gain the advantage in the "culture war" but in recent years—I've relaxed my position. Being "anti-supernatural" has become too vague of a position for most people to support. The proverbial frog is being boiled—people don't even realize that they've been introduced over many years to new ideas and paradigms that allow an open-mindedness that would have been non-existent a generation ago. Paranormal TV shows, despite their questionable material, dominate the ratings, "the other side" is in pop culture and firmly embedded. Being a harsh materialist skeptic now requires greater levels of work and cognitive dissonance. Times have changed, and while old institutions—whether TED or Wikipedia—cling to power, anyone on the front-lines can feel the air changing.

But does this mean we should do nothing? I wouldn't suggest that. Something I do believe is of critical importance is spreading the *right* ideas about afterlife topics. This involves promoting direct spirit communication, the works of arduous scientists like Gary Schwartz, impartial journalists like Leslie Kean, and removing the stigmas associated with practices like out-of-body travel (I still get asked, fairly often, silly questions like if it's possible to get stuck and never return to your body and thus die.)

Spreading correct and educated information is where the priorities should now lie. Because while skeptics and their denialism are a nuisance, the real threat lies within. There are countless people who monopolize the subject and use it for power and money. This has been happening for thousands of years—since ancient soothsayers—and it still happens today in the form of questionable celebrity psychics or authors prioritizing book deals over actual knowledge. While the topic is extremely vast, there's certain elements I believe are in opposition to "cosmic truth"—divine laws that exist in our objective reality. Whether it's ideas that our deceased loved ones are illusions created by a cosmic computer program, McSpirituality, or the fundamentalist religious ideas spun by the "Heaven is For Real" crowd—there are some interpretations that are flat wrong, and if they are not challenged then this whole level of reality risks being interpreted by our civilization in an incredibly skewed way.

Without fail, when I hear bad information being sent out to the masses, I see two things happen.

1.) The materialist skeptics receive ammo. The truthful stuff is harder to counter and receives less criticism—I think because people intuitively know there's strength behind it. The bad information, however, is how the materialists make sweeping generalizations to cast a bad light on *everything* and push public opinion to their favor.

2.) Fence-sitters and supporters alike begin to suffer grief. This is what burns me up inside and keeps me motivated. When a popular author releases a new idea that suggests to all his or her readers that the afterlife is NOT a place of reunions in another realm—without fail, heartbroken people flood the forums asking for clarification, or they start sending me personal e-mails. Authors who paint themselves as authority figures, and then publish their cynical pet opinions, are not aware that masses of people with deceased spouses, parents, children, and friends are counting on this information and follow the credible material closely as they desire hope or clarification about their own ADCs. It's a fragile process, and such people do not deserve untested theories to be spread as factual by people looking to carve a niche market or be trendy.

To combat bad information the best idea is to apply greater amounts of critical thinking—something that's almost always a positive no matter where it's applied. Reduce channels of information that do not have plausible direct spirit sources. For instance, an NDE account by an author with some clinical verifiability of his or her experience is more reliable than an unverified story. A mental medium with a proven track record of beyond-doubt communication (Susanne Wilson, Suzanne Geisseman, Allison Dubois or the late Maurice Barbanell come to mind) are probably more reliable than a psychic who is new on the scene and pushing hard for fame or TV show deals. A physical medium historically / scientifically scrutinized (Leslie Flint) will have better information than someone claiming to be a channeler and creating theories with no backing.

But, in addition, even if a source is well-known, if they begin saying things that defy your sense of reason, philosophical morality, or intuition—be especially cautious. Personally, I know my intuition is more than just guesswork. If something doesn't feel right, I can almost feel a transfer of information entering my mind—telling me to "watch out." It's never proven me wrong, and I suspect guides orchestrate this ability on the other side, if not directly my "higher self."

Most importantly, to tie everything in this chapter together, when you align toward accurate, truthful information—the picture that's painted is too powerful for even materialists to have much motivation to attack. They run out of ammo because it's usually a fight they don't want to engage. That's because who wouldn't want a world where we reunite with our loved ones, continue to progress as individuals, return to our prime ages and acquire perfect health? Where we can live in a superior version of this Earth and finally express ourselves in truthful ways, unhindered by struggles of economics? This is what the evidence suggests. This is what direct spirit communication—researched and compiled for at least 200 years dating back to Swedenborg in the 1700s—has shown us. It's only when people begin adding their own addendums or personal biases that this clear picture distorts. And it's that distorted picture which is the thing that's exploited by the enemies of spirituality.

Keep the picture adjusted in the right direction, and these problems will slowly become better.

How to Put Nails in Materialism's Coffin

What are the experiments of the future that will finally switch us out of the materialistic paradigm? It's not until the day comes that today's acolytes of the mainstream say, "Yes, of course, we knew this all along," will we finally be at the next stage of these changing global paradigms.

Alternative science outlets offer the hints of what might be occurring and the taboo subjects that are gaining in popularity. Unfortunately, this is also a messy subject to explore. Science, regardless, is a difficult institution to change. It's extremely rigid and typically controlled by special interests. A surefire cure to cancer could be discovered tomorrow, and because of bureaucracies and regulations, it wouldn't see the light of day for at least ten years. So, the idea of switching to a whole new mode of thinking is never going to be easy or fast. Further, while I sometimes disparage materialist critics and skeptics, this doesn't mean they're wrong in all their criticisms. So many areas in this field probably deserve the title of "pseudoscience" and it's hard to separate the wheat from the chaff.

However, I've been quite interested in certain alternative science areas that are cutting edge. Despite their current criticisms, what I am interested in are scientific breakthroughs that are easily repeatable and will—consistently—disprove materialist notions. This is the path to busting this paradigm out into the mainstream. As long as experimenters are open-minded enough to consider the possibility that the results they see are caused by "unthinkable" possibilities (psi, non-locality, extended consciousness, etc) then such experiments will be self-evident to the point that fence-sitters will change their positions.

So what are some of the potential breakthrough science experiments that could help drive a stake through materialism's heart? In the next chapter, we'll look at unusual, surprising areas of science that hold the potential of linking many non-material subjects together in a way that applies to the real, physical world.

XI – New Science That Could Change Everything

One of the reasons the afterlife is such a hard pill to swallow is that there is no foundational structure to support it. Para scientist "superstars" like Targ, Radin, and Sheldrake have done an excellent job of pushing ideas like psi and morphic resonance into the semi-mainstream, but how far can an idea go when it's believed it exists in contrast to the rest of nature? However, another perspective is that nature—including fields like biology—have energetic / psychic / resonant elements that our post-enlightenment world has grossly overlooked.

A New Non-Materialist Biology?

Since the beginning of science, there's been a great struggle to understand where life originated from. Theories of Darwinism and primordial ooze have maintained a lynchpin on the subject and are the go-to explanation by closed-minded skeptics to explain life; however, actual biologists realize there are serious holes in these ideas.

For one thing, recent discoveries have upended the commonly accepted ideas about evolution. Scientists, reporting in the journal *Proceedings of the National Academy of Sciences,* discovered in 2017 3.5 billion-year-old fossilized bacteria that were significantly more advanced than the earliest forms of life were supposed to be at that point. According to an Astronomy.com report, these fossilized microbes indicate that life can evolve rapidly, which could mean life is more abundant in the universe than previously thought[22], not just because of the rapid evolution but due to the fact such complex bacteria appeared while there was limited oxygen on the planet, before even the evolution of photosynthesis. The study also shows life originated at least 4-billion-years ago.

These discoveries poke more holes into the idea that life just randomly evolved due to molecules spinning together and somehow deciding to form into cells and DNA. Why does this process happen so fast? How come scientists cannot currently replicate this phenomenon?

This is adding more weight to the idea of panspermia, that our life piggy-backed off an asteroid that crashed and suddenly began populating our desolate, nearly oxygen devoid planet with single-celled organisms. Which of course leads to the question of how life evolved on the asteroid, where the asteroid came from, and just how much life is really in the universe. Skeptics who have long held on to the idea that we're alone in the universe and extraterrestrials are bunk (along with spirits and ghosts) are now sweating a little bit.

But there's another possibility that fits closer to the themes of this book: What if life appears out of "nothing" in a rapid yet natural process? What if this process defied what is understood via materialist science and requires some kind of trans-dimensional component or trans-dimensional nature to life? These are the questions raised by a series of unusual experiments reported by numerous scientists dating back to the 1930s, including recent experiments outlined in a 2011 journal by one of the world's most eminent scientists. These particular studies all seem to correspond to one another, with researchers arriving at very similar conclusions about the nature of life and astonishing properties of "inert" matter. Is somewhere in this complex, messy world of "pseudo-science" the keys to upending the materialist narrative about life and the universe?

Spontaneous Life Generation

In 2000, a surprising headline from the *Times of London* was released: "Dust 'comes alive' in space." Although it's been many years since this study was carried out, the results remain a mysterious and overlooked part of biology: Somehow, DNA double helixes could form out of non-organic matter, and there could even be some type of "memory" akin to life itself found in *non*-life. Obviously this has many implications for the way see the world. From the Times article[23]:

> An international panel from the Russian Academy of Sciences, the Max Planck Institute in Germany and the University of Sydney found that galactic dust could form spontaneously into helixes and double helixes and that the inorganic creations had memory and the power to reproduce themselves.
>
> A similar rethinking of prospective alien life is being undertaken by the National Research Council, an advisory body to the US government. It says NASA should start a search for what it describes as "weird life" - organisms that lack DNA or other molecules found in life on Earth.
>
> The new research, to be published this week in the New Journal of Physics, found nonorganic dust, when held in the form of plasma in zero gravity, formed the helical

> structures found in DNA. The particles are held together by electromagnetic forces that the scientists say could contain a code comparable to the genetic information held in organic matter. It appeared that this code could be transferred to the next generation.

This discovery would continue with new research. A Venezuelan neurobiologist named Ignacio Ochoa carried out a series of experiments claiming to show how, indeed, life can just "spontaneously generate" itself. Further, the life allegedly generated is a bit more detailed than the types of "weird life" that the research partnership advised to keep an eye out for: he observed the formation of relatively complex organisms that utilized actual DNA.

Ignacio's experiment was performed in the following way:

1.) Heat beach sand to white-hot luminescence. This kills all possible lifeforms or spores. Deposit into test tube with further sterilized distilled water.
2.) Hermetically seal with a Bakelite cover. Let the mixture cool, then use an autoclave device to further sterilize it. The autoclave uses temperatures and pressure scientifically proven to kill all forms of life—the same technique for sterilizing surgical equipment.
3.) Allow to sit for 24 hours. During this period, allegedly the natural "tortion energy fields" will begin to help the raw materials coalesce together. Somehow, amidst this process, non-organic particles will attract, forming the highly complex substance known as DNA.
4.) Skim a top layer of sediment. In Ignacio's paper, this is when the first signs of life were found—life generated from raw, inert non-organic matter that began naturally producing DNA.
5.) Ignacio would then sterilize the vial two more times to guarantee no contamination, wait a period of time, skim the surface and still find microbes newly "hatched" from the raw materials.

The results of this experiment were published in his paper titled "*Ultrastructural and light microscopy analysis of SAPA bions formation and growth in vitro.*"[24] This experiment was also an attempt to replicate the works of Wilhelm Reich and his research into bions—vesicules that are allegedly energetically powered proto-lifeforms, arising from the disintegration of matter. We'll talk more about Reich in a little bit.

From Ignacio's paper:

> "The present study demonstrates the formation, growth, motility, reproduction and organization of bions at the structural and ultrastructural level of microscopic resolution using experimental thermal conditions that normally destroy all organic components present in the structure of vegetative cells and spores. "

Here is a photo of one such microbe Ignacio discovered:

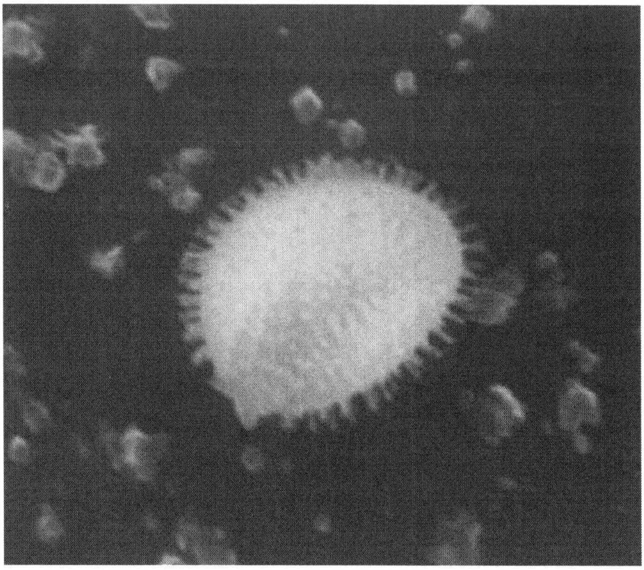

Huh? This Doesn't Make Any Sense

We are taught to believe that there is either life or non-life. Biologists have long claimed that life must, somehow, arise from "nothing"—in the crude materialist view. What they were not expecting is for discoveries to suggest this occurs rapidly and is guided by some power we could never imagine. The story doesn't end here, though. With this idea capturing the imaginations of different outside-the-box scientists, we continue to see research in this area, such as:

A Famous Scientist Also Makes DNA from Energy Signal

Eleven years after Ochoa's research, we saw a revolutionary scientist engaging in startlingly similar work—with eye-opening results. Although not an exact replication of Ochoa's, it fits in perfectly with the idea of a non-materialist basis in biology.

The experiments were undertaken by Nobel prize winning HIV researcher (he *discovered* the HIV-AIDS connection) Dr. Luc Montagnier. The following is from a January 14th *Popular Science* article[25]:

> A Nobel prize winning scientist who shared the 2008 prize for medicine for his role in establishing the link between HIV and AIDS has stirred up a good deal of both interest and skepticism with his latest experimental results, which more or less show that DNA can teleport itself to distant cells via electromagnetic signals. If his results prove correct, they would shake up the foundations upon which modern chemistry rests. But plenty of Montagnier's peers are far from convinced.

This experiment certainly dovetails with the prior work of Ochoa and the researchers who studied the spontaneous formation of the DNA double-helix in space vacuums. This work is a continuation of the idea that life—specifically DNA—is hard coded as a potentiality in inert molecules—and is transferable through a type of energy-based system. This experiment is somewhat different from Ochoa's approach as he attempts to study the creation of "bions" that lead to life generation in disintegrating matter; however, it could be easily tied together (both researchers assert DNA possesses a transcendent energetic property.)

To simplify: if there's the presence of existing life, then the components of that life may then replicate naturally in the environment. This is the DNA teleportation hypothesis—hardly embraced by the mainstream; however, this was not research performed by a low-level scientist or a quack, but someone whose reputation is so eminent it forced outsiders to take it seriously.

Investigating Montagnier's Claims

Montagnier's interest was related to his study of the HIV virus, and what he claims was the detection of electromagnetic energy in cells, inspiring him to go into the field of researching water memory—a field that has been known to kill careers and, according to a 2012 documentary[26], destroyed the career of an eminent predecessor. In the same documentary, Montagnier is quoted, "…These are my best years of research, I'm finding the most important phenomena today. It's a good thing to discover a virus [HIV,] but finding about the mechanisms of life, that's even more important."

In the 2012 documentary investigation, researchers arrived at his lab and developed a double-blind encoding protocol to observe the experiment being carried out while regulating against fraud or outside influence. The researchers carefully labeled the combination of test tubes that went through a thorough dilution process, resulting in the complete removal of DNA traces, mixed among 10 placebo tubes containing just water. In the experiment, Montagnier is testing to see whether the tubes containing merely the "memory" of prior existent DNA has the ability to "grow" the DNA again due to an electromagnetic imprint that it had placed upon the water. Due to the extremely sensitive equipment present, the documentary team must shut off their cell phones and switch to the lowest-EMF production equipment available.

The next stage involves the recording of electromagnetic frequencies emitted from the tubes. Using EMF-sensitive machines and software, the tubes begin the testing, with the results saved on a hard drive. If the tubes merely contain water, what could possibly be getting detected? The first two tubes fail to produce any signals. As they continue, they find electromagnetic signals present in tubes #10 and #3—while the rest contain no signal. These two tubes were the sixth and seventh dilutions—not the placebos. Montagnier successfully locates dilutions that are apparently imprinted with the DNA "signal." According to mainstream physics, water contains no signals. As Montagnier explains, there is no physical DNA present in the tubes; rather, it is the structure of the water itself that is emitting the signals.

The experiment continues, breaking into more ambitious grounds. The signal produced in the computer will then be reconstituted digitally, sent to a partnering lab in Italy, where they will attempt to expose new water to the digital copy which would, in theory, imprint the water with the same DNA signal. This occurs through exposing the water to the digital signal for an hour—the scientists describing it as water that's "listening to music." From that point, the experimenters will then use a PCR device—also known as a thermal cycler—which are "DNA amplifiers"—a phenomenal piece of modern equipment that reconfigures broken DNA molecules using a natural enzyme called polymerase. This technology is especially useful in the field of criminal forensics.

What would happen when adding water to the thermal cycler that was exposed to the DNA signal produced in a lab 1000km away? (The water contains some trace biological elements that could be used to create DNA, but no actual DNA strands.) According to materialist science, the answer should be "nothing." You can't digitally expose water to a signal that results in a physical object being grown. Life is hard and material—and the rules of physics are not akin to a giant computer program, after all.

But the results baffle the investigators. The PCR machine shows that the DNA from Montagnier's vial that was diluted in water to the point of non-existence but whose signal remained and was transferred digitally to a partnering lab, had now regrown itself in new water using some basic molecular building blocks. The final step was for a third party to analyze the DNA and compare its sequencing with the starter DNA, and they concluded the newly grown DNA is a 98% match. The DNA successfully teleported from one lab to the next, using an invisible signal that was transmitted on water.

What does this mean? Besides suggesting the long-ridiculed subject of homeopathy may be legitimate, it shows that DNA and the generation of life itself are based on electromagnetic signals that attach to the environment. Unsurprisingly, despite the concrete scientific evidence, this is not an idea that's being widely embraced. I've read a lot of armchair skepticism about this experiment, such as "The vials were contaminated, and the experiment was flimsy." As is often the case with pseudo-skeptical debunking attempts, these explanations are lackluster theories that are presented as the concrete and determined alternative explanation. With something this groundbreaking, we are in another make-or-break situation where if accepted, everything would be forced to be redefined and it would switch perspectives firmly in a non-materialist direction. This reason alone is why these experiments made waves in 2011 and 2012 and then promptly fizzled out. Theoretical chemist Jeff Reimers summarized it best, "If the results are correct, these would be the most significant experiments performed in the past 90 years, demanding a re-evaluation of the whole conceptual framework of modern chemistry."[27]

The experiment showed that DNA can originate out of inert materials using an electronic signal. It would explain why life has been found as early as 4 billion years. It would mean that a complex series of random mutations may not have been required to generate the vastly complex DNA structure. What if, instead, life is "coded" into nature itself, and through a kind of electrical stimulus combined with an existing energetic "signal"—DNA and subsequent lifeforms will erupt out of inert matter? This is a very different way of looking at the world than the randomness taught in school.

However, what if this experiment was just a small-scale demonstration of something more remarkable? The idea that life can spontaneously manifest itself dates back much further than this experiment, further than Ochoa's work, back to the 1930s. While Montagnier demonstrated the viability of energy-based systems of life in a mainstream, academic way—there are much "crazier" claims still floating around fringe science, summarily dismissed by virtually everyone on the mainstream, but which now appear less crazy than originally thought.

Wilhelm Reich – Science Pariah

How did this whole idea of life arising from nowhere begin? It was Wilhelm Reich and his theories of orgone energy that gave rise to this notion—and was the precursor to the previous experiments mentioned so far.

If you hear the words orgone energy and you are (unlike me) past the age of about 40, memories may come to mind about quack science dating back to the 60s and 70s—with hippies building "orgone boxes" to revitalize themselves by padding wool and steel together. Beyond this casual dismissal, the science of orgone energy developed by Wilhelm Reich was an attempt to underpin an energetic foundation to life itself, and it would seem to dovetail very closely with the discoveries of Montagnier. It was

Reich, the Austrian psychology pioneer and friend of Sigmund Freud, 70-80 years prior to Montagnier, who claimed that life can erupt as a result of energetic infusion within ordinarily inert matter. Could the electromagnetic fields produced by DNA, resulting in water memory and teleportation, be a manifestation of what Reich had already discovered?

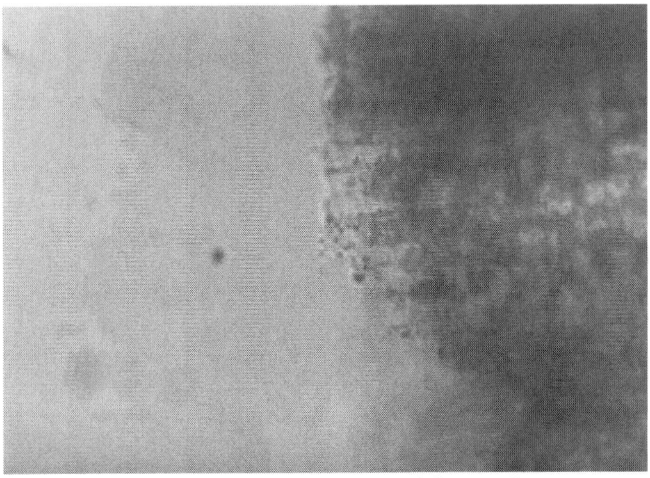

A bion allegedly forms out of destroyed grass.

It's easy to dismiss orgone energy because of the New Age gold-rush that it caused. Still today, countless crystals, medallions, helmets, and clothing are sold at conventions with claims they are imbued with orgone energy. "Why should I buy this quartz crystal for so much money? "Because it has ORGONE energy in it!" "Ah, okay, here's $75." As a pseudo-science, it's an easy way to cash in on something—as the presence of orgone energy is not provable in any of these items but for believers it will cure everything from hiccups to cancer.

However, outside of the capitalistic orgone market, we can look back at the way the subject is maintained and studied by various orgone institutes throughout the world. Orgone science often involves studying bions—small vesicles that allegedly carry an underlying energetic force throughout biological systems. The Orgone Institute of the UK explains it thusly[28]:

> "[Reich]discovered the process of bionous disintegration, by which dead matter swelled in water or a nutrient fluid and generated the growth of bions, tiny, highly-charged and very motile vesicles that were the transitional elements between life and non-life. (The Bion Experiments on the Origin of Life and The Cancer Biopathy .) These vesicles had a tendency to gather in clumps and even form organisms in some circumstances. Reich filmed these processes under the microscope. You can see some of them on C O R E's videos on YouTube.
>
> ...Reich found that some of his bion cultures in test-tubes gave out a form of radiation that produced sensations in observers and noticeable physical effects. He investigated this 'radiation' further and this led him to the discovery of the life energy, which he named orgone after its origin in his study of the orgasm function and organic processes in nature."

These extraordinary claims of a "life energy" include the notion that bion vesicles, energetic capsules, create life where there was previously no life. Orgonomic institutes claim independent researchers can observe this experiment and others, and they publish booklets so that people can see for themselves what were Reich's original experiments. Allegedly, bions themselves can be seen through a microscope and are about one micron in diameter, highly mobile, glowing blue and exist as a transitionary point between life and non-life. Think of them as shells of would-be organisms. While mainstream scientists dismiss these as irrelevant particulates, orgone scientists claim they are storage capsules of life energy.

The hardest claim for me to believe is that these bion vesicles—which can be produced not only from organic material but by exposing hard metals, sand, rocks, etc to intense heats—can then transform into single-celled life from where there was none previously, thereby explaining the origin of life itself deriving from energy systems imbued in nature. Skeptics claim it's just a misinterpretation of data, analyzing contaminated samples or misidentifying natural spores with non-living "bions." However, given Montagnier's work, is the alternative of imbedded energy systems entirely impossible? Or what about Ochoa's rigorous sterilization processes? How could contamination still occur in situations where no life is capable of being present?

Personally, I have neither the time, budget nor patience to start buying lab equipment and seeing for myself if protozoan lifeforms magically emerge out of an energy field (as fascinating as this sounds.) However, I can report on a typical style of orgone experiment as claimed by a couple of YouTube presentations I watched on the subject:

Change the World and Create Life out of "Nothing" According to Orgone Researchers

(Note the similarities to orgone / bion experiments to that of Ignacio and Montagnier's work.)

1.) Experimenters may first gather some green grass and distill it in water for several days.
2.) According to Reich's research, the act of disintegration of organic or even non-organic material can produce bions. After several days, using a 5000x microscope, bions are seen coming out of the grass.
3.) Bions are collected and added to a sterilized solution. Researchers wait for 2-3 months and discover the formation of bion "clumps."
4.) The clumps may then form into proto-versions of life, including very simplistic amoebae.
5.) Allegedly, this can be performed in a sterilized solution with control cultures in place.

What I am not so sure about, based my research, is the validity of the "life" produced. What I see are life-like structures. For instance, a yeast-looking formation amidst bions produced by exposing metal to an intense heat. However, how certain are we that it's not merely a contaminated sample? This general doubt is what's kept orgone research on the extreme fringe of science.

Nonetheless, there are elements of this research that are quite peculiar, and create reasons for consideration:

- Although physical objects, bions appear to be energetic as well (ethereal, perhaps?)

- They appear in a distinct blue color and allegedly glow.

- When released from matter, they're strangely mobile, spinning around wildly.

- Reich's research extended into bions being a fundamental component of matter, including their ability to electrically hold clouds together. He created a giant "bion sucking" gun—famously known as the Cloudburster. When directed at clouds, allegedly clouds would break apart.

- Orgone institutes make many claims that this life energy is a cornerstone of health and wellbeing. The "conspiracy narrative" surrounding orgone studies is that as Reich began curing patients of cancer using orgone boxes, the medical "cabal" saw him as a threat, prosecuted him for medical fraud, and sent him to prison in 1956—where he died of "heart failure" a year later.

- Proponents claim a negative form of orgone energy called Deadly Orgone Radiation can be responsible for crop decimation among other problems. Supporters claim orgone science has treated these issues, leading to successful crop rehabilitation and anomalous precipitation, making it an essential farming tool.

- Wilhelm Reich seemed unfairly persecuted, and this could have related to his linking of sexuality and orgone energy production ("orgone" deriving from organism and orgasm.) Reich was an early sex activist, encouraging sexual liberation, contraceptive use, sexual hygiene, and treatment of sexual neuroses[29]. During his highly conservative, relatively puritanical era, it could explain why he became a prime target by the "establishment" to be stopped.

- Orgone energy science comes with reported hazards. Sucking the orgone from an area can disrupt your natural balance, leading to sickness. Workers in this field claim to practice great caution with how they approach experiments, being careful not to have their orgone energy zapped out or getting flooded by negative orgone energy resulting in opposite effects (sickness and pain.)

- Finally, it all matches up with the works of Ignacio Ochoa, who successfully replicated these experiments with even greater stringent tests, and of course Montagnier who has demonstrated DNA's energetic power. Even if there are flaws in these individual subjects, it seems like all these experiments taken together as a whole are suggesting something is happening for real.

The common knowledge is that with millions of microbiologists on the planet, all peering into microscopes every day, someone else would have discovered these bions. How could they hide in plain sight? However, I remind myself that science is an institution, controlled by political forces, and not the neutral, benevolent force that idealists would like. If natural forces could usurp complex pharmaceutical solutions or energy-producing devices, then such studies will always fall mysteriously short of funding or acknowledgment. If we go back to the (admittedly hard to believe) testimonies of insiders from this book's earlier chapter on technology—this is exactly what they say—that forces like "orgone" (which is another word for Qi energy, prana, or various other words throughout the ages) provide technological solutions to most of our world's issues, ranging from free energy production to eliminating common deadly illnesses. Certainly, this has been the point of view heralded by the New Age movement for decades; however, it often manifests as questionable and ironically high-priced treatments that further discredit the non-mainstream approaches to science. Insiders claim the "real" treatments are carefully monitored and controlled by the "deep state." If, for instance, natural energy systems began seeing their true power used in technology, the scientists involved would quite literally start disappearing.

If any of this information is even partially true, it represents an untapped area of science that would kill materialist paradigms once for all, while also explaining the age-old baffling question about the origin of life itself. While it's true, Newtonian physics would have to be rewritten, and we'd see an existential crisis arise across all the world's scientific institutions, we'd come out the other side as a far different, much more advanced civilization.

Cultural Impact

A bigger point you may have surmised so far in this book is that there's no foundation in society—any society (eastern or western)—to accept a claim like an afterlife, which is why it's such a long and difficult process. That's because we are utterly transfixed by the ideas of rigidity, randomness, meaninglessness, and physicalism. Without even proper evidence to back it up, mainstream science *assumes* life arose from *random molecules randomly deciding to start randomly producing unbelievably complex DNA that will randomly evolve itself into cells to randomly make bigger cells and entire, thinking organisms.* Science already speculates that non-biological life magically became biological, but the big addendum is that 1.) It took billions of years, 2.) It happened randomly (have to emphasize this) and 3.) It's a completely unintelligent, clunky process. For instance, cells came into existence when pieces of matter got stuck in tiny "bubbles" randomly floating around in solutions, but after hundreds of millions of years, those bubbles decided to start adapting and fighting over resources from other bubbles.

Part of me actually finds these theories fascinating—imagine just regular old pieces of matter deciding one day to compete over other specs of carbon for more energy and resources. It's fun to think about pieces of useless debris obtaining rudimentary intelligence (even if it takes hundreds of millions of years.) I can never look at dust and soap bubbles the same way again.

But despite how fun it is to imagine, I know inside that it's all bullsh--. The science intelligentsia are totally clueless. But what if, hiding in plain sight, was the origin of life? What if life arises as a result of an energetic signal interacting with inert manner, helping it spring to life? Given the alternative of freakish coincidences and soap bubbles coming to life, is it really so strange?

This explanation, however, exists on a very different spectrum than materialism. The concept is an energy—a frequency or vibration—has the power to create life from basic building blocks. It would mean, firstly, that life is abundant in the universe. It would mean life existing on a planet like Mars isn't just possible but nearly certain. **It would also suggest some type of vast, cosmic intelligence**. While ancients have called it "qi" or "prana," science would be forced to examine an all-encompassing energy system that literally powers the universe.

Skepticism and Self-Sabotage

Upon researching all these different experiments into non-organic life generation, as well as the claims of orgone energy, I was surprised to learn about the rigor applied to the scientific research. In the DNA teleportation experiments referenced earlier, scientists worked with an independent team of researchers using blinded experimental protocols and a thorough analysis with state-of-the-art equipment. All that said, a quick Google of DNA teleportation yields a Wikipedia article that begins with, "DNA teleportation is the pseudo-scientific claim that..." Well, now we're back to the Wikipedia issues we talked about in the last chapter. With so much strong science to support these notions, including the research back in 2000 into DNA generation in the vacuum of space, how can all of this still be fringe?

Unfortunately, what I come to find is that some of these researchers—the orgone energy crowd included—are their own worst enemies and have been for many years.

The best example would be how the subject of orgone energy morphed into a subculture, with sets of values, especially in relation to sexual liberation, which were especially popular in the 1960s and 1970s but remain highly polarizing. An October 2011 article by Stephan Simonian, M.D., with *The Journal of Psychiatric Orgone Therapy*, is titled "On the Sexual Rights of Youth."[30] This article is itself not as bad as it sounds, as it seems to discuss Reich's work related to the libido and the need to recognize children will experience sexual feelings, and it must be addressed psychologically. However, the article boasts what may be the worst title I've ever seen. The gut reaction of most readers is: "Children shouldn't have sexual rights because it would be horrifically dangerous if they did; and further, I now want nothing to do with these orgone energy people whatsoever, as this type of talk is a stones-throw away from advocating pedophilia." I imagine these feelings are especially sensitive in the age of Pedogate scandals in the U.K., Hollywood, and other establishments.

Issues don't end there. Luc Montagnier, despite being the pioneering HIV researcher, made some strange bedfellows by appearing in the AIDS denialism movie *House of Numbers.* To summarize this strange field, there's a subculture of conspiracy theorists who believe that HIV is not a real, or at least not a dangerous, virus. They believe that instead of a virus it's the treatment of HIV—the drugs themselves—that cause AIDS to occur, forgetting how before appropriate antiretroviral drugs and HIV was left untreated, it was a virtual death sentence. However, like many murky conspiracy topics, information is cherry picked and arguments run in circles until critics give up. Similarly, Montagnier's words were cherry-picked to create a façade of his support for their position. Nonetheless, Montagnier demonstrated a lapse in judgment by appearing in the documentary.

A mystery to me is why people on the cutting edge allow themselves to become so vulnerable. If a new science is burgeoning on the edge of going mainstream, the vocal institution should not write an article about the sexual rights of children, and a lead scientist in a new field should not affiliate with fringe, dangerous groups. When I researched these topics, inevitably the skeptics used both of the above incidents to smear both subjects. No, it's not fair. Being interviewed in a documentary should not determine the nature of one's science experiments. It's highly illogical to imply such a thing. Nonetheless, that is how public opinion is formed: through ad homs and character assassinations.

Similarly, the subject of the afterlife requires care and attention to public relations. Psychics require magnanimous reputations to quell the backlash against fakes. Even writers like myself must remain vigilant about our reputations and whom we partner with lest we become guilty by association. The issue I see is that with all these subjects—the groups doing the research become marginalized by the mainstream, and this marginalization means moving closer to the alternative communities. And while alternative communities may hold some truth, these are also the environments where actual quack science and "crazy stuff" can spread. I would advise those researching these ideas to remain highly aware of what the public is capable of digesting. While the public is may accept that energetic blueprints can create DNA helixes from non-organic matter, and possibly even life itself, they may not be willing to hear ideas about orgone energy in talismans balancing your auras. A large part of the population (often rightfully) shuts their interest off as soon as ideas go into the areas of "crazy conspiracy" or "crazy New Age." Heck, even my mind still does that—and I write about meeting dead people while out of my body.

I hope these researchers stop playing their own worst enemies, and the information begins receiving serious budgeted efforts and mainstream scientific pursuits by numerous private entities, forcing attention on potential paradigms that would revolutionize biology—and force society to look long and hard at paradigms outside of materialism.

Or maybe "bions" are just random particles and the results prove how excitement and expectations can create bizarre results. Hey, even that is at least worth looking into.

XII – Connecting to the Afterlife

Many theories and wild ideas have been presented so far in this book, but can we bring it back to our own lives? The afterlife's influence upon us occurs among people to varying degrees. In this chapter, I am going to lay out some "how to" steps for engaging with the afterlife, especially for the purposes of reconnecting with deceased loved ones.

My own experiences have been life-changing, but the stories I hear people share on *Afterlife Topics and Metaphysics* and sister groups on Facebook like *Evidence for the Afterlife* are also life-changing. Connecting to the afterlife is possible for anyone, even among those who feel hopeless. Factors include bravery and dedication. For me, it took until my late-twenties before I mustered the courage to begin having out-of-body experiences, allowing me to relate to the apprehension of venturing into this territory fully. But there may come the point where you feel ready to go all-in, much as I did shortly before my exploration of OBEs.

What Does the Afterlife Matter if it's Not a Part of Our Lives?

I frankly hope a time will come when everyone can connect to their deceased loved ones. That's why I do this work. Already, we've seen great progress. Earlier, I spoke about how times have changed quite a lot since the "old days" when the subject of the afterlife was minimal in popular culture, the 'Skeptics' had full control of the airways, and few—if anyone—knew about the objective evidence.

What we see today is a convergence of different fields gaining popular interest, whether it's Sheldrake discussing morphic resonance or ghost hunting and psychic TV shows—all these different topics point in the same directions of non-materialism and the mind extending outside of the body. And once this is considered, the idea that maybe our deceased loved ones are not really dead starts to enter people's minds. As a result, so many people now are open to these ideas and actively practicing contact with the other side.

However, the most important thing to remember is that it takes work and dedication. Some of us have spontaneous "supernatural" experiences and become greatly disappointed if, afterward, there are no further experiences. This can be disheartening, but it's important to understand the reasons why further contacts are inhibited, which we will explain later.

How Contact Experiences Occur

In any contact with another dimension, they are either **expending energy** to reach through to you or **receiving energy** by means of your energy being expended. In any situation where a **manifestation** occurs (their sight, smell, audible presence, etc) they are using up their finite supply of energy to project themselves into this dimension. Numerous sources of mine state this act requires a considerable amount of work. The alternative is for a person to expend their own energy by appearing on their side. This includes astral projection and to a limited extent dream experiences.

"But I thought on spirit side, they were omnipotent and had infinite energy, I don't understand."

One would think, but that doesn't seem to be the case. Information I received through my mother stated that contacting us may require literally going through workshops to teach how it is done. Further, I've seen evidence of this among many who carry out ongoing relationships with the other side. According to a member of my forum, Kristine, who posts elaborate EVP and ITC-based communication attempts with her deceased spouse, learning a new technique may take an entire year of practice before it is fully manifested, and is very much a two-way process between both parties, requiring complex processes of energetic alignment. Kristine even claims her deceased spouse must "rest" after such contacts to recoup energy. Although on the astral it does not seem you must do activities like consume food to regain energy, this may not mean there is unlimited energy, and apparently manifesting into a "lower" vibrational realm like ours is a major consumer of such energy.

Another factor that seems to influence visitations concerns the element of "permission." This is a reoccurring theme that I hear about, that a particular spirit must be granted "access" to contact us. It does not seem the contacting of this plane is undertaken lightly, but there may be rules and stipulations involved. This was highly surprising to me, as I generally assumed those beyond have full autonomy without governing institutions, but it seems that many variables are taken into account, and authoritative structures exist.

Factors include whether a person is psychologically fit and ready to receive communication from the other side and whether such a manifestation may in some way interfere with our life plans or free will.

Also, there may be considerations about wider societal impact—some on that side may have the ability to just walk among us fully materialized, but that could disrupt our civilization. Similar to ET encounters, I sense there is a "prime directive" in place to avoid interfering in our world too drastically.

The Different Types of Contacts That Can Occur

Before attempting to create or request an ADC (after-death experience) from a loved one, it's important to be familiar with the types of experiences that can occur and to have the ability to recognize (and be prepared) for various things to happen. I'll list these in rough order of the most common experiences listed first, ending with the rarest types of encounters.

(Note: For my citation, please see the huge database of ADCs at ADCRF.org. Here you can browse hundreds of user-submitted experiences spanning the full breadth of different types of contacts.)

Dream Visitations

Probably the most common type of experience. In fact, it'd be rather unusual for a person who loses a loved one *not* to have such a visitation. Some notes:

- Such a visitation in a dream is much more real and crisp than a regular dream.

- There is a specific context about the person having died and delivering a message to you.

- You'll wake up feeling amazed by the experience, by comparison to a regular dream which may be a jumbled mix of images, sensations and ideas with not a lot of meaning behind it all (i.e.: hallucinations.)

So what *is* a dream visitation? This relates to the more complex subject of "what dreams are." One thing I am certain of is that astral projection and lucid dreaming are closely tied together, yet not entirely the same. It appears a dream world is a distinctive state where the mind creates a temporary plane around itself for some purpose of exploration or working out psychological issues. And, this sometimes involves nonsensical things that would be out of place in the "real" world as they are allegories and metaphors made manifest by the higher self. Nonetheless, this realm can be entered into by other minds and shared by more than one person (think *Inception,*) and on the other side, spirit people can enter dreams together quite easily.

A dream visitation may also be a guided, brief astral experience in a non-dream world. It's easy to confuse the two upon waking.

Physical Disruption

Another highly common occurrence. As an astral individual travels into the murky near-Earth astral to try and connect to us, they will do whatever it takes to make contact. As an out-of-body practitioner, I personally have been in this environment, seeing my hand pass through solid objects and realizing nobody notices my presence. For me, it's fiendishly fun to realize I'm literally a "ghost"—but for someone who is suddenly dead and desires to make contact, it's not so much fun—it's quite frustrating.

Out of that frustration, a deceased loved one may become "disruptive." As they desperately try to make contact, they will only successfully affect subtler energetic elements that are receptive to their presence. As an example, a lightbulb may burst, a clock may stop working, a TV may turn on and off, etc. These should be considered "early signs" of ADC contact—and a good sign your deceased loved one is working hard to make contact. It's not uncommon for these incidents to be precursors for much more elaborate contact. In the event you begin experiencing odd electrical disruption or other "problems" after a loved one's death, I suggest speaking out loud and encouraging their presence. Say something like, "Is that you? Please, keep trying to make contact. I'm here and ready to experience any method that you can make your presence known." Keep them encouraged to continue the work.

Also keep an eye out for familiar objects being manipulated—old music boxes, watches, cell phones, any activatable objects that belonged to the deceased or which may possess a significance.

Physical disruption does NOT mean your loved one is "earthbound." This is a misnomer (I spoke of this much earlier in the book.) Often, an ethically misaligned medium will tell a grieving person such things and request a hefty fee to help the loved one "go to the Light." In most cases, this is a huge insult to the deceased loved one.

A Presence

One of the most basic but prevalent experiences is the feeling that your loved one is close. It may include a whiff of a familiar scent, a physical sensation, or just a non-physical "feeling" that is distinct. Similar to a dream visitation, it's unlikely that someone will *not* experience something like this at one point after a loved one passes away. Like other topics, however, the ability to detect this type of ADC may also depend on sixth-sense abilities. With no attunement or awareness whatsoever of the other side, a presence may be harder to be felt.

An Audible Encounter

In my experience, these most commonly occur upon waking, and may even happen in conjunction with the prior two experiences (a dream or a presence.) As you wake up, you will hear your deceased loved one's voice call out to you. In my own case when my mom did this, I awoke to her yelling out, crystal clear, "Hey Cyrus!"

This does not mean however such experiences are limited to waking up. I'm familiar with many stories of this occurring unexpectedly, like while cooking in your kitchen or outside gardening. In other words, it's best to be prepared for an encounter like this happening at any time, anywhere.

Photo Anomalies

Unusual light patterns in photos are common as an initial ADC, as are orbs. The orb phenomenon is explored by my friend Virginia Hummell, author of *The Orb Whisperer*. It's also the subject I am caught criticizing the most. That's because people constantly identify false orbs, including dust particles, and post photos all over paranormal Facebook groups looking for confirmation that they're spirits. And, of course, many people enthusiastically exclaim "Yes! It's a spirit! Congratulations!" … No, some dust particles were in the air after you opened a door or puffed a pillow, and a bit of light reflected on them. While fake contact with the other side can be "comforting" I don't have much patience for it—because in life duping oneself is NEVER a sustainable way to live.

That said, real orb contact can occur when there is distinctive, complex orbs present that may include imagery such as faces. Another sign the orb is authentic is if it appears to interact with the environment as opposed to just existing on the lens. And, obviously, if an orb is seen with the naked eye—it's probably paranormal.

So, just what *are* orbs? Contrary to popular opinion, I do NOT think orbs mean we exist on the other side *as* orbs. I think our world is very hard to manifest in physically, so becoming an orb may be the only way to appear here. They may also be just a type of energy that manifests when a spirit is inhabiting the near-Earth astral. I am not certain.

Animal Visitations

It appears possible for an astral individual to manipulate or "take over" the motor function of small creatures like insects. People report unusual encounters with innocuous household insects like butterflies, crickets, moths, etc. Is an insect behaving strangely, continually hopping up to you and making contact? If that insect dies, does another take its place and continue the strange behavior? This could be a person on the astral side using the insect as an instrument. There are also reports of this occurring among small animals (squirrels, chipmunks, birds, even dogs.) However, smaller insects like butterflies seem a bit more common—and the most distinctive as, typically, insects do not behave in friendly or complex ways.

Visual Anomalies

This is a very interesting subject. It is possible for an astral individual (likely with help) to manipulate our environment's lighting or reflections to create a specific image. This can be identified as a "supernatural" occurrence when the lighting phenomenon would never occur naturally or does not have a recognizable external source.

One of the best examples of this I've seen comes from a member of *Afterlife Topics and Metaphysics*, Wendi Henry-Herbst, who received an eye-opening visual sign shortly after her son passed away. She describes this below:

> I lost my son on June 11th 2018. I have been begging him to help me with my grief and show me a sign. My son was a very intelligent individual with a high I.Q. My microwave quit

working, light bulbs burned out, TV shuts off for no reason. Such is life, I didn't think anything of it. My son knew he would have to go above and beyond. He used the reflection of light to appear on my wall!

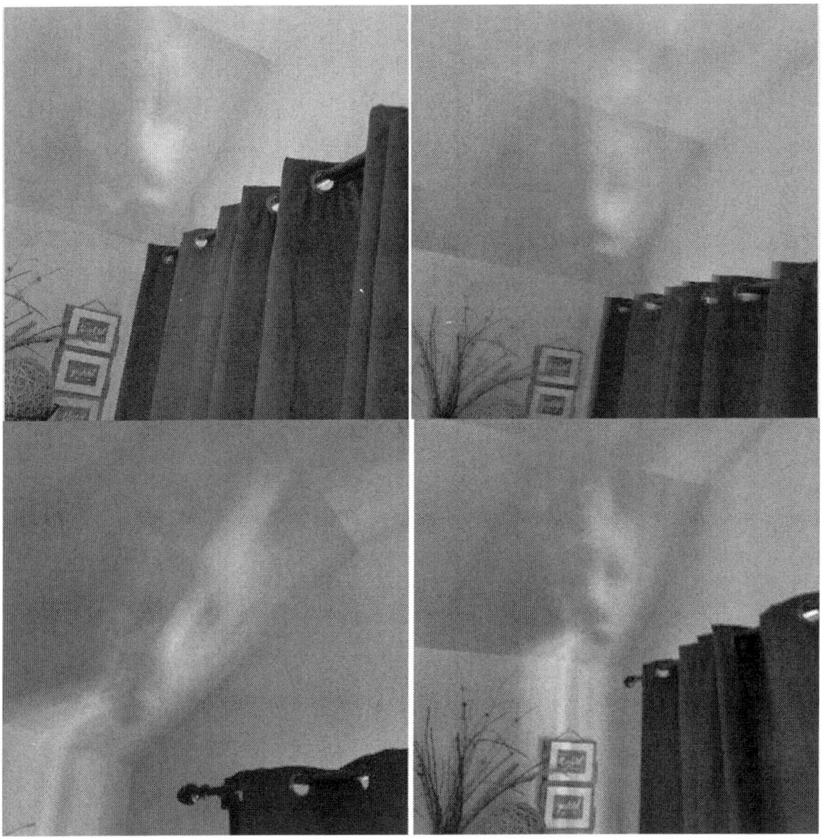

Here we can see a light phenomenon in the house being manipulated into the rough shape of her son's face. It appears almost holographic in nature and is highly anomalous.

Off-Site Physical Engagement

For some reason I am unsure about, it appears easier for an individual in a higher frequency to make manifest in our environment or alter it when no one is directly observing it.

I am reminded of a friend in Los Angeles who told me a story about an ADC. He had been preparing in the microwave one of those frozen pot pies. He left the room before the microwave went off. When he returned to the kitchen, the pot pie had been taken out of the microwave and prepared for him on a plate. He ate the pot pie as he tried to put his brain back together from the extremely bizarre experience. Later, he had a strong sense it was his recently deceased grandmother.

Synchronicities

In ways this author is clueless about, it seems possible for rules of time and action to be manipulated to create unusual phenomena. These types of events may increase in volume upon the death of a loved one. A few examples include:

- An important date, like a birthday, repeatedly occurring in strange places (the numbers on a receipt, then later the numbers scroll by on a TV.)

- Let's say your deceased connection is named Roger. Suddenly, you meet several people named Roger in unlikely situations on the same day.

- You may even meet someone who physically looks just like the deceased connection.

Those are just examples, but there are many more ways this strange type of ADC can occur.

While most of the phenomena outlined in this chapter I can rationalize—or even talk to a deceased person to understand how it's done—this one eludes my common sense and logic. Perhaps these types of things are orchestrated on a much higher level.

EVP Contact

Electronic voice phenomenon was pioneered by Latvian radio pro and author of *Breakthrough*, Konstantine Raudive—however, the unusual history of the practice dates back as far as Thomas Edison who believed he could create a communicative system to the beyond. Today, anyone watching a ghost-hunting show is familiar with the practice of using a normal recorder to pick up faint voices. However, not everyone is aware that it can also be a form of ADC. Like with ITC contact (below)—anomalous voices may occur unexpectedly. For instance, I hear reports of vocal contact occurring in normal recorded audio—like a vacation video shot with a smartphone. When an initial anomalous voice is picked up, this is a signal for an individual to begin more directive communication attempts as part of an overall ADC strategy.

I was once skeptical of EVP contact. If you listen to a few EVPs that sound like garbled gobbledygook, the skepticism may overwhelm you. Although, similarly to orbs, people become desperate for signs and will report crude sounds as contact. In addition, people use Ghost Box apps that string together pieces of radio frequencies. Such apps CAN result in communication with the other side, but initially they spit out various words and phrases randomly, so it's highly illogical to interpret a piece of a syllable as a contact when such "contact" occurs by simply leaving the app on unattended.

Therefore, to take EVP seriously, it's best conducted without any outside interference (including such apps) using a normal recording apparatus. It should be acceptable, however, to use some background noise like water running to help a spirit manipulate the sounds a bit. It may take a long time to develop a direct contact, but once you are hearing speech being generated in an isolated room without variables, and responding to your questions, the paranormal becomes the clearest explanation.

ITC Contact

ITC, or instrumental transcommunication, is commonly practiced by experienced researchers such as Rinaldi and the Scole experimenters including Sandra and Robin Foy as well as Diana and Alan Bennett. Experiments often include taking digital photos of specific light-reflection apparatuses (mirrors, reflective crystals) or digital "noise" (like the waving lines of a TV screen.) The photo will show a message or a face that is highly distinguished. Below is an example of a woman's face procured during an ITC experiment performed by the Bennetts (http://atransc.org/visual-itc-bennett/)

While these experiments may seem exclusive to investigators, it's also possible for ITC contact to occur spontaneously. An astral person may be able to manipulate a visual phenomenon that is only seen after taking a photo. As an example, a holiday photo is taken and the face of a deceased family member is seen projected onto the fuzz of a TV screen in the background.

The best idea is to begin private ITC experiments after a deceased loved one has already made their presence known. For instance, you can try Fiorella Lattaruli's Reflective Paper Image ITC Method (http://itcvoices.org/lattaruli-reflective-paper-itc/). I've seen some impressive instances of this among grieving persons. Like in many situations, results may not occur if there is no definite contact happening—if the deceased individual isn't making a concerted effort to make contact then no amount of experiments will yield success.

Bedside Astral Communication

Astral communication is a broad category, and it occurs less commonly due to the general inability for most of us to astral project. However, for those of us who do hone this ability, we'll often find our loved ones are eager to come to us when we are the ones entering into their domain—it's much easier for them because, in these types of visits, we're doing most of the work!

Bedside astral communication is distinctive because it's easier to occur, even among people without so much astral projection ability. A baseline astral experience may occur upon waking, or within a partial waking / sleep state. As an out-of-body explorer, I can testify that many who are sleeping are actually asleep in their astral bodies. Their Earth-plane body will be on the bed, their astral body (which appears like a carbon copy) is standing a few feet from the sleeping Earth-body, in a trance akin to a sleep-walker. If I'm out-of-body, it's futile trying to get the attention of a sleeping person.

However, upon the return of the consciousness and re-assimilation between Earth and astral bodies, there is a brief period of disconnection. Have you ever had a curious experience where you open your eyes, look around the room, think you're awake—then your eyes "really" open? This occurs when your consciousness is accidentally operating its astral counterpart,

This is also the period a loved one can appear and make contact. If they can catch you at the precise moment where you're laying on your bed but tuned to your astral consciousness, you may find yourself in a state of "sleep paralysis" (physical body immobility) while your loved one's voice manifests or you feel him / her laying or sitting beside you. The physical sensation and lucidness are no different from our normal waking reality. Therefore, I'd consider this one of the best possible ADC contacts. It's a chance to speak in a direct, frank way to a deceased person and even feel them physically holding you. If you regain some motor function of your astral body, you may find yourself able to physically see him / her and sit together in a "normal" way.

Advanced Astral Communication

Astral projection is the act of either leaving the body and entering consciously into the other side or reconnecting your consciousness to an experience already happening in that realm that you'd normally be unaware of. Understand that many of us have adjacent lives occurring astrally while we sleep, which is part of the theory of concurrent lives discussed at length in this book. If we astral project, our minds on Earth are temporarily synced up to the minds possessed by our dual selves.

Whether consciously or not, we may find ourselves with our deceased loved ones while we sleep. An astral practitioner may come into awareness of a situation where he or she is right alongside a deceased person in a foreign environment. To the deceased person, they may have been spending time with you in a normal fashion—your astral parallel self—when suddenly you are "possessed" by the consciousness of your

Earth-self and begin babbling frantically that you're out-of-body while becoming overcome by emotion because of the reunion (see Chapter 5 for more info.) When the experience ends, "you" will still be on that side but no longer connected to your Earthly brain (perhaps you'll be apologetic about the sudden spell that came over you.) The whole process may seem a very strange thing to happen, but your deceased loved one will understand how it all works.

Direct Electronic Communication

One of the most exciting developing fields is that of direct electronic communication. Truly a branch of ITC phenomena, we see spirit contact entering the modern age. I have countered numerous reports of Facebook messages and phone calls from deceased persons (I talk about this a bit more elsewhere in this book.) If you've experienced such things, in particular contact via social media, and have a story to share please e-mail me (cyrus@cyruskirkpatrick.com.)

In regard to this subject, I suggest taking seriously anomalous phone calls after the death of a loved one. This experience may begin as disconnected calls or picking up a phone and hearing nothing but a collection of static. This could potentially evolve into calls where you actually hear a voice talking to you and trying to deliver a message.

Even more interesting are the alleged Facebook communications. This subject, albeit sporadic and not yet fully researched, may add new meaning to the existence of memorial pages. (Can you imagine a future where memorial pages to deceased loved ones may commonly become active again?)

Spontaneous Mediumship Development

Not everybody is a true medium. In my opinion, it's a somewhat rare gift. However, the death of a loved one may open a special, one-on-one connection to a deceased person via either mediumistic impressions (the direct transmission of data / knowledge) or an ability like clairaudience. Likely, some level of mediumistic ability would have to already exist, but the intimate connection explodes this minor inert power into a full-fledged communication.

Physical Materialization on Our World

This is one of the least common ADCs to occur yet not at all unheard of. It seems to depend on two variables:

- The sheer skill and talent of the communicating spirit person.
- The energetic resonance of the receiver of the experience.

If these two factors are aligned together, this may happen. It's happened to my father allegedly on a frequent basis involving my mother, his sister, and his mother. He claims my mother appeared in full waking consciousness in early 2018 in the kitchen for approximately 5 minutes. "I held her hand and she was completely solid. It was just like she was alive again and visiting from out of town or something. We talked until I guess the energy was no longer strong enough and she just disappeared."

Death and dying pioneer Elizabeth Kubler-Ross and author of *On Life After Death* has also made claims about direct materializations, including the famous elevator incident whereupon a spirit visitor (a deceased colleague) greeted her in an elevator and left a sample of handwriting behind[31].

These are bold claims, and even I feel like a video would do such claims a lot of justice. However, like most areas in this field, I believe this phenomenon is a lot more complex than what meets the eye.

- We don't know if these materializations are occurring fully in our world. To an outsider, maybe the materialized person would appear invisible and is only solid to the recipient.

- There may be stipulations against this type of thing. See prior points in this book or in "Understanding Life After Death" about the "prime directive" assumptions—it may go against some level of cosmic ethics for that side to begin interacting physically with us with the exception of very personal, 1-on-1 encounters. If these visitations are allowed for only personal grief support, it's unlikely we'll be seeing YouTube videos of deceased materializations anytime soon.

Complex Synchronicities and Encounters

Synchronicities that further boggle the mind to a much higher degree are what I would call complex ADCs or complex synchronicities.

In the book *Awakened by Death*—a collaboration between myself and podcast host KAren Swain—a chapter was featured about Scarlett Lewis, who lost her son Jesse in the Sandy Hook school massacre. As she embarked on a road trip with her remaining son to Orlando, she noticed a sky-writer operating a plane, creating a message in the air: *Jessie and Jesus Together Forever.* However, the strangeness didn't end there. Young Jessie always wrote his name with a backwards "J." The skywriter, too, made sure the "J" was written how Jessie wrote his name.

This creates a lot of questions: who was the skywriter who made this message? Was it a synchronicity—with someone else named Jesse who was being memorialized—or was it a message specifically for Scarlett? If it was for Scarlett, did a spirit entity perhaps "possess" a pilot's mind to compel him or her to create the message at that time? Who knows—these are not easy questions to answer, and maybe there is no answer we can understand.

If you have any other examples of this type of advanced ADC, shoot me an email (cyrus@cyruskirkpatrick.com.)

No ADCs? Opening a Connection

Despite what appears to be a lengthy list of ADCs I've compiled, I still hear from people all the time who do not experience any such phenomena—except for an uncertain dream or disruption-based encounter which is not that convincing. This can leave a mourner feeling frustrated by the lack of contact. They often ask, "What can I do to hear more often from my deceased loved one?"

This is a hard question because, sometimes, the deceased may not be actively trying to communicate. If this is the case, one cannot force their hand. Despite what certain pop mediums may have you believe, the deceased are not 100% always available for contact and willing to work with us (don't you love those "mediums" who, when challenged can contact anyone, at any time for any reason immediately? Trying to talk to Genghis Khan? Why, of course, let me just close my eyes for three seconds…)

In fact, what capitalistic on-demand mediums won't reveal is that spirit people may have actual *lives*, issues, guilts, and problems like we do. As a result, they may not be available for instant communication, and for whatever reason—a person might not be ready to start producing ADCs. This is especially possible if a person is deceased as a result of a traumatic event that could involve guilt or personal grief—for instance, suicide. A spirit person may simply not have the energy or motivation to begin making contact. In other words, it may not be your fault.

However, at other times a person in spirit may be motivated to contact you, but the issue is more related to your inability to energetically connect. In this case, there's things that can be done to hopefully increase your connection to our neighboring realm. The following are some guidelines that may help:

- **Routine Consciousness-Based Meditation**

Meditation of a transcendental quality is what allows a person to cut through barriers of consciousness. It's not so much that one hasn't learned an ability to tune to the other side—but one hasn't sufficiently removed barriers; in other words, mental clutter that is preventing awareness. In this case, the goal should be more about learning to tune to the moment and become extremely present rather than making a stressed, forced desire to connect with a loved one. As a byproduct of continual meditation, you will find consciousness-related tasks to be easier, including out-of-body experiences as well as general contact.

My recommendation is to meditate with incense, a pleasant odor which you can focus your intention on. In a dimly lit room, stay in a comfortable position but not to the point where your body desires to fall asleep (this is why people sit cross-legged.) Your goal should be the elimination of every wayward thought or stress with the exception of the smell of the incense. When ready, begin practicing the induction of "positive vibrations"—thoughts that bring joy, excitement or loving feelings. Learn to control those feelings and bring them into your thought-space. An hour meditation focusing on creating these positive vibrations will greatly assist anyone's health—and expand consciousness-related abilities.

- **Setting Intentions at Sleep**

One of the best ways to begin having astral-related experiences, in my experience, involves overcoming the fear of the experience enough to set a strong intention at sleep. As far as overcoming the fear, the previously mentioned meditation steps are an excellent way to work on this. The more comfortable you feel in peaceful states of consciousness, and the more easily you can enter positive, loving states of mind—the easier it is to get past the initial fear of astral-experiences that virtually everyone experiences.

Tell yourself the following: "Upon waking, I will first be in my astral body before my consciousness returns to my physical body." It may take some time, but with enough intention and training, you may incur an out-of-body experience. In my experience, one's first OBE opens a doorway for many more. Much like any sport or hobby, the fear fades and then it's easier a second time.

- **Using OBEs to Make Contact**

Sometimes the nature of OBEs differs between people, but there are common characteristics. If you find you obtain motor control of a second "duplicate" limb (like an arm) while you are laying on your bed—this means you've successfully switched to astral consciousness. If you can rise up out of your physical body in this state, then you've entered a mobile out-of-body state (go spy on friends or learn to fly.) If you come into consciousness in a foreign environment that feels real and solid—you're successfully astral projecting. From any of these points it's possible to establish a powerful link to a deceased loved one, usually just via the intention to do it.

There is one possible issue with this strategy: *the dark side*. As I've discussed elsewhere in this book, not every OBE is positive in nature. Sadly, this reinforces people's pre-existing fears and paranoia about the practice (spurred on further by movies like *Insidious*.) Earlier in this book, I mentioned my roommate's encounter with a cadre of shadow people upon his first out-of-body venture. Some of those reading this book probably got the heebie-jeebies so bad they've sworn off ever going out-of-body.

The thing is: I don't like to sugarcoat information. There are books elsewhere that claim other realms are always safe, sunshine, flowers, and fairies. This just isn't so. In fact, if you wish to make contact with a deceased loved one and become adept at out-of-body work, you must tackle the potentially negative side and approach the subject from a strong, fearless stance.

The way to do this is through knowledge and understanding: **if you are in a positive, loving mood when you are out-of-body, the odds of attracting or dealing with negative entities is zero**. Armed with this knowledge, and by practicing the first point (meditation / raising your loving energy) you can practice OBE-contact fearlessly.

-

- **Releasing Anguish and Grief**

We can file this under "easier said than done," nonetheless, in my experience intense grief will either spur ADCs (those on the other side will feel desperate to contact and help the grieving person) OR it will ward them away (if the astral individual is emotionally fragile at all, a guide may suggest against entering the Earth-plane and being exposed to the intense emotions of loved ones.)

For the latter reason, it is possible that ADCs will remain elusive until proper time has passed. If during great grief no ADCs have occurred, it may be necessary to work on the inner-growth needed to piece one's life back together upon the death of a close loved one. As this occurs, and a grieving person reaches a healthy emotional level again, this may be when that person is ready to begin experiencing phenomena.

Of course, the big question is "how." There is no easy answer, and I am not a grief therapist. I can, however, offer general life advice and pointers that may assist—which I will elaborate on in the next chapter. But for grief in particular, I am a firm believer that **knowledge combats grief**. The very fact of knowing about the afterlife is grief's biggest enemy.

Sadly, those I've known the most consumed by grief have also been those with nihilistic materialist beliefs. Western materialism has created a frightening sorcery in the modern age, where a complete lack of understanding about the afterlife propagates division, sorrow, and further death in the form of suicide. The doubt about the afterlife is fostered by agents of materialism—in the media and in our lives, and it's extremely easy to buy into the narrative that the universe—and our lives—are meaningless. **See this idea for what it is: a malevolent darkness, dismiss it and explore the afterlife instead—leaning**

toward the truth that our loved ones are fine, versus the superstition of materialism.

- **Opening a Third Eye**

Holy vagueness, Batman—what am I talking about now? Well, I mean literally going to a mystic or shaman and having them perform astral work where they help attune your consciousness energetically to the other side.

I don't recommend this for everyone. In fact, I don't exactly recommend doing this at all (lots of variables, including what a self-purported shaman may charge for the service.) Nonetheless, as a reporter of information, I hear of this process helping some people. In fact, for one of my friends, a third-eye reversal process greatly benefited her. A woman I knew in Indonesia (a devout Muslim) was plagued by seeing crossed over individuals everywhere, from the age of three until about 17. When she was 17, she went to see a village mystic (in a rural part of Indonesia) who performed a "closing of the third eye" ceremony. From this point on, she never saw a deceased person again.

It's possible what's happening is that the strong belief that a "third eye" is closed is what created the effect—a spiritual placebo. However, even placebos are a medically viable phenomenon—and if it works, why not?

- **Going on a Retreat or Making a Major Life Change**

Just like high stress damages your health and well-being on numerous levels, it may create "spiritual constipation." If all your worldly thoughts are occupied with clients, customers, bosses, and angry family members—you may not be in a receptive lifestyle at all to receive contact.

To this I ask a question I frequently ask: how much can you downsize? Can you reduce material clutter (sell a lot of possessions) and move out to the mountains for a while? Maybe even switch to a lower stress job? This is unthinkable in the West, where work is life, but there are some things more important in life than money—including our spiritual happiness. For someone grieving badly yet consumed by stress and work, if they can afford to do it without creating additional stress—it may be time to take a break from Western consumerism for a while.

Rent a cabin for a month or two in a nice, high-vibration woodland environment, meditating daily and enjoying alone time. This combination of solitary time and a low-stress environment could be the perfect conduit for enabling spirit communication to occur.

- **Creating a Habit of Communication**

For your deceased loved one—you must make them into a part of your continued life. Ask them to join you within your plane for special events. At dinner, set a chair aside for them. Talk to them casually. Keep them around—keep alerting them that you're paying attention to them, trying to talk to them, and don't give up. Make it known that you are not going to "shut up" until an effort is made by the deceased to make solid contact.

In Summary

There's so much more we could go into, learn or teach (for that I suggest Afterlife University: www.afterlifetopics.com/university.) Undoubtedly, there are many more types of ADCs we can receive—I am merely listing the ones I'm familiar with or that could logically occur. What more will we discover as we go into the future? As those on the other side and our side learn together about new methodologies of communication?

XIII – Life Guidance

This necessary chapter includes ***my personal*** advice for "getting your sh-- together." It may not apply to everyone, but I feel it's very important for certain readers. I've noticed many focus on an afterlife as a solution to their problems in life—and this is not healthy, as it means *literally waiting to die*. I hope what I share in this chapter will round out the value I've hopefully provided to you elsewhere in this book.

Yes, there's an afterlife. But guess what? On the astral plane **sometimes we have the same damn problems**. I know this to be true because my "second self" (see Chapter 5) has traveled all over the astral side. Lots of cities, lots of realms, lots of cool places—meeting countless people, and my takeaway is that the human experience doesn't fix itself. Everyone must discover who they really are—we must all come into power eventually. The process of discovering ourselves—discovering our true individualities—is supposed to be the greatest adventure of all; yet, out of fear, many skip this concept entirely, living lives of utter, horrific mediocrity where self-development is completely ignored. This just won't do.

Sometimes we even fall into wayward spiritual paths where we try to deny individuality is real—or we cling to the idea that we become perfect at death, and the universe wipes us of who and what we once were (see Chapter 6.) **This is all mythology. The universe isn't wiping you. Your ass is STUCK as "you" for the foreseeable future—there's no cheating around this fact. It's time to get used to that and start making it work!**

"What do you do after your dreams come true?"

Earlier in this book, I wrote about Anthony Bourdain and why such a soul would necessitate a diversified afterlife experience. Only later, after I wrote that section, did Tony commit suicide by hanging[4]. This tragedy occurred only weeks after fashionista Kate Spade also took her life, and a number of months since Linkin Park's frontman Chester Bennington killed himself. And this was not long after Audioslave frontman Chris Cornell took his life—also by hanging.

[4] Of course, there is also a chance Tony was murdered. See: https://www.youtube.com/watch?v=rJ6F5W88rlw

TIME Magazine writer Belinda Luscombe wrote a moving analysis about Bourdain and Spade's deaths—and the dangerous inaccuracy of having envy about other people's lives:[32]

> It's not much of a solace, but perhaps one thing these deaths could remind us of is the uselessness of envy. As with many of the behaviors once considered vices — greed, sloth, lust — envy reflects a miscalculation in the relative worth of things. When we look at lives like Spade's and Bourdain's, it can make our own feel wanting. We haven't started our own companies, or turned our work experience into a book. They're happier and more fulfilled, because we are not as hardworking or talented as they are. Their lives look better than ours, therefore they must be better people than we are.
>
> Our desire to turn Bourdain and Spade's success into a judgment on our own stems from a flawed comparison due to incomplete data. Many lives are not as they appear. Happiness is not the end result of a sum of accomplishments. The person whose wealth/wardrobe/job/talent you wish you had has his or her own struggles, and they could at least equal our own. Bourdain seemed to hint at his, when during an episode shot in Sardinia, he asked in a voiceover, "What do you do after your dreams come true?"

I don't know how often people think about this problem. Clearly, not enough. This existential threat faces many successful people. Even those with a great deal of money and worldly possessions, who seem to "have it all," are not necessarily happier than a motorbike driver in Jakarta, Indonesia making $8 a day.

This is not to say money doesn't provide opportunity, security and the potential for happiness through those things; however, without a deeper foundation it seems the rich and successful are attacked by a depression even deeper than what may affect regular people: because they come to a grim conclusion that after so much effort to accomplish "dreams," what happens when those dreams do not provide the magical, sustainable feeling of happiness and contentment? The inevitable conclusion for some is that their life has been a lie. That's a horrific thing for a person to face.

On the flipside, I'm all about accomplishing dreams. I've accomplished a few of mine. Not necessarily dreams of riches but of traveling to exalted places around the world and having particular types of adventures. This has been done through remote work, budgeting, and ambitious travel planning. However, throughout the fulfillment of these dreams, I've kept a drumming voice in the back of my mind: **the TRUE path to contentment is not in the obvious obtainment but it lies somewhere else**.

And where would that "somewhere else" be? The answer is right in front of us: *OTHER PEOPLE.*

To illustrate, I always wanted to explore Istanbul, Turkey. Firstly, I arrived in a stuffy hotel by myself. I'd go out, enjoy the sights, take photos of the famous mosques, eat Baklava, and return to my hotel. Sleeping alone, I'd wake up with a lingering sense of isolation. Yes, I'd explore the beautiful city, but where was the fun? The connection? The adventure? Where was the "feeling" that we all strive to achieve? We know the essence of the "feelings" we desire because we remember the excitement of being children—when everything had the potential to be joyous, and our imaginations ran wild. But as adults trying to accomplish "dreams" we often grow frustrated because a kid going to a stream and collecting bugs out of the dirt will have a 10x more exciting time than an adult going to a 5-star hotel in an exotic city, attending interesting restaurants, riding in a hot air balloon, paragliding off a mountain or any other activity. What's going on? The problem is materialistic, goal-setting philosophies (that no amount of fake smiles on Instagram can make seem meaningful) leave people feeling empty inside. And if there's anything I notice in Western, Californian culture it's people desperately trying to hide their deep emptiness as a way to fit in with everyone else.

In Istanbul, I was only in the hotel a few days as a "splurge." When I was finished, I relocated to a hostel near Taksim Square. I stayed in a dormitory for nearly a month. At the time, early 2015, the hostel was populated by mostly Syrian refugees. I befriended a bunch of them and heard their stories.

One man was a doctor who was about to embark on a long, extremely dangerous journey to reach his family in Sweden.

Another man was a fashion designer from Damascus whose business and home were destroyed. He was waiting indefinitely in

Turkey for things to get better in his country. Despite having lost everything, he always knew how to dress very sharp.

A third man was refugee from Libya, and we fast became friends. He was an entrepreneur who made a surprisingly high amount of money from his online services. He was hoping to use that money to convince the people at the U.S. embassy to grant him a visa so he could go to San Diego—his dream.

A fourth man, unrelated to the rest, was a French man in his late 20s—handsome and stylish but with a constant stutter. He went on a voyage to ponder his relationship with his girlfriend back home in Lyon—a "time out" period. His personality was completely different from everyone else, but it created a fun contrast.

For a month, we'd all go to the night markets and I got to see a lot of the "real Istanbul." We'd venture into areas the staff told us never to go—because they were bad areas of town controlled by the mafia. Without batting an eyelash, my group would stroll into these sections as late as midnight. Instead of thugs and gangsters, we saw families buying fish and yogurt late at night—with little kids running around and old ladies. We'd return to the hostel with all the fresh ingredients, and they'd prepare Syrian dishes and basic local foods of a Mediterranean nature—flatbread, olives, dates, yogurt, Feta cheese, hummus, eggplant.

Many sub-plots happened in between. A beautiful Turkish girl broke my heart by rejecting me after we had an intimate evening together (no, not sex—but a lot of cuddling and kissing.) When I found her taking an interest in the French man—after deleting me from Facebook—I experienced something I hadn't felt in a very long time: jealousy mired by anger. The Syrians helped me get over my subsequent personal crisis about her. When I think back about that whole debacle, I just have a good laugh about it all.

You may have caught on to a larger theme here: none of what I describe could have happened in a stuffy hotel room by myself. That month tops the list among adventures, but I've had many comparable experiences: taking a bus across communist North Korea for 11 hours operated by a rag-tag group of government agents, staying in a hostel in Macedonia run by a crazy old man and a forlorn, pretty receptionist looking for a life purpose, or most recently a hostel in Singapore where a 50-something year-old sheikh from India would tell stories for all the travelers in the communal lobby every afternoon.

Do these adventures create happiness? Not by themselves. I am sure Tony Bourdain was the king of such experiences. But it's incomparably more fulfilling than how tourists typically travel—wrapped in cocoons of personal comfort and a lingering xenophobia of the culture they're experimenting with. I think this is an important first-step, because while many people can have countless fun, exciting experiences to load their memories with incredible stories, a pizza with only half the proper ingredients is still not a proper pizza but an imitation of something that could be much better.

The second step concerns coming into full acceptance of ourselves during or through these experiences, and from that position of acceptance being able to love and enjoy other people (as well as other experiences) from a much greater level. This is a one-two formula for greater fulfillment, excitement, and joy in regard to the Earthly experience. The one-two process involves **adventurism** and what I call **elemental acceptance** or **elementalism** which is a philosophy of immersing into experiences. I'll now go into greater detail of these concepts:

A Guide for Having Adventures

"Adventure" is one of those ideas that so many people want—rarely do people say "I need less adventure in my life"—but few can define what it means. It seems to be a kind of alchemy between the experience of discovering people, and a situation or storyline that unfolds. This nourishes our creative process and fuels attempts to recreate such experiences through song, theater or the written word. Adventure never arrives forced—it must occur naturally, and it will never happen among those who rarely leave their houses. When it does happen, it may not be immediately apparent, but in retrospect we may say, "Wow, that was such an adventure." When this is said, what a person is really saying is: "I experienced something fulfilling on a deep, soul-level that made me remember what living is truly about."

"Adventures"—dynamic situations with other people are also extremely important for self-development and introspection. Show me a person whose life is entirely routine, and I'll show you a personality that is equally monotonous. In Western culture, I am aghast to what extent people sit on bad habits, and this is completely attributable to fears of change and / or material obsession. If we learn and develop, while putting ourselves in new situations, it's almost inevitable that some of our bad habits will be eliminated. Reading self-help books is a nice start, but it takes real-world experiences to learn about yourself and other people—necessary components of enjoying life.

While adventures must occur naturally, I believe there are certain steps we can take to put ourselves in situations where adventures are inevitable. **If you are in a situation in your life where things feel awfully predictable, monotonous, there is no growth, and / or a pervading sense of loneliness, my non-professional suggestion is to try the following**:

Take Some Time to Practice an Acceptance Attitude

Before you can go on any type of adventure, you have to do the hard work to enter a mindset where it's possible. You need to be extremely honest with yourself in regard to how you approach other people. Are you judgmental? Quick to anger? We can file this (once again) under "easier said than done" but it's necessary to work these issues out. **You must enter an experimental mindset where you tell yourself: "I will have no pre-judgments about anyone or anything. I will just listen or experience**." This is critical if you are not a very social person. The origins may be deep—stemming from past traumas and negative mindsets. But we can worry about fixing all that later (or your therapist can worry about it.) For now, our goal is to revitalize your life (without requiring an out-of-body or other mystical experience—here on the Earth plane.)

Temporarily Liquidate and Leave

Many lifestyle-revamping gurus suggest to literally sell all your worldly belongings. However, their target audiences are 20-something millennials having identity crises. I understand my readership is much older and this strategy may be a no-go when you have sheds full of antique furniture that you inherited from some relative and have promised to give to your kids. That said, there are still ways to transcend our material attachments long enough that we don't feel bogged down by them.

Plan an unorthodox trip **where you take the minimal necessary goods**. The point is to get into the habit of taking trips where your attention is focused on other people you meet along the way, experiences, and character-building situations. Not worrying about suitcase after suitcase. Before such a trip, you should also do what you can to minimize stresses and responsibilities. Tell yourself: **I will do the most I can to deal with X, Y, Z issues to the best of my abilities, and then it's time to let them go**. Do you owe a massive payment from medical debt (not applicable outside of the USA)? Are you in hot water with a boss who may not even let you get away for a couple of weeks? These may be things to work out first. Do what it takes, but the idea here is to do something for YOU—necessary time out to get perspective.

In the event you have a spouse who is unwilling to go on such a character-building trip, it may be necessary to go alone. I am not here to ruin people's marriages, but **a marriage is not an excuse for a life that completely lacks personal development**. I have seen this occur so often among people in my life: marriage becomes a union of non-activity, and neither party develops or changes in any meaningful way ad infinitum (until death do each other part.) This may be a lot to ask: *but we have to work on ourselves. It's a type of spiritual mission that literally applies to everyone, and it's MORE important than what family thinks*. The point is to take some time out and then return to your life as normal later on (a harmless proposition.)

Although, keep in mind that when taking out time to work on yourself, objections you may receive will likely come from a place of low-vibration emotions (envy, selfishness, etc) among friends or family who are offended that you are disrupting the status quo or going against the common and the established. Be prepared.

Finally, **do consider taking a HARD look at your material finances**. Will the $50,000 you've saved for a boat really make you so happy? Because I can almost guarantee the boat's not going to do much for your life in the long-term—once you stop pretending you're that guy Marvin from University whose parents were rich and owned a boat (and he was way more popular than you)—you'll realize it's just a giant chunk of polyester requiring obscene upkeep fees. On the other hand, $50,000 can keep you going for an awfully long time as you explore and travel while potentially finding a more meaningful job opportunity if you happen to be one of the 80% of Westerners who despise their jobs. (Hey, you may be in the 20%--if so, good for you, don't change anything. If not, I suggest my first book from 2014—*How to Quit Your Job* available on Amazon.)

Seek an Uncomfortable Situation Around Many New People

You're not planning a vacation but a situation. This doesn't have to be uncomfortable or uninteresting—it could be in some fabulous foreign country you've always wanted to visit. But the backdrop—the beautiful location—must be secondary to something that is social and preferably tests or challenges you.

Ideas include hitchhiking in a distant country, going on a week-long retreat in the woods (with a sizable group) with no electricity or communication to the outside world, volunteering with an NGO, participating in a communal farm in France for a summer, or what I like to do—stay in some traveler's dorms within a totally alien / exotic culture, meeting locals.

Some people, after watching "Eat Pray Love," especially middle-aged ladies, like to make trips like this via going to Bali, Indonesia. I recommend thinking of a more original idea as Bali is now overridden with people on cliché "voyages of self-discovery" which turn out to be rather narcissistic social media romps where they return with nothing but dozens of new Instagram pictures of eating vegan food and using hashtags like #blessed in yoga positions. The sheer annoyance of dealing with these people could interrupt your *legitimate* voyage of self-discovery.

The truth be told, you can fulfill the criteria I outline without even leaving your home city; however, I do recommend going someplace far away.

Make Friends: This is Important

Something so simple and basic is at the heart of having a sense of purpose and fulfillment in life. No matter what situation you find yourself in, the big picture is to make connections with other people. If you do not easily make connections with others—this is an even greater reason to do it. Being able to make friends has everything to do with meeting people from a mindset that is non-judgmental and accepting of them. If you feel "antisocial" or there is something that blocks you from meeting new people—consider if you are either judging people you meet, or if you are scared of being judged—perhaps projecting your own propensity for judgment as a character trait onto others. You must muse and meditate on these issues, especially as you meet and discover new people.

This is also why I suggest to go somewhere that you literally feel prejudiced against. My trips to North Korea may be an extreme example, but you could plan somewhere that is crime-ridden to help as a volunteer if you feel especially prejudiced against lower-class people in "criminal" neighborhoods. This gives you an eye-opening opportunity to change your mindsets and overcome that nagging, egotistical habit of judgments that interrupts our social abilities.

When you find you can easily and fluidly make friends with people wherever you go, I guarantee it means you have your "sh--together" more than many other people. It's a hallmark of an emotionally centered person—an external indicator of a spiritual equilibrium. This is a primary goal of this whole mission.

Learn to Implement Adventure in Your Normal Life

When your voyage is finished, you should figure out a way to incorporate elements of your experience / adventure into your "normal" life. What are interesting situations you can be involved in within your home city? Where can you continue to meet people in your community? How can you continue to explore your ability to make connections with others while analyzing your own shortcomings? Can you continue to eliminate judgmental tendencies and other blocks to how you relate to others? These are the important elements to having a life of adventure that you can learn and improve from.

Part 2: Elementalism

Living and learning from an adventurous lifestyle is one thing, but I suggest a second aspect: a philosophy I have dubbed *elementalism* designed to help you, in a meditative way, fully appreciate new experiences—in a way similar to being a kid again. As you evolve as a person through your new, sometimes challenging experiences—a full appreciation of what's happening around you helps to keep your spirit centered in a positive and fulfilling way. Without this, your adventures may pass as memories, and your lessons could become forgotten as those memories fade. This is not acceptable, as you risk not really developing in any substantive way.

What is Elementalism?

Elementalism is the opposite of reductionism. It's a theory that everything that creates an explicit, unique feeling is part of an *elemental concept* in the universe that will always exist. This includes individual people, works of art, and specific experiences that become like stories that arouse nostalgia. Elementalism is the ability to tap into the essence of particular things to fully experience it. In a spiritual way, when we meditate/ tap into the essence of an individual person, this is like sending a direct message to that spirit—which can be felt if they're deceased (and sometimes even while they're still on this plane.) Likewise, tapping into the essence of a situation or a work of art can create a full sensory merging process—something that is more intimately practiced on the astral side, but can still have powerful effects down here.

Note: We often think of meditation as entering a state of "blankness" of the mind. This concept takes traditional meditation in a different direction. Rather than entering thoughtlessness, we focus our mind upon the essence of a particular experience or a specific set of emotions or feelings generated by an experience. This allows us to more deeply appreciate the experience.

A Few Interesting Examples

- A video game you loved when you were four-years-old may evoke specific nostalgic feelings. This video game is imbued with an essence passed down from its creators.

- A long-lost friend or significant other. Even if this person is no longer in your life, the essence and feelings this person creates can be appreciated as a specific set of energies that can exist nowhere else except through that person's existence. You can meditate on this person and fully experience the energy of who they are.

- A movie or story, when absorbed as a whole, may leave behind a very specific feeling in your mind and body. This means the story became an elemental concept that is etched into the universe's fabric. I know whenever I watch *Indiana Jones* it creates a very specific set of feelings.

- Something completely basic may have its own elemental sensation. Think about a literal element like fire or water. What feeling does fire evoke for you? What about water? Can you generate that feeling at will to "experience" this energy?

What Elementalism Can Do in Practice

In my earlier example of living in a hostel in Turkey, every day had that *sensation* of being on an adventure, and it was extremely linked to the unique aspects of the situation. This included the context of how we were all together, the food, the weather, the morning calls to prayer in Istanbul. The story that accompanied these specific events had become elemental—it developed its own energy.

As I realized the experiences were elemental in nature, it became possible to fully absorb these experiences and meditate on their importance, as well as fully enjoy everything around me—good or bad.

This is the key component: a story or experience, when its elemental in nature, *may not always be positive*. This is the same way a book is filled with contrasting negative and positive elements. *The Lord of the Rings* would not be a moving story if it were the tale of a bunch of hobbits on a quest to an elf city to have some parties, drink mead, and return home (although it could make for an interesting Paul Thomas Anderson movie.) Instead, we had orcs and the corrupt wizard Saruman and the archangel-turned-demigod Sauron who wants to see the world burn. The hardship is necessary for the hobbits, by the end of the story, to become completely changed individuals. It's also necessary for the story to be of substance, to hit on valuable archetypes, and create an elemental essence that we can tap into every time we pick up Tolkien's book or watch Peter Jackson's adaptation.

Elementalism means the power to *see such a story occurring in your own life*. When you can do this, it becomes possible to separate yourself from the "bad" situations that happen as you zoom out and appreciate the much bigger picture. Maybe you're lost in Beijing, someone stole your phone and wallet, and you have to knock on people's houses to find food and shelter (this never happened to me, but I've heard of similar things happening to friends.) At the time, it may seem awful—

and a regular Joe Schmoe may have a near panic-attack, but if you are meditating on the essence of an entire experience, then any experience—including adversity, can become something highly enjoyable.

This is what elementalism is to me: finding the essence of a situation, good or bad, and finding a way to both enjoy it and learn from it. The end result is being able to enjoy life with fewer stresses and thus adopt a more fluid approach to life. I am not well-versed in the tenants of eastern religious monks, but when I saw a Buddhist monk once meditating at a hectic bus stop in downtown Chicago, I imagine he was practicing a similar philosophy.

Part 3: Individual Self Obtainment

The next important part is to attune oneself to their own elemental essence. Understand, this is in contrast to philosophies that may suggest we should eliminate or shrug off the so-called personality. I've always found this a curious suggestion, and it ties into other themes explored earlier in this book—a desire that some possess to rid themselves of "themselves"—to absorb into something that can literally eat whatever they once were. Advocates of this belief suggest our personalities are constructs, impermanent and unimportant.

However, those who have explored realms beyond this one—and spoken to the souls residing on such planes—will find a different perspective, and it's a perspective I've long suspected just from my own life experience. It's that every person you meet—while their personalities may have some fabricated or egoistic elements that are not genuine—at the core a personality is part of a much bigger *essence* that every soul possesses. While the "watcher"—God or the universe that animates consciousness may be omnipresent and singularly created ("we are all God",) wherever God consciousness chooses to reside (currently, inside of you) means existing fully as an elemental essence also created by the universe and as fundamental as the colors red, blue, yellow or green. The personality that is you has always existed, and will always exist. It does not, and never can, extinguish itself into an amorphous blob, despite even if a personality has an individual desire to self-exterminate.

That being said, since your personality is fundamental, it should be your job to perfect your individuality and come into essence. Left-hand philosophies would refer to this as coming into individualized

Godhood. Silver Birch, the esteemed communication team that was brought through Maurice Barbanell, described it best[33]:

> Another question that crops up many times is the thought of returning to God. There is a certain fear that you lose your individuality in this return. A. The ultimate is not attainment of Nirvana. All spiritual progress is towards increasing individuality. You do not become less of an individual, you become more of an individual. You develop latent gifts, you acquire greater knowledge, your character becomes stronger, more of the divine is exhibited through you. The Great Spirit is infinite and so there is an infinite development to be achieved. Perfection is never attained, there is a constant striving towards it. You do not ever lose yourself. What you succeed in doing is finding yourself.... [Y]ou get to conditions and spheres that are beyond language. They consist of states of consciousness and awareness. This is something you will not understand until you attain it. You do not lose your individuality in a sea of greater consciousness, but that depth of the ocean becomes included in your individuality."

To apply this idea to your everyday life, it's important to recognize things like your personality and desires, and understand that the more attuned you are to your "essence"—which we superficially refer to as the things we enjoy or love, the "happier" you become. As simple as this advice is, most people don't follow it. Or worse, they are crippled by existential depression—namely, the fear of death—that they never allow themselves to explore who they are and enjoy life to any greater extent. Additionally, any soul who's mired by conditions like low self-esteem or feelings of unworthiness will find their individuality being suppressed, including the state of joy that comes with attunement to who and what you are. When joyless, there is a spiritual toll that is also taken on the body: increased aging, greater susceptibility to illness and a degeneration of appearance (sudden weight gain, skin complexion changes, etc.) People attuned properly, confident in who and what they are, by contrast, begin to adopt a radiance which is unmistakable. Working to enter this latter category of "radiance" is as good a life purpose as anything else I could imagine. Remember: although it's true your money and possessions may follow you into the astral plane (my silver ring is still on my finger when I project,) there they have no substantial worth beyond your own value for them. The eternal worth comes through self development and our relationships and love of others.

And while you figure out your own essence, we also discover the joy of existence: discovering other people's essences. In this way, for all eternity, meeting new people becomes an adventure that can never get old. And the more refined an individual personality is—the more radiant—the more pristine the experience is. Surely, there are people you've met in life, if only briefly, that you discovered a magnetism about and you can't forget them.

Concerning Physical Appearance

On the astral side, with a little work, we can begin regressing to our prime physical embodiments. How we look between the ages of 25-35 seems to be how we are "designed" to look. From there onward, as we age, our appearance is being subjected to entropy and rules that don't apply to other realms. An old man without teeth and in a wheelchair is just a malformed version of a soul's vessel and should not be considered the true physical appearance.

However, physical appearance has tolls. I've met so many people who have lost all confidence to go out, explore the world and explore themselves because their appearances have declined. Maybe people who are overweight, old, and have grown extremely shy about facing the public. It creates a cycle where that shyness prevents fulfillment of one's essence, leading to existential crises (depression) which perpetuates a further decline in physical appearance, further weight gain, and so forth.

Obviously, the hard path is to break the cycle and, somehow, push beyond self-consciousness through hard work. We work hard to make money, yet few of us work hard to overcome pressing psychological issues. As I've mentioned elsewhere, the best way is to go out and meet people, whether via solo travel or some other strategy. You have to throw yourself into the fire and let it burn you before you can relearn who you are. Ancient ceremonies that involve walking on coals or being subjected to painful processes manifest this idea literally.

You may find, concerning issues like weight gain or other effects common with older age, this process provokes a desire to lose such weight and become healthier, and the very act of working out psychological issues may also manifest greater health.

Concerning Your Psychological Health

I cannot create a full roadmap for whatever your individual problems are, and "solo travel" is not a cure-all by any means. Your problem may be that you have an abandonment complex after your parents threw you on the street at age 14, and you automatically view strangers with distrust that they don't like you, which sometimes causes you to lash out at them as a preemptive response. Or maybe you experienced sexual assault, and you eat fatty food to destroy your physical appearance so no one else will ever find you physically attractive out of fear of another assault. Or maybe you never said goodbye to your parents and were angry at them before they died, so every day you tell yourself what an awful person you are and it prevents even reasonable functionality among other people.

Whatever the case may be, you're quite disconnected from your individual self-essence, and your life is never going to be up to its full potential again until some of these problems are sorted out. A closely attuned spiritual quest of some type may help you, but a psychotherapist who has integrity may be an even more important route. It depends. What I can say, though, is these problems **have at least some possibility of carrying with you into other planes after you die**. Even joining with your "higher self" and being aware of your 400 other incarnations and your past life as Nefertiti of Egypt is not going to fix this particular existing incarnation that's heavily damaged. In fact, it may be the damage from this incarnation could affect the psychological welfare of all 400 other incarnations. That wouldn't be good, would it?

That means it's extremely important that you work these things out. Not doing so is irresponsible to you, those you care about, and your greater self in the grand scheme of things.

Concerning How You Treat Other People

How far along you've come in your personal progress and psychological health is, of course, a personal matter. Nonetheless, how you treat other people is still your responsibility, and no amount of past traumas or issues will morally condone how you treat others.

I have to be a bit blunt: in the "spirituality" communities **I've met some of the worst people of my life**. While hiding behind a stack of Eckhart Tolle and Deepak books, I've seen the most judgmental people of my life, sometimes with plastered on smiles as they explain their state of enlightenment that's greater than yours is. They'll basically tell you that you're human garbage for something they disagree with you about, and finish the sentence with "Namaste" as if that nullifies the venom. In addition, I've met "spiritual seekers" who never resolved their lack of social functionality. They do not approach people with a sense of understanding or open-mindedness or curiosity, but with a jaded demeanor or instant distrust. As a result, such people live in a constant cycle of self-fulfilling prophecies: distrusting and disliking people, and therefore attracting energy that leads to betrayal or further reasons to distrust people. Yet, such individuals claim to be spiritual or may even try to become like spiritual teachers.

If you don't work this stuff out, I don't care how many New Age books you read (including this one) you're no more "spiritual" than a nematode in the ocean. Although at least the nematode exists in a peaceful, non-judgmental state, so I take that back.

You're also not "spiritual" by abandoning your individuality and becoming like a doorknob. Oh, I've seen this one, too. Do you remember what Silver Birch said about our individuality being perpetual, yet others seem intent on destroying it? Well, some are so eager to dissolve themselves they begin practicing in this life early—by walking around in a constant stupor, maybe popping mushrooms or other psychotropic drugs like M&Ms or just generally not being receptive to the world around them. All these people are doing is hiding from life and the pain of self-developmental work.

Finally, I'll add that if you find it virtually impossible to make friends and people don't want much to do with you: **it's time to take a long hard look at yourself because I assure you, it's NOT everyone else—it's YOU.**

Actual people I meet whom I sense are "developed" in a proper, healthy way are immediately identifiable to me: they have a relaxed demeanor, they have a strong presence—they cannot be pushed around—but have a loving sense of accommodation. They see the best in you first and foremost and are easy to talk to. I feel like I'm more likely to meet a person like this changing my oil—some happy middle-aged father telling a few jokes—than some would-be erudite of spiritual books. **To summarize, people are in desperate need of life experience and social interaction to develop these abilities.**

Below is my own roadmap, combining different concepts together to help you tackle your life, your attitude, your social skills, and your individual essence.

Cyrus' Quick Guide to Actual "Spiritual Development"

- Face your shortcomings.

- Realize your fears. Do it intentionally if you have to by going out to do what you don't want to do.

- Accept your individuality (rather than trying to hide from or eradicate it.)

- Figure out what your individuality means (what the divine essence of "you" really is about and what it represents—and not buying into the false eastern-religious premise that the personality is some illusion you need to get rid of to rejoin a homogenous mass.)

- Taking responsibility, even for sh-- like your victim-complexes that you want to blame on others like politicians, family members, society, etc.

- Try to stop lying to yourself, including about things like your own shortcomings.

- Learn to forgive yourself.

- Then learn to forgive others.

- Learn to empathize and love in a healthy way. Not in a possessive, overly-attached, needy, co-dependent or vampiric way.

- Which means learning to socialize and get along with other people (You won't progress spending your life huddled in a room or an office, talking to no one and claiming you're introverted as an excuse.)

- Learn to enjoy every moment, even the small ones, as opposed to constantly looking for the next-best-thing (finding the elemental essence of places, situations, etc.)

- Learn how to handle conflict without losing your frame or hurting your self-esteem: being mature about dealing with other people's temperamental shortcomings, standing up for yourself and defending what's right without buckling.

- Come to terms with nasty things you've done—and find personal redemption. (Buddhists may call this clearing your karma.)

- Begin to see the best in other people to the point where you can quickly love those you meet, but (again) without it being a clingy or obsessive love.

Self-development is the key to creating a paradigm shift in society; big changes begin first with YOU. As you develop on the personal path, you can start to think more about the big picture, such as:

- Educating yourself about important subjects (like what this book is about.)

- Being objective and rational-minded—while still defending what you hold in your heart to be true.

- Performing actions with the big picture in mind—maybe quitting your job if your daily actions at such a job are doing absolutely nothing to benefit society.

- Seeking change WITHOUT putting yourself on a high-horse and becoming a social justice warrior with a sense of political superiority. In other words, being dedicated to helping mankind while TRYING to be humble and understanding. Egotistical moral superiority completely undoes good intentions.

- Being a CRITICAL THINKER—not taking information that's fed to you at face value, INCLUDING from cherished sources—questioning everything (including this book!)

- Take ACTION where it's needed. Perhaps joining communities and spreading awareness in ways that are APPROPRIATE (what is NOT appropriate is preaching to people who are not yet ready to learn. Or alienating your friends by going on and on about topics they view as totally crazy.)

At a certain point, the self development process begins to switch to a longing desire to be of assistance to other people. This often requires adopting an important cause where you can focus your energy and help others. In my own life, I've found the subject of life after death to be one of the best causes, because not only does it support a new paradigm of enormous benefit, but on a practical level it assists monumentally with grief.

The following are some reasons why, considering everything that was written in this book, the afterlife makes the most sense as a subject to help change the world:

- The afterlife is loaded with verifiable, objective and even scientifically scrutinized information to confirm its existence in ways that are more substantial than any other so-called paranormal topic.

- Contacting "the beyond" can be learned by virtually anyone, which can immediately reduce fear of death (and with it, the fear of life.)

- The existence of a greater, multi-dimensional reality (or greater planar reality, as I discuss in my first book,) immediately calls into question standard Newtonian physics, and the death-grip materialists have had on society for centuries.

- The realization that your loved ones are still around—living in superb conditions and they are still themselves—is an extraordinary boost of morale. I've seen this revelation transform many lives since I began my "career" in afterlife research over 15 years ago.

- The existence of other dimensions primitively called the "spirit world" helps open people's minds to how the so-called "supernatural" really works—everything from Bigfoot to UFO sightings can be explained by inter-dimensional fluctuations and astral "bleed through" from other realms.

- Learning empathy and decreasing selfish behavior in society is much easier with the revelation that life isn't a meaningless path to personal extinction.

- It's easier to relate to people as souls inhabiting bodies than robots pretending to be souls. The latter belief system—that we thoroughly picked apart earlier in this book—feels unnatural (probably because we know inside its bullsh--) and alienates us from each other.

In Summary

Put the books down and get to work on yourself.

XIV – What's Beyond the Afterlife?

This book has been about the afterlife, its reality, effects on society, and how it affects your life in practical ways. But we must face that the afterlife itself a red herring subject. It's necessary terminology, but do you remember how I mention that on astral planes, they don't use the prefix "astral" for their communities? In the same way, they do not call their world "the afterlife."

The Earth life / afterlife cycle is a strange, temporary and perhaps a bit traumatic period of your existence. It's not something to place all your mental abilities upon. Really, we must learn about the afterlife, accept its existence, then transcend beyond it.

I try not to spend my whole life dwelling on the afterlife. It comes as a shock to many when they find out what subject exactly I author books on. I travel, work other jobs, meet many people and learn from everyone's different perspectives and viewpoints. For me, travel is not about taking photos of some temple in Bali, but it's about meeting people and exploring other people's essences.

This is something that continues after we die. That's because we're in "the afterlife" right now—the same "spirit world" that comprises physical or semi-physical existences. Although, in this instance, nature has done an excellent job of making us forget anything about who we really are. It's up to us, the "meaning of life" perhaps, to rediscover our greater selves. Incarnation appears to be a process of rediscovery—almost like a game we play where we are thrown into a new situation, forgetting all our past knowledge, and being forced to rediscover who we are and survive.

Many disagree with my work, because I argue that we exist as ourselves upon death. The alternative would mean we merge with God or become angelic beings. If this were true, then there is truly no "after" life that occurs after this one, as it is separated from anything about our current selves. I do not believe this is accurate. Instead, life flows from one period to the next.

And what I've discovered about the astral universe has shown that possibilities never seem to stop. Imagine how lifeless planets in our universe are filled with life on the astral side. And on any such planet, there exists new realms, civilizations, species. We may incarnate astrally just as we incarnate in this domain. Therefore, far beyond the scope of your current incarnation, you may desire a new life on one of countless billions of planets. As unique as human Earth life may seem to you—something fundamental---it's not unique. There's a lot, *a lot* out there. It's the materialists who have tried to have us believe that our planet with life is the sole such planet in the cosmos, and that parallel dimensional frequencies with life also do not exist. If you believe this, you've been brainwashed.

Going beyond the afterlife means, eventually, not having to worry about the afterlife—especially not having to worry about whether or not it exists. It would mean accepting how life and death really operates and then using that in a bigger context as we lead our own lives.

Our civilization is not yet ready. But, I think there may be something on the horizon.

Earlier in this book we talked about the rumors of a "coming shift" in consciousness. I stay vigilant about many of these claims. But sometimes, I think what happens is if a general message is being conveyed—we wildly misinterpret that message and mix it with a hearty amount of our imaginations (which, of course, is a problem in spiritual communities.) But there may be a fundamental truth being expressed which is that, even though grandiose claims of 2012 ascensions go nowhere, a lot is still going to change in the near future. The afterlife subject is one piece of that puzzle. But when the blinders come off, it's not just about the existence of other planes of reality (a normal and common thing to the rest of the denizens of the universe, but bizarre to us,) it's about realizing how vapid elements of pop culture consume our lives almost as badly as vapid consumerist jobs that don't add anything to society. And the glue that binds the meaninglessness together is the philosophy of materialism—which, of course, I spoke at length about in this book.

With materialism as a philosophy, an idea is enforced that the superficial things matter more than they do. If there are no parallel planes, extraterrestrials, powers of the mind, or any other number of topics in our vast universe, then we must plug our minds with something where there is otherwise a void desperate for greater meaning and discovery.

We may find substance to plug the void via our imaginations—video games, movies, and stories. Or we find it through distraction—drinking alcohol and making money.

The above habits, by themselves, are not always so bad. But when we take on any activity as a supplementation for greater meaning, we place ourselves at risk of depression. The alcoholic never finds a long-term happiness via the bottle. A person who reads fiction novels all day, every day will never find much happiness beyond fictional worlds if the outside world feels like a dark place, devoid of meaning.

But there is another pleasure nearly as powerful as knowledge of greater realities: it's the pleasure created by power and domination. The people with the most to gain are those who are conscious of materialist philosophy, conscious it's wrong, but using it to their advantages. Domination is, too, a hollow pursuit. But, its intoxicating enough that powerful people walk this path with great determination.

The next time you believe that nothing discussed in this book is true, or can be true, ask yourself if those thoughts are your own or if they were planted into your consciousness. Ask yourself what the benefits of annihilation are. What are the benefits of a population that believes in extinction of the personality—devoid of hope? The benefits of a society that sees no hope anywhere else but enjoys the temporary thrill of buying consumer goods? The answer is that the greater the hopelessness, the greater the need to distract through easy purchases. And with every purchase, someone makes money. It's not the girl at the counter who benefits but her bosses' bosses' bosses' boss. And that boss may have a couple of bosses, too, that are not readily apparent but gaining even more power. And with all that power, think about the intoxicating thrill of dominating an entire society.

Whomever they are, they don't want this information to be universal. The existential depression of non-existence at death, contrary to all evidence of the beyond, is not an accident. It's has all been setup this way. As isolated and lonely as your thoughts may feel, you're not alone in them. If our society were designed differently, what was discussed in this book would not be on the fringe. But if that were the case, our civilization would be very different.

It's up to us to choose logic over fear and evidence over superstition. Materialism itself is, in fact, a superstition. Non-existence at physical death is impossible—it's an urban legend supported by no actual evidence, but continually reinforced.

Today, we see materialism's stronghold breaking. The barrier has already been breached. We can now move forward, beyond our fear and existential depression, to learn about realms beyond this one and, in time—stretch beyond even the afterlife into the greater horizons that were meant for humans to achieve. When the day comes that the afterlife is no longer something to stress about or try to prove—but is accepted—then we can move toward truly optimizing our existences on this plane with full knowledge of who we are.

What is your role in this saga?

Thank you for buying this book.

I wonder, then, what you have learned?

If anything, at all, then I suppose I performed my job.

Maybe you love me, maybe you hate me.

But what I do cannot continue without the help of others.

A review on Amazon means the world. Because without them, authors are marginalized to only major publishers. The voice of many is constricted to the influence of a few. Do we want that?

So, please help me continue with what I do, and kindly consider a review.

- *Cyrus*

P.S.: Do you want to get in touch with me? cyrus@cyruskirkpatrick.com may just be the way.

About the Author

Cyrus Kirkpatrick, based in Los Angeles, CA and Tucson, AZ, is prone to frequent bouts of buying one-way tickets and living out of a backpack, sometimes in hostels for $6 a day—as it's an excellent way to have adventure, socialize, explore new cultures, and learn from the world. Currently, Cyrus works primarily as an editor and publishing assistant for various clients, while also spending a considerable amount of free time studying life after death, authoring books, updating personal websites, and generally staying glued to the laptop even while traveling in exotic locations (being on a beach in Indonesia does not mean having a vacation, just a nicer view while still working all day.) Cyrus grew up deep in the Sonoran desert and as such, the desert will always remain a part of his heart. He enjoys Andalusian music, Turkish food, staying up late, Salsa dancing, and still playing an old computer game from 1999 called *EverQuest.*

REFERENCES

[1] "My Platonic Sweetheart." *Wikipedia*, Wikimedia Foundation, 27 July 2018, en.wikipedia.org/wiki/My_Platonic_Sweetheart

[2] "'I Could See My Body': Researchers Probe Near-Death and Out-of Body Experiences | CBC News." *CBCnews*, CBC/Radio Canada, 9 Oct. 2014, www.cbc.ca/news/health/patients-near-death-experiences-during-cardiac-arrest-tested-1.2793068

[3] "Time and the Near-Death Experience ." *Near-Death.com*, www.near-death.com/science/research/time.html

[4] "Love After Life: How I Defeated Grief and Developed a Fulfilling Relationship with My Soul-Mate after She Passed from the Physical. - Kindle Edition by William Murray. Religion & Spirituality Kindle EBooks @ Amazon.com." *Amazon*, Amazon, www.amazon.com/dp/B078GL4ZSN/

[5] Becker, Ernest. "The Denial of Death." *Google Books*, Google, books.google.co.uk/books?id=G67wXZ94JmoC&dq=the denial of death&source=gbs_navlinks_s

[6] Williams, Kevin. "Carl G. Jung's Near-Death Experience." *Near-Death.com*, www.near-death.com/experiences/notable/carl-jung.html

[7] "Carl Jung and the Shadow: The Hidden Power of Our Dark Side." *Academy of Ideas*, 14 June 2018, www.academyofideas.com/2015/12/carl-jung-and-the-shadow-the-hidden-power-of-our-dark-side

[8] "Aftereffects of the Near Death Experience." *Psychology Today*, Sussex Publishers, www.psychologytoday.com/us/blog/understanding-grief/201803/aftereffects-the-near-death-experience

[9] Keaten, Jamey. "104-Year-Old Australian Promotes Right to Assisted Suicide." *U.S. News & World Report*, U.S. News & World Report, www.usnews.com/news/world/articles/2018-05-08/104-year-old-australian-promotes-right-to-assisted-suicide

[10] "9 Circles of Hell (Dante's Inferno)." *History Lists*, 2012, www.historylists.org/art/9-circles-of-hell-dantes-inferno.html

[11] Donahue, Molly. "Frozen In Time: 7 Celebrities Who Are Taking Steps to Live Forever." *New Hampshire Public Radio*, www.nhpr.org/post/frozen-time-7-celebrities-who-are-taking-steps-live-forever#stream/0

[12] Woodruff, Bob, et al. "Former Alcor Employee Makes Harsh Allegations Against Cryonics Foundation." *ABC News*, ABC News Network, 7 Oct. 2009, www.abcnews.go.com/Nightline/alcor-employee-makes-harsh-allegations-cryonics-foundation/story?id=8764331

[13] Newton, Casey. "When Her Best Friend Died, She Used Artificial Intelligence to Keep Talking to Him." *The Verge*, The Verge, 6 Oct. 2016, www.theverge.com/a/luka-artificial-intelligence-memorial-roman-mazurenko-bot

[14] Frances, Karen. "The Ongoing Quest to Build Life from Scratch." *TED,* Ideas.ted.com, 9 Mar. 2017, www.ideas.ted.com/the-ongoing-quest-to-build-life-from-scratch/

[15] "Is It Possible to Attain Yogic Superpowers?" *Gaia*, Gaia.com, June 2017, www.gaia.com/lp/content/is-it-possible-to-attain-yogic-superpowers/.

[16] Delhi, Dean Nelson in New. "Man Claims to Have Had No Food or Drink for 70 Years." *The Telegraph*, Telegraph Media Group, 28 Apr. 2010, www.telegraph.co.uk/news/worldnews/asia/india/7645857/Man-claims-to-have-had-no-food-or-drink-for-70-years.html.

[17] Edamaruku, Sanal. "India's Man Who Lives on Sunshine | Sanal Edamaruku." *The Guardian*, Guardian News and Media, 18 May 2010, www.theguardian.com/commentisfree/belief/2010/may/18/prahlad-jani-india-sunshine.

[18] Harris, Sam. "The Mystery of Consciousness." *SamHarris.org*, 17 July 2018, www.samharris.org/the-mystery-of-consciousness/

[19] revolutionloveevolve. "Graham Hancock - The War on Consciousness BANNED TED TALK." *YouTube*, TED X White Chapel - Reposted by Revolution Love Evolve, 15 Mar. 2013, www.youtube.com/watch?v=Y0c5nIvJH7w

[20] Taylor, Suzanne. "Ex TEDx West Hollywood." *SUE Speaks*, www.suespeaks.org/ex-tedx-west-hollywood/

[21] "Jordan Peterson and Ben Shapiro: Frontline of Free Speech (LIVE)." *YouTube*, The Rubin Report, 31 Jan. 2018, www.youtube.com/watch?v=iRPDGEgaATU.

---

[22] Schopf, J. William, et al. "SIMS Analyses of the Oldest Known Assemblage of Microfossils Document Their Taxon-Correlated Carbon Isotope Compositions." *PNAS*, National Academy of Sciences, 13 Dec. 2017, www.pnas.org/content/early/2017/12/12/1718063115

[23] Kyuuketsuki. "Dust Comes 'Alive' in Space." *The Times & The Sunday Times*, 12 Aug. 2007, www.timesonline.co.uk/tol/news/uk/article2241753.ece.

[24] Hernando, Jose Alfonso. "Experiment Shows How Life Can Spontaneously Appear Wherever It Can." *Noticias Selección Valdeandemágico*, 1 Jan. 1970, www.noticiasseleccionvaldeandemagico.blogspot.com/2014/04/experiment-shows-how-life-can.html

[25] Dillow, Clay. "Can Our DNA Electromagnetically 'Teleport' Itself? One Researcher Thinks So." *Popular Science*, Popular Science, 13 Jan. 2011, www.popsci.com/science/article/2011-01/can-our-dna-electromagnetically-teleport-itself-one-researcher-thinks-so

[26] "Water Memory Documentary of Luc Montagnier." *YouTube*, Sexual Alchemy, 4 Sept. 2017, www.youtube.com/watch?time_continue=77&v=k2NuZhRlWCc

[27] Coghlan, Andy. "Scorn over Claim of Teleported DNA." *New Scientist*, New Scientist, 12 Jan. 2011, www.newscientist.com/article/mg20927952-900-scorn-over-claim-of-teleported-dna/.

[28] "What Is Orgonomy? A Brief Explanation for Newcomers." *Orgonomyuk.org.uk*, www.orgonomyuk.org.uk/What is Orgonomy.html. The most poorly designed website I've ever seen. Did they make this in 1996?

[29] "A Brief History of Wilhelm Reich's Discoveries and the Developing Science of Orgonomy." *Orgonelab.org*, http://www.orgonelab.org/wrhistory.htm.

[30] Simonian, Stephen. "On the Sexual Rights of Youth | The Journal of Psychiatric Orgone Therapy." *Kleptomania, a Case Discussion | Journal of Psychiatric Orgone Therapy*, The Journal of Psychiatric Orgone Therapy, 11 Oct. 2011, www.psychorgone.com/history/on-the-sexual-rights-of-youth.

[31] Jade. "The Mysterious Case of Mrs. Schwarz." *GriefandMourning.com*, www.griefandmourning.com/kubler-ross-schwarz

[32] Luscombe, Belinda. "Anthony Bourdain, Kate Spade and the Dangers of Envy." *Time*, Time, 8 June 2018, www.time.com/5305955/anthony-bourdain-kate-spade-death-envy/

---

[33] Ballard, Stan A.. The Silver Birch Book of Questions & Answers" Spiritual Truth Press, 1998.

46021376R00143

Printed in Poland
by Amazon Fulfillment
Poland Sp. z o.o., Wrocław